What to Look for in a Classroom

What to Look for in a Classroom

... and Other Essays

Alfie Kohn

Jossey-Bass Publishers
San Francisco

Jossey-Bass books and products are available through most bookstores. To contact Jossey-Bass directly, call (888) 378-2537, fax to (800) 605-2665, or visit our website at www.josseybass.com.

Substantial discounts on bulk quantities of Jossey-Bass books are available to corporations, professional associations, and other organizations. For details and discount information, contact the special sales department at Jossey-Bass.

TCF Manufactured in the United States of America on Lyons Falls Turin Book. This paper is acid-free and 100 percent totally chlorine-free.

Library of Congress Cataloging-in-Publication Data

Kohn, Alfie.
    What to look for in a classroom : and other essays / Alfie Kohn. — 1st ed.
    p.   cm.
    Includes index.
    ISBN 0-7879-4453-X (cloth)
    1. Teachers.   2. Teaching.   3. Classroom management.   4. Learning.
5. Teacher-student relationships.   6. School management and organization.
I. Title.
    LB1775.K643 1998
    371.1—ddc21

                                 98-25426

FIRST EDITION
HB Printing 10 9 8 7 6 5 4 3 2

To three wise, caring, irreverent educators
who left too soon but whose influence lingers

John Nicholls (1940–1994)
Sylvia Kendzior (1936–1997)
Herb Lovett (1949–1998)

Contents

—ᶜᵛ— Introduction

From 1979 until 1985, I taught a course on existentialism to high school students. It was not my only teaching experience but it was far and away my favorite. Between terms I fine-tuned the reading list and perfected the lectures, looking forward to the next year when I could teach it again—rather as one might tinker with a new car in the garage before proudly bringing it out. It wasn't until years later that I began to realize just how little I understood about teaching. The idea of a teacher with a ready-made course just waiting to be taught to students makes about as much sense as a young, single person with a ready-made marriage who needs nothing more than a partner to have it with.

Once I was out of the classroom, I came to understand that a course is created *for* and *with* a particular group of students. I didn't see it that way before because I wasn't thinking about learning, only about teaching. I was trying to find the most efficient way of giving students the knowledge and skills I already had, which meant that I was treating the students as interchangeable receptacles—as rows of wide-open bird beaks waiting for worms, if you will. (Some beaks are defiantly closed, of course, but there are plenty of in-service workshops available on how to "motivate" those birds to open up.)

I would like to be able to say that my current ideas about education spring directly from my own classroom experience, but they really don't. They spring from watching teachers who are better than I ever was, from reading remarkable research, from talking and listening and thinking. My own classroom experience serves mostly to make me wince in retrospect. It's the basis for a lesson not in pedagogy but in humility—and it reminds me how hard it is for even reasonably smart, humanistic, well-intentioned people to put the good stuff into practice.

This book is not an account of how I learned but an indication of what I'm learning. It is a collection of nineteen essays that have appeared in *Phi Delta Kappan, Educational Leadership, Education Week,* the *Boston Globe,* and other publications; all but one were written in the 1990s, and the majority since 1995. The shortest essay is the title piece, which appears at the end and consists mostly of a chart; the longest is a discussion of self-esteem (Chapter Eleven) that identifies the two major schools of thought on the issue and then proceeds to criticize both of them. With the exception of some minor tweaking, I've left the original text of these articles alone. I have, however, added a postscript to the oldest piece in the bunch, "Suffer the Restless Children" (Chapter Ten). One article, "Television and Children" (Chapter Twelve) appears for the first time in this anthology.

When I look at these essays together, the strongest impression they leave me with is the diversity of topics. Unlike people who devote their entire careers to a single issue, such as discipline or assessment, I have pursued whatever questions seemed compelling to me. There was no Ten Year Plan informing this process, no calculated decision to write on specific topics in pursuit of a grand unifying theory, no predictable linear sequence laid out in advance. After all, children rarely learn that way (although they are often taught as if they did), and evolution, too, is more a conglomeration of accidental connections and dead ends— more a bush than a ladder, as Stephen Jay Gould likes to say. So, too, is this collection. Although some of these articles led to others, the whole is identifiable primarily in the sense that the parts were all written by the same person.

Yet when I try to look at this book as a reader, I think that one can discern an agenda, a sensibility, that runs through it. It offers an invitation to reconsider some of our most basic practices and premises as educators (and, incidentally, as parents). Thus the chapters ask such questions as Will kids really act better if we teach them social skills? Do some kids really "have" something called attention deficit disorder? Is the very act of watching television really bad for you? The operative word in each case is *really:* How sure are we of what we have assumed?

At least as often, though, these essays are not asking Is X true? so much as Have we asked the right question here, or asked it the right way? What I think I've been trying to do is reframe the way controversies are presented and suggest more meaningful questions than the ones we tend to ask. For me, the meaningful questions are generally the radical ones—and I use *radical* in the sense suggested by the word's original Latin meaning, which is "of the root." Thus, to take just a few examples of what follows in this book, I argue that:

- We ought to call a moratorium on our national frenzy to "raise standards" and ask what assumptions about children and schools are built into that endeavor.

- We ought to refrain from conducting elaborate, time-wasting discussions about how to stem grade inflation, because the real problem is not the number of students who get A's but the number who are taught that getting A's is the point of school.

- We ought to reflect on the well-intentioned quest to get kids to read more and ask what the usual strategies are doing to *how* kids read and *why* they read.

- We ought to rethink the search for better methods of assessing students' work—because our motives for assessment matter more than our methods, because too much attention to student performance threatens to undermine learning, and because there are disturbing implications to construing what goes on in classrooms as "work."

A few years ago, I received—and accepted—an invitation to speak to a fourth grade class that had just finished reading excerpts from one of the articles included in this book (Chapter Seven, "Grading"). A week or so after my visit, a batch of thank-you letters and reflections from the students arrived in the mail. One boy's note read as follows:

Dear Mr. Kohn,
I'm glad you came in because it helped me understand your theory. I was wondering though why you disided to spend you life time doing this I mean I disigrie with [some] things but I woulden't spend my life-time disigrying.

When I finally stopped laughing, I started to take this letter seriously, accepting a nine-year-old's challenge to think about what I'm spending my life doing—and what most of the essays in this book are about. Only the articles in Part Five explicitly talk about what I think we should do (as opposed to what we should stop doing): turn classrooms into caring communities, give students more opportunities to participate in making decisions, and so on. But I feel obliged to remind myself periodically that the criticism of popular practices, the "disigrying" with conventional wisdom that characterizes most of these articles and much of my career, is also informed by a vision of what should be. Though I will own up to having something of a contrarian streak, I rail against a lot of what goes on in schools chiefly because those practices threaten to eclipse the values I am trying to affirm. Rewards trouble me because of what they do to intrinsic motivation; traditional discipline and character education offend me because of how they derail moral development and fail to meet children's needs.

This process of opposing in order to affirm began in the early 1980s, when I was thinking through the destructive consequences of competition. When my study of that subject was published by Houghton Mifflin in 1986 (as *No Contest: The Case Against Competition*), I was led off in three separate directions, all of which had the effect of pulling me toward the field of education (as opposed to social criticism and human behavior more generally, where I had dwelled to that point).

First, the search for practical alternatives to competitive structures led me to cooperative learning, which just happens to take place in schools. Beginning with a commonsense recognition that students are likely to benefit if they can exchange their insights and information, I eventually realized that collaboration is even more important as a means of facilitating how people think, and that took me off in the direction of constructivism. In the late 1980s, if you had told me that cooperative learning was a big part of your classroom, I would have grinned and congratulated you. By the early 1990s, I was starting to reply, "Hmmm. What kind?"—wary of the versions that I came to call "group grade grubbing" (because of their reliance on artificial inducements for teamwork) and suspicious of a model of cooperative learning that simply spices up the traditional curriculum and fails to challenge a teacher-centered, behaviorist model of instruction.[1]

Second, the research I had uncovered suggesting that excellence and competition are not only different ideas in theory but actually pull in opposite directions in practice—that is, all the studies showing that people work or learn less effectively when they are competing—forced me to come up with some explanations for this counterintuitive finding. One reason that competition typically backfires is its status as an extrinsic motivator, an attempt to use something outside a task (namely, the possibility of winning a contest) to get people to try harder. Extrinsic motivators are not only less successful than intrinsic motivation (that is, interest in the task itself) but they also tend to *undermine* intrinsic motivation, along with the quality of one's performance. All of this took up scarcely half a dozen paragraphs in *No Contest* but eventually led me to wonder whether extrinsic motivators are counterproductive even when no competition is involved.

I published the answer in 1993 as *Punished by Rewards,* which looks at the failure of our ceaseless attempts to "motivate" people by dangling goodies in front of them at school, at work, and at home. All three arenas interested me, but I was particularly drawn to what I was finding out about schools—and to the alternatives to using rewards (or punishments) to get students to work harder or behave themselves. I came to see the problems of traditional grades, as well as the promise of some alternative forms of assessment (if used sparingly and for the right reasons). I started to think about the tendency to overemphasize the teaching of skills, the influence of behaviorism on contemporary character education, the absurdity of reading incentives, and the limits of "positive reinforcement" along with other troubling aspects of popular discipline programs—and I addressed all of these topics in articles that appear in this volume.

Third, I looked hard at the commonplace assumption that we compete because it's "just human nature" to do so and found not a shred of evidence to support it. Instead, logic and research strongly suggest that we compete because we're raised that way rather than born that way—an inconvenient conclusion insofar as we then face the responsibility of doing something about the institutions in our culture that compel us to work against each other. But again, an answer triggers more questions: What else do we attribute to human nature because it's convenient rather than because it's true? Is there good evidence to support our casual belief that competitiveness, aggression, selfishness, and laziness are more natural than cooperativeness, nurturance, generosity, and curiosity?

The result of that research project was a relatively academic book published in 1990 called *The Brighter Side of Human Nature: Altruism and Empathy in Everyday Life,* which I don't mind telling you has sold *dozens* of copies. But again, the practical side of me was unsatisfied. Having laboriously attempted to prove that it is as natural for humans to help as to hurt, I wanted to say something useful, to offer some way of actively promoting the prosocial. This immediately led me to think about children and schools. I had been invited in 1988 and 1989 to speak about competition at the annual conference of the National Association of Independent Schools, but in 1990 I switched gears and prepared a talk entitled "Caring Kids." I then published an expanded version of that lecture in the March 1991 issue of *Phi Delta Kappan*. The article resulted in an invitation to develop one- and two-day workshops for Phi Delta Kappa, which I conducted, on and off for several years, all over the country. From how to help students become compassionate, empathic people, it was a short jump to a number of related educational topics, such as those addressed in this collection.

Before I sign off, I want to thank three people who found something worthwhile in my stumbling attempts to make sense of schools, and in my presumptuous efforts to challenge mainstream assumptions. Phil Harris at Phi Delta Kappa, Pauline Gough at *Kappan,* and Ron Brandt at the Association for Supervision and Curriculum Development may not agree with everything I write or say in public, but their backing over the last eight years or so is responsible for the existence of many of these articles, and for the fact that someone actually thought there would be interest in publishing a collection of them. That someone was Lesley Iura at Jossey-Bass, to whom I am also indebted.

Note

1. Two of my publications on cooperative learning are not included in this book: "Learning Together," which is Chapter Ten of the revised (1992) edition of *No Contest;* and "Group Grade Grubbing vs. Cooperative *Learning,*" *Educational Leadership,* Feb. 1991, pp. 83–87, my first article to appear in an educational periodical. I have, however, included a discussion of why cooperative learning has so often failed to take root, which appears as Chapter Five.

PART ONE

Classroom Mismanagement

CHAPTER ONE

The Limits of Teaching Skills

We are in love with skills. Not any specific skills, mind you, but the very idea that children's problems can be remedied by teaching them skills. The model is so simple and familiar to us that we do not even think of it as a model. It is just common sense that people who thrash about in the water need to work on their swimming skills. Likewise, we assume, if children do not pay attention to what someone else is saying, they could benefit from some remedial work in listening skills. If they fail to lend a hand to a fellow human being in distress, they need to hone their helping skills. If they are reluctant to stand up for themselves, they are candidates for assertiveness training.

But along comes early childhood specialist Lilian Katz to remind us that most kids already know how to listen; what they sometimes lack is the inclination to do so. (In many classrooms, they have to do altogether too much listening, but that's another story.) Along comes Ervin Staub, an expert in altruism, to suggest that we should be less

---

Originally published in *Reaching Today's Youth* in 1997.

concerned with giving people instructions on how to help others and more concerned with fostering a "prosocial orientation"—that is, a disposition to help. And along comes Robert Deluty at the University of Maryland with research showing that submissive kids as well as aggressive kids are usually able to describe the appropriately assertive way to respond to any number of situations. In other words, they know how to be assertive; the question is why they aren't.

None of this is meant to suggest that skills do not matter, or that many students might not derive some benefit from becoming more skillful in all sorts of endeavors. But even where this is most obviously true, such as in learning how to read and write, the question of motivation may still be decisive. Children who are excited about what they are doing tend to acquire the skills they need to do it well, even if the process takes a while. When interest is lacking, however, learning tends to be less permanent, less deeply rooted, less successful. Performance, we might say, is a by-product of motivation. (The implication is that we ought to be spending our time making sure classrooms preserve and enrich kids' desire to learn. The call for "higher standards," which typically skips over the question of how students feel about what they are doing, would thus seem to be fatally misguided.)

Now consider attempts to promote respect and responsibility. Our first obligation is to think about how these words are being used. When some educators complain that children are "disrespectful," what they mean is that children talk back rather than doing what they are told. Similarly, it often turns out that a "responsible" student (or one who "takes responsibility") is one who unthinkingly complies with an adult's demand. Students are typically expected to follow the rules regardless of whether the rules are reasonable and to respect authority regardless of whether that respect has been earned. Given these connotations, I would argue that the most pressing question is not how we can make children more respectful or responsible, but whether these goals, as currently defined, are even legitimate.

But let's assume we have in mind a more reasonable, less autocratic understanding of respect and responsibility. Once again, we find ourselves facing the limits of a skills-based approach. Most students know how to treat someone respectfully. What we want to find out is why they sometimes fail to do so. Apart from simple carelessness, one logical explanation is that they do not feel respected themselves. One is struck repeatedly by the number of adults who criticize children for acting disrespectfully—all the while setting an example of precisely what they are complaining about: they talk *at* students rather than listening, fail to take students' needs and points of view seriously, try to control students' behavior by dangling rewards in front of them or threatening them with punishments, and make little or no effort to involve them in decision making.

It is widely understood that people learn by example. But adults who are respectful of children are not just modeling a skill or behavior; they are meeting the emotional needs of those children, thereby helping to create the psychological conditions for children to treat others respectfully. I once visited a kindergarten classroom where the teacher, about to begin a class meeting, paused to ask whether it was OK to erase a childish scrawl on the blackboard. It is the accumulation of such small gestures of respect that create a climate where kids are inclined to act likewise—with the teacher and with each other.

Another example: a high school math teacher suggested that it might be time for a test on Friday, and the students objected that they were not ready. The teacher's response was to ask when they would be ready, and after some discussion they decided to take the test the following Wednesday. Many teachers would assume that asking their students to suggest a good time for a test would prompt a sarcastic response such as "Never!" But these students would not think of answering that way for the simple reason (as one of them explained to me) that their teacher respected them.

By the same token, if we want students to act responsibly, we have to give them responsibilities. We have to provide them with a classroom where they are encouraged and helped to make decisions. If students are unable to weigh the arguments carefully, anticipate long-term consequences, or take others' needs into account, that may mean they need help figuring out how to do these things. They may have little experience making meaningful choices. Indeed, the same paradox appears: many of the teachers and parents who grumble that kids "just don't take responsibility" spend their days ordering kids around—as though children could learn how to make good decisions by following directions. Once again, though, the question is not just whether we have taught children a list of relevant skills, but whether we have worked with them to create an environment where their needs and preferences matter, where their voices are heard and valued.

Why, then, is there such a disproportionate emphasis on teaching skills? First, this way of thinking implies that it is the students who need fixing. If something more complicated than a lack of know-how

is involved, we might have to question our own practices and premises, which can be uncomfortable. Moreover, a focus on skills allows
us to ignore the structural elements of a classroom (or school or family). If students insult each other, it is easier for us to try to make each
student act more courteously than it is to ask which elements of the
system might have contributed to the problem. Practices such as
awards assemblies and spelling bees teach students that they must
triumph over each other to be successful. Indifference to others'
needs—or even active efforts to put each other down—may be rational responses to a dysfunctional system. But it is obviously more convenient for us to address each individual who says something insulting
than it is to track down the structural contributors to such behaviors.
(Likewise, it is less ambitious and more conservative to teach children
the skills of "dealing with" competition than to figure out how to eliminate competitive practices. The status quo has no more reliable ally
than the teacher of coping skills, because whatever is to be coped with
is treated as something to be accepted rather than changed.)

Second, a skills-based approach is compatible with behaviorism,
whose influence over our schools (and indeed all of American society) is difficult to overstate. Behaviorism dismisses anything that cannot be reduced to a discrete set of observable and measurable
behaviors. This dogma lies behind scope-and-sequence approaches to
teaching reading as well as other segmented instructional techniques,
but its footprints are also discernible in character education, classroom management, and virtually the entire field of special education.

Consider two children in separate classrooms, each of whom gives
away half his lunch to someone else. The two behaviors are identical;
the two children are evidently both skilled at helping. But why did these
kids share their food? The first one, let us imagine, was hoping the
teacher would notice and shower him with praise. ("What a nice thing
to do, Robert! I'm so proud of you for sharing like that!") The second
child neither knew nor cared whether the teacher saw—he gave away
some of his sandwich because he was worried that his classmate might
go hungry. Virtually all of us are more impressed by the second child's
motive, but a preoccupation with behavior—and, by extension, with
skills—distracts us from attending to motives.

Put these two factors together (an emphasis on fixing the child and
a focus on behavior) and you have what might be called the transmission approach to learning. Here, academic instruction is construed
as a matter of pouring facts into empty containers, while character ed-

ucation involves transmitting values to—or instilling them in—passive receptacles. The emphasis on skills is reassuringly consistent with this model. We know how to do something, and we transfer this knowledge to a student so he or she can do it, too. To some extent this transaction may be successful. We may be able to get students to replicate an action (making eye contact while speaking) or recite an algorithm ("To divide by a fraction, flip it upside-down and multiply"). But replication does not imply commitment, and recitation does not mean understanding.

What's more, the student may be able to do something, but may not want to do it. And this brings us back to where we started. The management theorist Douglas McGregor once remarked that corporate executives like to dangle money in front of their employees because—well, because they can. They have control over how much people are paid, whereas they cannot control how people will feel about their work, and whether they will want to do it, and why. Likewise, we educators gravitate to the things we can do something about, things like teaching skills. Unfortunately, that process can be of only limited use when it comes to helping children become altruistic or assertive, responsible or respectful.

The Trouble with School Uniforms

Satire became obsolete, Tom Lehrer remarked, on the day that Henry Kissinger was awarded the Nobel Peace Prize. We might add that the redundancy of satire is confirmed every time people earnestly propose ideas like this one: the best way to help children learn—or to improve their character—is to force them to dress alike.

The appeal of school uniforms is based less on the likelihood of realizing any long-term benefits than on the nostalgic yearning for a simpler and less dangerous age. To imagine that telling students what to wear will bring back those days is to engage in wishful, if not fuzzy, thinking.

For some people, however, the good old days symbolized by uniforms were characterized not only by simplicity but by obedience: those were the days when kids did what they were told and kept their mouths shut. Here the question is not so much whether uniforms can make this happen but whether the goal itself is legitimate.

Originally published in *The Boston Globe* in 1996.

If we want students to grow into critical thinkers and ethical people, then we have to aim higher than mere conformity. We have to join them in asking, "What kind of school do we want to create?" Thus, if T-shirts contain slogans that offend us, or gang colors threaten to be inflammatory, school administrators might invite students to participate in analyzing the problem and constructing a solution. Apart from being more respectful, this approach is also more effective over the long run (and better preparation for life in a democratic society) than issuing a decree ("Wear this").

Just as the proponents of "school choice" never talk about how much choice students have about what happens in the classroom, so the advocates of uniformity assume that the only objection to dress codes is that kids want the freedom to wear whatever they wish. Overlooked is the more substantive argument, that kids don't learn much of value in an environment where they are excluded from decision making.

A search for data supporting the use of uniforms turns up a single study finding that teachers and others *believed* students in uniforms were more successful than their peers. But this suggests nothing more than a prejudice on the part of these observers, analogous to attributing various qualities to students on the basis of race or gender.

In the absence of real research, many news stories have cited anecdotal claims, notably from Long Beach, California, where school uniforms are alleged to have instantly produced positive results. However, as the district's superintendent acknowledged to the *Harvard Education Letter* this year, programs to promote conflict resolution, peer mediation, and parental involvement have also been implemented there recently and "it is really hard to know exactly what is producing the positive effect"—assuming that a meaningful effect really does exist, and persists.

Is it even reasonable to expect uniforms to solve the problems for which they are recommended? Can violence be reduced by borrowing an idea from the military? Can class differences be smoothed over by making kids dress identically? (In any case, those very real differences ought to be addressed openly rather than camouflaged.)

And what about the pressure some students feel to dress better than their friends, which can drive parents to distraction (if not bankruptcy)? This is just a symptom of a broader social disease called competition. If we were serious about dealing with the underlying pressure on students to triumph over their peers, we might begin by challenging school-sponsored practices such as awards assemblies and spelling bees.

Complex problems will not disappear just because we demand that students wear what we tell them. Relying on power to induce conformity rarely produces lasting solutions. The alternative to uniforms is not merely to allow different styles; it is to work with students to transform schools into democratic communities where everyone's voice counts.

CHAPTER THREE

Beyond Discipline

A few years ago, I received a letter from a woman who was working on a book about a progressive educator. She said she was considering devoting a chapter of her manuscript to a discussion of a program called Assertive Discipline, which was at best only indirectly related to her subject. But she knew my stomach reacted the same way hers did to the sight of marbles in a jar, or a hierarchical list of punishments on a classroom wall, and she wanted to know whether I thought she should bother with this digression.

It didn't seem a particularly complicated question, and yet the more I thought about it, the more I found my response shifting. At first, I was simply going to say, "Hell, yes! Help the hundreds of thousands of teachers who have been exposed to this program to reflect on how pernicious it really is." Assertive Discipline, after all, is essentially a collection of bribes and threats whose purpose is to enforce rules that the teacher alone devises and imposes. The point is to get the trains to run on time in the classroom, never mind whom they run over. Everything,

---

Originally published in *Education Week* in 1996.

including the feelings of students, must be sacrificed to the imperative of obedience: "Whenever possible, simply ignore the covert hos-
tility of a student. By ignoring the behavior, you will diffuse [sic] the
situation. Remember, what you really want is for the student to comply with your request. Whether or not the student does it in an angry
manner is not the issue."[1]

As I prepared to write this to her, however, and as I recalled Lee
Canter's disclaimer in the *Teachers College Record* several years ago that
"there is nothing new about Assertive Discipline," that it is "simply a
systematization" of common behavior-management strategies, I realized that it was too easy to single out one person as the Darth Vader
of American education. At least Canter is candid about the authoritarian (and behaviorist) thrust of his methods. No one could possibly
confuse his program for an attempt to engage students in ethical reflection, or to build caring relationships with them; teachers are urged
simply to tell students "exactly what behavior is acceptable. . . . No
questions. No room for confusion."

But the same cannot be said of many other programs on the market that wrap themselves in words like *cooperative* and *dignity* and even
love. While rejecting the most blatant forms of coercion, they too are
ultimately about getting students to comply, and they too rely on carrots and sticks. These programs unhesitatingly recommend that we
dangle rewards in front of students when they act the way we want:
praise and privileges, stickers and stars, and other examples of what
has been called "control through seduction."

The groovier programs, following the lead of Rudolf Dreikurs, prefer not to talk about punishing students. Instead, punishment is
repackaged as "logical consequences." The student is still forced to do
something undesirable (or prevented from doing something desirable), but the tone of the interaction is supposed to be more reasonable and friendly, and the consequence itself must have some
conceptual connection to the child's act: the punishment fits the
crime. Thus:

• If a second grade student is guilty of "talking out of turn, squirm-
  ing, and so on," he might be ordered not only to leave the room
  but also to spend time back in a kindergarten class. This is a
  "logical consequence," and therefore appropriate, as long as the
  teacher strikes the right tone by saying that she wonders whether

the boy is "ready to continue in second grade" and suggesting that therefore "it might be better for [him] to try and go back to kindergarten for a while."[2]

- If a student makes a spitball, the teacher should force him to make five hundred more spitballs so that his throat becomes "increasingly parched." If a student tips her chair back, "she can be asked to stand for the rest of the period."[3]

- "Each student who violates a rule [must] write his own name on the blackboard"—or, in another approach, must have his name written there by an elected class "sheriff" who is "responsible for keeping the behavioral records."[4]

Is it more reasonable to make a child stand for the rest of the period than, say, for the rest of the week? Unquestionably. It is also more reasonable to paddle a child than to shoot him, but this does not offer much of an argument for paddling. Is there a connection between tipping back a chair and not being able to sit in it? Yes, but does it really matter to the child? The issue is not the specific features of the punitive response so much as the punishment itself: "You didn't do what I wanted, so now I'm going to make something unpleasant happen to you." We would not expect the child to be less resentful (or less likely to retaliate) just because the teacher used what amounts to Punishment Lite.

In trying to answer the woman who was considering a chapter about Lee Canter, I came to conclude that the problem is not just with his program but with the use of rewards and punishments per se, regardless of what they are called or how they are embellished. Even when children are "successfully" reinforced or consequenced into compliance, they will likely feel no commitment to what they are doing, no deep understanding of the act and its rationale, no sense of themselves as the kind of people who would want to act this way in the future. They have been led to concentrate on the consequences of their actions to themselves, and someone with this frame of reference bears little resemblance to the kind of person we dream of seeing each of our students become.

Gradually, though, I began to wonder whether even this was the last word. Rewards and punishments are instruments for controlling people, and the real problem, I began to suspect, was the belief that the teacher should be in control of the classroom. If all these discipline programs disappeared tomorrow, a new one would pop up like the next Kleenex in the box if teachers were determined (or pressured) to remain in control and needed methods for making sure that happened.

This recognition offered a fresh way of looking at my own experiences as a classroom teacher, and at what I had seen in countless classrooms over the last few years. Students are far less likely to act aggressively, intrusively, or obnoxiously in places where the teacher is not concerned with being in charge—and, indeed, is not particularly interested in classroom-management techniques. I realized that the discipline problems I had experienced with some of my own classes were not a function of children who were insufficiently controlled but of a curriculum that was insufficiently engaging. (The students weren't trying to make my life miserable; they were trying to make the time pass faster.) It occurred to me that books on discipline almost never raise the possibility that when a student doesn't do what he is told, the problem may be with what he has been told to do—or to learn.

Of course, none of this would make sense to someone who believed the only alternative to control was chaos. Even if such a teacher found continuing problems in a strictly controlled classroom—especially when she was absent—that might lead her to blame the students and to answer with more discipline, tougher consequences, tighter regulation. And the worse things got, the more "unrealistic" it would seem to her to give up control, the less likely that she would consider bringing the students in on the process of thinking about the kind of classroom that *they* would like to have, and how to make that happen.

No wonder the advice of Rudolf Dreikurs and his followers often seems interchangeable with that of Lee Canter. For example, if a student argues with anything we say, Dreikurs advises us to do the following: "First, you simply reply, 'You may have a point.' Second, you do whatever *you* think is right."[5] No wonder Canter recommends Dreikurs' work and quotes from it. Dreikurs may have talked about democracy, but what he apparently meant was the use of meetings and other "modern" techniques to get students to do what they are told: "It is autocratic to force, but democratic to induce compliance," he and his colleagues wrote.[6]

Classroom-management programs invariably urge teachers to begin the year by taking control and laying out their expectations for student behavior—along with what will be done to those who disobey. But no child ever became more likely to think for herself, or to care about others, in such an environment. To "manage" students' behavior, to make them do what we say, doesn't promote community or compassion, responsibility or reflection. The only way to reach those goals is to give up some control, to facilitate the tricky, noisy, maddening, unpredictable process whereby students work together to decide what respect means or how to be fair.

To help students become ethical people, as opposed to people who merely do what they are told, we cannot merely tell them what to do. We have to help them figure out—for themselves and with each other—how one ought to act. That's why dropping the tools of traditional discipline, like rewards and consequences, is only the beginning. It's even more crucial that we overcome a preoccupation with getting compliance and instead involve students in devising and justifying ethical principles.

And that's why I suggested to my correspondent that a critique of Assertive Discipline made a lot of sense—as long as it was more than a critique of Assertive Discipline.

Notes

1. L. Canter, and M. Canter, *Lee Canter's Assertive Discipline* (Santa Monica, Calif.: Lee Canter & Associates, 1992), p. 180.

2. R. Dreikurs and L. Grey, *Logical Consequences: A New Approach to Discipline* (New York: Plume, 1968/1993), pp. 143–44.

3. L. Albert, *A Teacher's Guide to Cooperative Discipline* (Circle Pines, Minn.: American Guidance Service, 1989), pp. 34, 78.

4. R. L. Curwin and A. N. Mendler, *Discipline with Dignity* (Alexandria, Va.: ASCD, 1988), p. 76.

5. R. Dreikurs and P. Cassel, *Discipline Without Tears* (New York: Plume, 1972/1991), p. 69.

6. R. Dreikurs and others, *Maintaining Sanity in the Classroom,* 2nd ed. (New York: HarperCollins, 1982), p. 67.

CHAPTER FOUR

How Not to Teach Values

A Critical Look at Character Education

Teachers and schools tend to mistake good behavior for good character. What they prize is docility, suggestibility; the child who will do what he is told; or even better, the child who will do what is wanted without even having to be told. They value most in children what children least value in themselves. Small wonder that their effort to build character is such a failure; they don't know it when they see it.

—*John Holt,* How Children Fail

Were you to stand somewhere in the continental United States and announce, "I'm going to Hawaii," it would be understood that you were heading for those islands in the Pacific that collectively constitute the fiftieth state. Were you to stand in Honolulu and make the same statement, however, you would probably be talking about one specific island in the chain—namely, the big one to your southeast. The word *Hawaii* would seem to have two meanings, a broad one and a narrow one; we depend on context to tell them apart.

The phrase *character education* also has two meanings. In the broad sense, it refers to almost anything that schools might try to provide outside of academics, especially when the purpose is to help children

---

Originally published in *Phi Delta Kappan* in 1997.

grow into good people. In the narrow sense, it denotes a particular style of moral training, one that reflects particular values as well as particular assumptions about the nature of children and how they learn.

Unfortunately, the two meanings of the term have become blurred, with the narrow version of character education dominating the field to the point that it is frequently mistaken for the broader concept. Thus educators who are keen to support children's social and moral development may turn, by default, to a program with a certain set of methods and a specific agenda that, on reflection, they might very well find objectionable.

My purpose in this article is to subject these programs to careful scrutiny and, in so doing, to highlight the possibility that there are other ways to achieve our broader objectives. I address myself not so much to those readers who are avid proponents of character education (in the narrow sense) but to those who simply want to help children become decent human beings and may not have thought carefully about what they are being offered.

Let me get straight to the point. What goes by the name of character education nowadays is, for the most part, a collection of exhortations and extrinsic inducements designed to make children work harder and do what they're told. Even when other values are also promoted—caring or fairness, say—the preferred method of instruction is tantamount to indoctrination. The point is to drill students in specific behaviors rather than to engage them in deep, critical reflection about certain ways of being. This is the impression one gets from reading articles and books by contemporary proponents of character education as well as the curriculum materials sold by the leading national programs. The impression is only strengthened by visiting schools that have been singled out for their commitment to character education. To wit:

• *A huge, multiethnic elementary school in Southern California uses a framework created by the Jefferson Center for Character Education. Classes that the principal declares "well behaved" are awarded Bonus Bucks, which can eventually be redeemed for an ice cream party. On an enormous wall near the cafeteria, professionally painted Peanuts characters instruct children: "Never talk in line." A visitor is led to a fifth grade classroom to observe an exemplary lesson on the current character edu-cation topic. The teacher is telling students to write down the name of the person they regard as the "toughest worker" in school. The teacher then asks them, "How many of you are going to be tough workers?" (Hands go up.) "Can you be a tough worker at home, too?" (Yes.)*

• *A small, almost entirely African American school in Chicago uses a framework created by the Character Education Institute. Periodic moti-vational assemblies are used to "give children a good pep talk," as the principal puts it, and to reinforce the values that determine who will be picked as Student of the Month. Rule number one posted on the wall of a kindergarten room is, "We will obey the teachers." Today, students in this class are listening to the story of "Lazy Lion," who orders each of the other animals to build him a house, only to find each effort unacceptable. At the end, the teacher drives home the lesson: "Did you ever hear Lion say thank you?" (No.) "Did you ever hear Lion say please?" (No.) "It's good to always say—what?" (Please.) The reason for using these words, she points out, is that by doing so we are more likely to get what we want.*

• *A charter school near Boston has been established specifically to offer an intensive, homegrown character education curriculum to its over-whelmingly white, middle-class student body. At weekly public cere-monies, certain children receive a leaf that will then be hung in the Forest of Virtue. The virtues themselves are "not open to debate," the headmas-ter insists, because moral precepts in his view enjoy the same status as mathematical truths. In a first grade classroom, a teacher is observing that "it's very hard to be obedient when you want something. I want you to ask yourself, 'Can I have it—and why not?'" She proceeds to ask the students, "What kinds of things show obedience?" and, after collecting a few suggestions, announces that she's "not going to call on anyone else now. We could go on forever, but we have to have a moment of silence and then a spelling test."*

Some of the most popular schoolwide strategies for improving stu-dents' character seem dubious on their face. When President Clinton mentioned the importance of character education in his 1996 State of the Union address, the only specific practice he recommended was re-quiring students to wear uniforms. The premises here are, first, that children's character can be improved by forcing them to dress alike, and second, that if adults object to students' clothing, the best solu-tion is not to invite them to reflect together about how this problem might be solved but instead to compel them all to wear the same thing.

A second strategy, also consistent with the dominant philosophy of character education, is an exercise that might be called "If It's Tuesday, This Must Be Honesty." Here, one value after another is targeted, with each assigned its own day, week, or month. This seriatim approach is unlikely to result in a lasting commitment to any of these values, much less a feeling for how they may be related. Nevertheless, such programs are taken very seriously by some of the same people who are quick to dismiss other educational programs, such as those intended to promote self-esteem, as silly and ineffective.

Then there is the strategy of offering students rewards when they are "caught" being good, an approach favored by right-wing religious groups[1] and orthodox behaviorists but also by leaders of—and curriculum suppliers for—the character education movement.[2] Because of its popularity and because a sizable body of psychological evidence germane to the topic is available, it is worth lingering on this particular practice for a moment.

In general terms, what the evidence suggests is this: the more we reward people for doing something, the more likely they are to lose interest in whatever they had to do to get the reward. Extrinsic motivation, in other words, is not only quite different from intrinsic motivation but actually tends to erode it.[3] This effect has been demonstrated under many different circumstances and with respect to many different attitudes and behaviors. Most relevant to character education is a series of studies showing that individuals who have been rewarded for doing something nice become less likely to think of themselves as caring or helpful people and more likely to attribute their behavior to the reward.

"Extrinsic incentives can, by undermining self-perceived altruism, decrease intrinsic motivation to help others," one group of researchers concluded on the basis of several studies. "A person's kindness, it seems, cannot be bought."[4] The same applies to a person's sense of responsibility, fairness, perseverance, and so on. The lesson a child learns from Skinnerian tactics is that the point of being good is to get rewards. No wonder researchers have found that children who are frequently rewarded—or in another study, children who receive positive reinforcement for caring, sharing, and helping—are less likely than other children to keep doing those things.[5]

In short, it makes no sense to dangle goodies in front of children for being virtuous. But even worse than rewards are *awards*—certificates, plaques, trophies, and other tokens of recognition whose numbers have been artificially limited so only a few can get them. When some children are singled out as "winners," the central message that every child learns is this: "Other people are potential obstacles to my success."[6] Thus the likely result of making students beat out their peers for the distinction of being the most virtuous is not only less intrinsic commitment to virtue but also a disruption of relationships and, ironically, of the experience of community that is so vital to the development of children's character.

Unhappily, the problems with character education (in the narrow sense, which is how I'll be using the term unless otherwise indicated) are not restricted to such strategies as enforcing sartorial uniformity, scheduling a value of the week, or offering students a "doggie biscuit" for being good. More deeply troubling are the fundamental assumptions, both explicit and implicit, that inform character education programs. Let us consider five basic questions that might be asked of any such program: At what level are problems addressed? What is the underlying theory of human nature? What is the ultimate goal? Which values are promoted? And finally, How is learning thought to take place?

1. At what level are problems addressed? One of the major purveyors of materials in this field, the Jefferson Center for Character Education in Pasadena, California, has produced a video that begins with some arresting images—quite literally. Young people are shown being led away in handcuffs, the point being that crime can be explained on the basis of an "erosion of American core values," as the narrator intones ominously. The idea that social problems can be explained by the fact that traditional virtues are no longer taken seriously is offered by many proponents of character education as though it were just plain common sense.

But if people steal or rape or kill solely because they possess bad values—that is, because of their personal characteristics—the implication is that political and economic realities are irrelevant and need not be addressed. Never mind staggering levels of unemployment in the inner cities or a system in which more and more of the nation's wealth is concentrated in fewer and fewer hands; just place the blame on individuals whose characters are deficient. A key tenet of the "Character Counts!" Coalition, which bills itself as a nonpartisan umbrella group devoid of any political agenda, is the highly debatable proposition that "negative social influences can [be] and usually are overcome by the exercise of free will and character."[7] What is presented as common sense is, in fact, conservative ideology.

Let's put politics aside, though. If a program proceeds by trying to "fix the kids"—as do almost all brands of character education—it ignores the accumulated evidence from the field of social psychology demonstrating that much of how we act and who we are reflects the situation in which we find ourselves. Virtually all the landmark studies in this discipline have been variations on this theme. Set up children in an extended team competition at summer camp and you will elicit unprecedented levels of aggression. Assign adults to the roles of prisoners or guards in a mock jail and they will start to become their roles. Move people to a small town and they will be more likely to rescue a stranger in need. In fact, so common is the tendency to attribute to an individual's personality or character what is actually a function of the social environment that social psychologists have dubbed this the "fundamental attribution error."

A similar lesson comes to us from the movement concerned with Total Quality Management, associated with the ideas of the late W. Edwards Deming. At the heart of Deming's teaching is the notion that the "system" of an organization largely determines the results. The problems experienced in a corporation, therefore, are almost always due to systemic flaws rather than to a lack of effort or ability on the part of individuals in that organization. Thus, if we are troubled by the way students are acting, Deming, along with most social psychologists, would presumably have us transform the structure of the classroom rather than try to remake the students themselves—precisely the opposite of the character education approach.

2. What is the view of human nature? Character education's "fix-the-kids" orientation follows logically from the belief that kids need fixing. Indeed, the movement seems to be driven by a stunningly dark view of children—and for that matter, of people in general. A "comprehensive approach [to character education] is based on a somewhat dim view of human nature," acknowledges William Kilpatrick, whose book *Why Johnny Can't Tell Right from Wrong* contains such assertions as, "Most behavior problems are the result of sheer 'willfulness' on the part of children."[8]

Despite—or more likely because of—statements like that, Kilpatrick has frequently been invited to speak at character education conferences.[9] But that shouldn't be surprising in light of how many prominent proponents of character education share his views. Edward Wynne says his own work is grounded in a tradition of thought that takes a "somewhat pessimistic view of human nature."[10] The idea of character development "sees children as self-centered," in the opinion of Kevin Ryan, who directs the Center for the Advancement of Ethics and Character at Boston University as well as heading up the character education network of the Association for Supervision and Curriculum Development.[11] Yet another writer approvingly traces the whole field back to the bleak worldview of Thomas Hobbes: it is "an obvious assumption of character education," writes Louis Goldman, that people lack the instinct to work together. Without laws to compel us to get along, "our natural egoism would lead us into 'a condition of warre one against another.'"[12] This sentiment is echoed by F. Washington Jarvis, headmaster of the Roxbury Latin School in Boston, one of Ryan's favorite examples of what character education should look like in practice. Jarvis sees human nature as "mean, nasty, brutish, selfish, and capable of great cruelty and meanness. We have to hold a mirror up to the students and say, 'This is who you are. Stop it.'"[13]

Even when proponents of character education don't express such sentiments explicitly, they give themselves away by framing their mission as a campaign for self-control. Amitai Etzioni, for example, does not merely include this attribute on a list of good character traits; he *defines* character principally in terms of the capacity "to control impulses and defer gratification."[14] This is noteworthy because the virtue of self-restraint—or at least the decision to give special emphasis to it—has historically been preached by those, from St. Augustine's day to the present, who see people as basically sinful.

In fact, at least three assumptions seem to be at work when the need for self-control is stressed: first, that we are all at war not only with others but with ourselves, torn between our desires and our reason (or social norms); second, that these desires are fundamentally selfish, aggressive, or otherwise unpleasant; and third, that these desires are very strong, constantly threatening to overpower us if we don't rein them in. Collectively, these statements describe religious dogma, not scientific fact. Indeed, the evidence from several disciplines converges to cast doubt on this sour view of human beings and instead supports the idea that it is as "natural" for children to help as to hurt. I will not rehearse that evidence here, partly because I have done so elsewhere at some length.[15] Suffice it to say that even the most hardheaded empiricist might well conclude that the promotion of prosocial values consists to some extent of supporting (rather than restraining or controlling) many facets of the self. Any educator who adopts this more balanced position might think twice before joining an educational movement that is finally inseparable from the doctrine of original sin.

3. What is the ultimate goal? It may seem odd even to inquire about someone's reasons for trying to improve children's character. But it is worth mentioning that the whole enterprise—not merely the particular values that are favored—is often animated by a profoundly conservative, if not reactionary, agenda. Character education based on "acculturating students to conventional norms of 'good' behavior . . . resonates with neoconservative concerns for social stability," observed David Purpel.[16] The movement has been described by another critic as a "yearning for some halcyon days of moral niceties and social tranquillity."[17] But it is not merely a *social* order that some are anxious to preserve (or recover): character education is vital, according to one vocal proponent, because "the development of character is the backbone of the economic system" now in place.[18]

Character education, or any kind of education, would look very different if we began with other objectives—if, for example, we were principally concerned with helping children become active participants in a democratic society (or agents for transforming a society *into* one that is authentically democratic). It would look different if our top priority were to help students develop into principled and caring members of a community or advocates for social justice. To be sure, these objectives are not inconsistent with the desire to preserve certain traditions, but the point would then be to help children decide which traditions are worth preserving and why, based on these other considerations. That is not at all the same as endorsing anything that is traditional or making the preservation of tradition our primary concern. In short, we want to ask character education proponents what goals they emphasize—and ponder whether their broad vision is compatible with our own.

4. Which values? Should we allow values to be taught in school? The question is about as sensible as asking whether our bodies should be allowed to contain bacteria. Just as humans are teeming with microorganisms, so schools are teeming with values. We can't see the former because they're too small; we don't notice the latter because they're too similar to the values of the culture at large. Whether or not we deliberately adopt a character or moral education program, we are always teaching values. Even people who insist that they are opposed to values in school usually mean that they are opposed to values other than their own.[19]

And that raises the inevitable question: Which values, or whose, should we teach? It has already become a cliché to reply that this question should not trouble us because, while there may be disagreement on certain issues, such as abortion, all of us can agree on a list of basic values that children ought to have. Therefore, schools can vigorously and unapologetically set about teaching all of those values.

But not so fast. Look at the way character education programs have been designed and you will discover, alongside such unobjectionable items as "fairness" or "honesty," an emphasis on values that are, again, distinctly conservative—and to that extent, potentially controversial. To begin with, the famous Protestant work ethic is prominent: children should learn to "work hard and complete their tasks well and promptly, even when they do not want to," says Ryan.[20] Here the Latin question *Cui bono?* comes to mind. Who benefits when people are trained not to question the value of what they have been told to do but simply to toil away at it—and to regard this as virtuous?[21] Similarly, when Wynne defines the moral individual as someone who is not only honest but also "diligent, obedient, and patriotic,"[22] readers may find themselves wondering whether these traits really qualify as *moral*—as well as reflecting on the virtues that are missing from this list.

Character education curricula also stress the importance of things like "respect," "responsibility," and "citizenship." But these are slippery terms, frequently used as euphemisms for uncritical deference to authority. Under the headline "The Return of the 'Fourth R'"—referring to "respect, responsibility, or rules"—a news magazine recently described the growing popularity of such practices as requiring uniforms, paddling disobedient students, rewarding those who are compliant, and "throwing disruptive kids out of the classroom."[23] Indeed, William Glasser observed some time ago that many educators "teach thoughtless conformity to school rules and call the conforming child 'responsible.'"[24] I once taught at a high school where the principal frequently exhorted students to "take responsibility." By this he meant specifically that they should turn in their friends who used drugs.

Exhorting students to be "respectful" or rewarding them if they are caught being "good" may likewise mean nothing more than getting them to do whatever the adults demand. Following a lengthy article about character education in the *New York Times Magazine,* a reader mused, "Do you suppose that if Germany had had character education at the time, it would have encouraged children to fight Nazism or to support it?"[25] The more time I spend in schools that are enthusiastically implementing character education programs, the more I am haunted by that question.

In place of the traditional attributes associated with character education, Deborah Meier and Paul Schwarz of the Central Park East Secondary School in New York nominated two core values that a school might try to promote: "empathy and skepticism: the ability to see a situation from the eyes of another and the tendency to wonder about the validity of what we encountered."[26] Anyone who brushes away the question "Which values should be taught?" might speculate on the concrete differences between a school dedicated to turning out students who are empathic and skeptical and a school dedicated to turning out students who are loyal, patriotic, obedient, and so on.

Meanwhile, in place of such personal qualities as punctuality or perseverance, we might emphasize the cultivation of autonomy so that children come to experience themselves as "origins" rather than "pawns," as one researcher put it.[27] We might, in other words, stress self-determination at least as much as self-control. With such an agenda, it would be crucial to give students the chance to participate in making decisions about their learning and about how they want their classroom to be.[28] This stands in sharp contrast to a philosophy of character education like Wynne's, which decrees that "it is specious to talk about student choices" and offers students no real power except for when we give "some students authority over other students (for example, hall guard, class monitor)."[29]

Even with values that are widely shared, a superficial consensus may dissolve when we take a closer look. Educators across the spectrum are concerned about excessive attention to self-interest and are committed to helping students transcend a preoccupation with their own needs. But how does this concern play out in practice? For some of us, it takes the form of an emphasis on *compassion;* for the dominant character education approach, the alternative value to be stressed is *loyalty,* which is, of course, altogether different.[30] Moreover, as John Dewey remarked at the turn of the century, anyone seriously troubled about rampant individualism among children would promptly target for extinction the "drill-and-skill" approach to instruction: "The mere absorbing of facts and truths is so exclusively individual an affair that it tends very naturally to pass into selfishness."[31] Yet conservative champions of character education are often among the most outspoken supporters of a model of teaching that emphasizes rote memorization and the sequential acquisition of decontextualized skills.

Or take another example: all of us may say we endorse the idea of "cooperation," but what do we make of the practice of setting groups against one another in a quest for triumph, such that cooperation becomes the means and victory is the end? On the one hand, we might find this even more objectionable than individual competition. (Indeed, we might regard a "We're Number One!" ethic as a reason for schools to undertake something like character education in the first place.) On the other hand, "school-to-school, class-to-class, or row-to-row academic competitions" actually have been endorsed as part of a character education program,[32] along with contests that lead to awards for things like good citizenship.

The point, once again, is that it is entirely appropriate to ask which values a character education program is attempting to foster, notwithstanding the ostensible lack of controversy about a list of core values. It is equally appropriate to put such a discussion in context—specifically, in the context of which values are *currently* promoted in schools. The fact is that schools are already powerful socializers of traditional values—although, as noted above, we may fail to appreciate the extent to which this is true because we have come to take these values for granted. In most schools, for example, students are taught—indeed, compelled—to follow the rules regardless of whether the rules are reasonable and to respect authority regardless of whether that respect has been earned. (This process isn't always successful, of course, but that is a different matter.) Students are led to accept competition as natural and desirable, and to see themselves more as discrete individuals than as members of a community. Children in American schools are even expected to begin each day by reciting a loyalty oath to the Fatherland, although we call it by a different name. In short, the question is not whether to adopt the conservative values offered by most character education programs, but whether we want to consolidate the conservative values that are already in place.

5. What is the theory of learning? We come now to what may be the most significant, and yet the least remarked on, feature of character education: the way values are taught and the way learning is thought to take place.

The character education coordinator for the small Chicago elementary school also teaches second grade. In her classroom, where one boy has been forced to sit by himself for the last two weeks ("He's kind of pesty"), she is asking the children to define tolerance. When the teacher gets the specific answers she is fishing for, she exclaims, "Say that again," and writes down only those responses. Later comes the moral: "If somebody doesn't think the way you think, should you turn them off?" (No.)

Down the hall, the first grade teacher is fishing for answers on a different subject. "When we play games, we try to understand the—what?" (Rules.) A moment later, the children scramble to get into place so she will pick them to tell a visitor their carefully rehearsed stories about conflict resolution. Almost every child's account, narrated with considerable prompting by the teacher, concerns name-calling or some other unpleasant incident that was "correctly" resolved by finding an adult. The teacher never asks the children how they felt about what happened or invites them to reflect on what else might have been done. She wraps up the activity by saying, "What we need to do all the time is clarify—make it clear—to the adult what you did."

The schools with character education programs that I have visited are engaged largely in exhortation and directed recitation. At first one might assume that this is due to poor implementation of the programs on the part of individual educators. But the programs themselves— and the theorists who promote them—really do seem to regard teaching as a matter of telling and compelling. For example, the broad-based "Character Counts!" Coalition offers a framework of six core character traits and then asserts that "young people should be specifically and repeatedly told what is expected of them." The leading providers of curriculum materials walk teachers through highly structured lessons in which character-related concepts are described, and then students are drilled until they can produce the right answers.

Teachers are encouraged to praise children who respond correctly, and some programs actually include multiple-choice tests to ensure that students have learned their values. For example, here are two sample test questions prepared for teachers by the Character Education Institute, based in San Antonio, Texas: "Having to obey rules and regulations (a) gives everyone the same right to be an individual, (b) forces everyone to do the same thing at all times, (c) prevents persons from expressing their individually [sic]"; and "One reason why parents might not allow their children freedom of choice is (a) children are always happier when they are told what to do and when to do it,

(b) parents aren't given a freedom of choice; therefore, children should not be given a choice either, (c) children do not always demonstrate that they are responsible enough to be given a choice." The correct answers, according to the answer key, are (a) and (c) respectively.

The Character Education Institute recommends "engaging the students in discussions," but only discussions of a particular sort: "Since the lessons have been designed to logically guide the students to the right answers, the teacher should allow the students to draw their own conclusions. However, if the students draw the wrong conclusion, the teacher is instructed to tell them why their conclusion is *wrong*."[33]

Students are told what to think and do not only by their teachers but by highly didactic stories, such as those in the Character Education Institute's "Happy Life" series, which end with characters saying things like "I am glad that I did not cheat," or "Next time I will be helpful," or "I will never be selfish again." Most character education programs also deliver homilies by way of posters and banners and murals displayed throughout the school. Children who do as they are told are presented with all manner of rewards, typically in front of their peers.

Does all of this amount to indoctrination? Absolutely, says Wynne, who declares that "school is and should and must be inherently indoctrinative."[34] Even when character education proponents tiptoe around that word, their model of instruction is clear: good character and values are *instilled in* or *transmitted to* students. We are "planting the ideas of virtue, of good traits in the young," says William Bennett.[35] The virtues or values in question are fully formed, and, in the minds of many character education proponents, divinely ordained. The children are—pick your favorite metaphor—so many passive receptacles to be filled, lumps of clay to be molded, pets to be trained, or computers to be programmed.

Thus, when we see Citizen-of-the-Month certificates and "Be a good sport!" posters, when we find teachers assigning preachy stories and principals telling students what to wear, it is important that we understand what is going on. These techniques may appear merely innocuous or gimmicky: they may strike us as evidence of a scattershot, let's-try-anything approach. But the truth is that these are elements of a systematic pedagogical philosophy. They are manifestations of a model that sees children as objects to be manipulated rather than as learners to be engaged.

Ironically, some people who accept character education without a second thought are quite articulate about the bankruptcy of this

model when it comes to teaching academic subjects. Plenty of teachers have abandoned the use of worksheets, textbooks, and lectures that
fill children full of disconnected facts and skills. Plenty of administrators are working to create schools where students can actively construct meaning around scientific and historical and literary concepts.
Plenty of educators, in short, realize that memorizing right answers
and algorithms doesn't help anyone to arrive at a deep understanding
of ideas.

And so we are left scratching our heads. Why would all these people, who know that the "transmission" model fails to facilitate intellectual development, uncritically accept the very same model to promote
ethical development? How could they understand that mathematical
truths cannot be shoved down students' throats but then participate in
a program that essentially tries to shove moral truths down the same
throats? In the case of individual educators, the simple answer may be
that they missed the connection. Perhaps they just failed to recognize
that "a classroom cannot foster the development of autonomy in the
intellectual realm while suppressing it in the social and moral realms,"
as Constance Kamii and her colleagues put it not long ago.[36]

In the case of the proponents of character education, I believe the
answer to this riddle is quite different. The reason they are promoting
techniques that seem strikingly ineffective at fostering autonomy or
ethical development is that, as a rule, they are not *trying* to foster autonomy or ethical development. The goal is not to support or facilitate children's social and moral growth, but simply to "demand good
behavior from students," in Ryan's words.[37] The idea is to get compliance, to *make* children act the way we want them to.

Indeed, if these are the goals, then the methods make perfect
sense—the lectures and pseudo-discussions, the slogans and the stories that conk students on the head with their morals. David Brooks,
who heads the Jefferson Center for Character Education, frankly states,
"We're in the advertising business." The way you get people to do
something, whether it's buying Rice Krispies or becoming trustwor-
thy, is to "encourage conformity through repeated messages."[38] The
idea of selling virtues like cereal nearly reaches the point of self-parody
in the Jefferson Center's curriculum, which includes the following activity: "There's a new product on the market! It's Considerate Cereal.
Eating it can make a person more considerate. Design a label for the
box. Tell why someone should buy and eat this cereal. Then list the
ingredients."[39]

If "repeated messages" don't work, then you simply force students to conform: "Sometimes compulsion is what is needed to get a habit started," says William Kilpatrick.[40] We may recoil from the word *compulsion*, but it is the premise of that sentence that really ought to give us pause. When education is construed as the process of inculcating *habits*—which is to say, unreflective actions—then it scarcely deserves to be called education at all. It is really, as Alan Lockwood saw, an attempt to get "mindless conformity to externally imposed standards of conduct."[41]

Notice how naturally this goal follows from a dark view of human nature. If you begin with the premise that "good conduct is not our natural first choice," then the best you can hope for is "the development of good habits"[42]—that is, a system that gets people to act unthinkingly in the manner that someone else has deemed appropriate. This connection recently became clear to Ann Medlock, whose Giraffe Project was designed to evoke "students' own courage and compassion" in thinking about altruism, but which, in some schools, was being turned into a traditional, authoritarian program in which students were simply told how to act and what to believe. Medlock recalls suddenly realizing what was going on with these educators: "Oh, *I* see where you're coming from. You believe kids are no damn good!"[43]

The character education movement's emphasis on habit, then, is consistent with its view of children. Likewise, its process matches its product. The transmission model, along with the use of rewards and punishments to secure compliance, seems entirely appropriate if the values you are trying to transmit are things like obedience and loyalty and respect for authority. But this approach overlooks an important distinction between product and process. When we argue about which traits to emphasize—compassion or loyalty, cooperation or competition, skepticism or obedience—we are trafficking in value judgments. When we talk about how best to teach these things, however, we are being descriptive rather than just prescriptive. Even if you like the sort of virtues that appear in character education programs, and even if you regard the need to implement those virtues as urgent, the attempt to transmit or instill them dooms the project because that is just not consistent with the best theory and research on how people learn. (Of course, if you have reservations about many of the values that the character educators wish to instill, you may be *relieved* that their favored method is unlikely to be successful.)

I don't wish to be misunderstood. The techniques of character education may succeed in temporarily buying a particular behavior. But they are unlikely to leave children with a *commitment* to that behavior, a reason to continue acting that way in the future. You can turn out automatons who utter the desired words or maybe even "emit" (to use the curious verb favored by behaviorists) the desired actions. But the words and actions are unlikely to continue—much less transfer to new situations—because the child has not been invited to integrate them into his or her value structure. As Dewey observed, "The required beliefs cannot be hammered in; the needed attitudes cannot be plastered on."[44] Yet watch a character education lesson in any part of the country and you will almost surely be observing a strenuous exercise in hammering and plastering.

For traditional moralists, the constructivist approach is a waste of time. If values and traditions and the stories that embody them already exist, then surely "we don't have to reinvent the wheel," remarks Bennett.[45] Likewise an exasperated Wynne: "Must each generation try to completely reinvent society?"[46] The answer is no—and yes. It is not as though everything that now exists must be discarded and entirely new values fashioned from scratch. But the process of learning does indeed require that meaning, ethical or otherwise, be actively invented and reinvented, from the inside out. It requires that children be given the opportunity to make sense of such concepts as fairness or courage, regardless of how long the concepts themselves have been around. Children must be invited to reflect on complex issues, to recast them in light of their own experiences and questions, to figure out for themselves—and with one another—what kind of person one ought to be, which traditions are worth keeping, and how to proceed when two basic values seem to be in conflict.[47]

In this sense, reinvention is necessary if we want to help children become moral people, as opposed to people who merely do what they are told—or reflexively rebel against what they are told. In fact, as Rheta DeVries and Betty Zan add (in a recent book that offers a useful antidote to traditional character education), "If we want children to resist [peer pressure] and not be victims of others' ideas, we have to educate children to think for themselves about all ideas, including those of adults."[48]

Traditionalists are even more likely to offer another objection to the constructivist approach, one that boils down to a single epithet:

relativism! If we do anything other than insert moral absolutes in students, if we let them construct their own meanings, then we are saying that anything goes, that morality collapses into personal preferences. Without character education, our schools will just offer programs such as Values Clarification, in which adults are allegedly prohibited from taking a stand.

In response, I would offer several observations. First, the Values Clarification model of moral education, popular in some circles a generation ago, survives today mostly in the polemics of conservatives anxious to justify an indoctrinative approach. Naturally, no statistics are ever cited as to the number of school districts still telling students that any value is as good as any other—assuming the program actually said that in the first place.[49] Second, conservative critics tendentiously try to connect constructivism to relativism, lumping together the work of the late Lawrence Kohlberg with programs like Values Clarification.[50] The truth is that Kohlberg, while opposed to what he called the "bag of virtues" approach to moral education, was not much enamored of Values Clarification either, and he spent a fair amount of time arguing against relativism in general.[51]

If Kohlberg can fairly be criticized, it is for emphasizing moral reasoning, a cognitive process, to the extent that he may have slighted the affective components of morality, such as caring. But the traditionalists are not much for the latter either: caring is seen as an easy or soft virtue (Ryan) that isn't sufficiently "binding or absolute" (Kilpatrick). The objection to constructivism is not that empathy is eclipsed by justice, but that children—or even adults—should not have an active role to play in making decisions and reflecting on how to live. They should be led instead to an uncritical acceptance of ready-made truths. The character educator's job, remember, is to elicit the right answer from students and tell those who see things differently "why their conclusion is *wrong.*" Any deviation from this approach is regarded as indistinguishable from full-blown relativism; we must "plant" traditional values in each child or else morality is nothing more than a matter of individual taste. Such either/or thinking, long since discarded by serious moral philosophers,[52] continues to fuel character education and to perpetuate the confusion of education with indoctrination.

To say that students must construct meaning around moral concepts is not to deny that adults have a crucial role to play. The romantic view that children can basically educate themselves so long as grown-ups don't interfere is not taken seriously by any constructivists

I know of—certainly not by Dewey, Piaget, Kohlberg, or their followers. Rather, like Values Clarification, this view seems to exist principally as a straw man in the arguments of conservatives. Let there be no question, then: educators, parents, and other adults are desperately needed to offer guidance, to act as models (we hope), to pose challenges that promote moral growth, and to help children understand the effects of their actions on other people, thereby tapping and nurturing a concern for others that is present in children from a very young age.[53]

Character education rests on three ideological legs: behaviorism, conservatism, and religion. Of these, the third raises the most delicate issues for a critic; it is here that the charge of *ad hominem* argument is most likely to be raised. So let us be clear: it is of no relevance that almost all of the leading proponents of character education are devout Catholics. But it is entirely relevant that, in the shadows of their writings, there lurks the assumption that only religion can serve as the foundation for good character. (William Bennett, for example, has flatly asserted that the difference between right and wrong cannot be taught "without reference to religion."[54]) It is appropriate to consider the personal beliefs of these individuals if those beliefs are ensconced in the movement they have defined and directed. What they do on Sundays is their own business, but if they are trying to turn our public schools into Sunday schools, that becomes everybody's business.

Even putting aside the theological underpinnings of the character education movement, the five questions presented in this chapter can help us describe the natural constituency of that movement. Logically, its supporters should be those who firmly believe that we should focus our efforts on repairing the characters of children rather than on transforming the environments in which they learn, those who assume the worst about human nature, those who are more committed to preserving than to changing our society, those who favor such values as obedience to authority, and those who define learning as the process of swallowing whole a set of preexisting truths. It stands to reason that readers who recognize themselves in this description would enthusiastically endorse character education in its present form.

The rest of us have a decision to make. Either we define our efforts to promote children's social and moral development as an *alternative* to "character education," thereby ceding that label to the people who have already appropriated it, or we try to *reclaim* the wider meaning of the term by billing what we are doing as a different kind of character education.

The first choice—opting out—seems logical: it strains the language to use a single phrase to describe practices as different as engaging students in reflecting about fairness, on the one hand, and making students dress alike, on the other. It seems foolish to pretend that these are just different versions of the same thing, and thus it may be unreasonable to expect someone with a constructivist or progressive vision to endorse what is now called character education. The problem with abandoning this label, however, is that it holds considerable appeal for politicians and members of the public at large. It will be challenging to explain that "character education" is not synonymous with helping children to grow into good people and, indeed, that the movement associated with the term is a good deal more controversial than it first appears.

The second choice, meanwhile, presents its own set of practical difficulties. Given that the individuals and organizations mentioned in this article have succeeded in putting their own stamp on character education, it will not be easy to redefine the phrase so that it can also signify a very different approach. It will not be easy, that is, to organize conferences, publish books and articles, and develop curricular materials that rescue the broad meaning of "character education."

Whether we relinquish or retain the nomenclature, though, it is vital that we work to decouple most of what takes place under the banner of "character education" from the enterprise of helping students become ethically sophisticated decision makers and caring human beings. Wanting young people to turn out that way doesn't require us to adopt traditional character education programs any more than wanting them to be physically fit requires us to turn schools into Marine boot camps.

What does the alternative look like? Return once more to those five questions: in each case, an answer different from that given by traditional character education will help us to sketch the broad contours of a divergent approach. More specifically, we should probably target certain practices for elimination, add some new ones, and reconfigure still others that already exist. I have already offered a catalogue of examples of what to eliminate, from Skinnerian reinforcers to lesson plans that resemble sermons. As examples of what to add, we might suggest holding regular class meetings in which students can share, plan, decide, and reflect together.[55] We might also provide children with explicit opportunities to practice "perspective taking"—that is, imagining how the world looks from someone else's point of view. Activities that promote an understanding of how others think and feel, that support the impulse to reach imaginatively beyond the self, can provide the same benefits realized by holding democratic class meetings—namely, helping students to become more ethical and compassionate while simultaneously fostering intellectual growth.[56]

A good example of an existing practice that might be reconfigured is the use of literature to teach values. In principle, the idea is splendid: it makes perfect sense to select stories that not only help students develop reading skills (and an appreciation for good writing) but also raise moral issues. The trouble is that many programs use simplistic little morality tales in place of rich, complex literature. Naturally, the texts should be developmentally appropriate, but some character educators fail to give children credit for being able to grapple with ambiguity. (Imagine the sort of stories likely to be assigned by someone who maintains that "it is ridiculous to believe children are capable of objectively assessing most of the beliefs and values they must absorb to be effective adults."[57])

Perhaps the concern is not that students will be unable to make sense of challenging literature, but that they will not derive the "correct" moral. This would account for the fact that even when character education curricula include impressive pieces of writing, the works tend to be used for the purpose of drumming in simple lessons. As Kilpatrick sees it, a story "points to these [characters] and says in effect, 'Act like this; don't act like that.'"[58] This kind of lesson often takes the form of hero worship, with larger-than-life characters—or real historical figures presented with their foibles airbrushed away—held up to students to encourage imitation of their actions.

Rather than employ literature to indoctrinate or induce mere conformity, we can use it to spur reflection. Whether the students are six–year–olds or sixteen–year–olds, the discussion of stories should be open-ended rather than relentlessly didactic. Teachers who refrain from tightly controlling such conversations are impressed again and again by the levels of meaning students prove capable of exploring and the moral growth they exhibit in such an environment. Instead of announcing, "This man is a hero; do what he did," such teachers may involve the students in *deciding* who (if anyone) is heroic in a given story—or in contemporary culture—and why.[59] They may even invite students to reflect on the larger issue of whether it is desirable to have heroes. (Consider the quality of discussion that might be generated by asking older students to respond to the declaration of playwright Bertolt Brecht: "Unhappy is the land that needs a hero.")

More than specific practices that might be added, subtracted, or changed, a program to help children grow into good people begins with a commitment to change the way classrooms and schools are structured—and this brings us back to the idea of transcending a fix-the-kid approach. Consider the format of classroom discussions. A proponent of character education, invoking such traditional virtues as patience or self-control, might remind students that they must wait to be recognized by the teacher. But what if we invited students to think about the best way to conduct a discussion? Must we raise our hands? Is there another way to avoid having everyone talk at once? How can we be fair to those who aren't as assertive or as fast on their feet? Should the power to decide who can speak always rest with the teacher? Perhaps the problem is not with students who need to be more self-disciplined, but with the whole instructional design that has students waiting to be recognized to answer someone else's questions. And perhaps the real learning comes only when students have the chance to grapple with such issues.

One more example: A proponent of character education says we must make students understand that it is wrong to lie; we need to teach them about the importance of being honest. But why do people lie? Usually because they don't feel safe enough to tell the truth. The real challenge for us as educators is to examine that precept in terms of what is going on in our classrooms, to ask how we and the students together can make sure that even unpleasant truths can be told and heard. Does pursuing this line of inquiry mean that it's acceptable to fib? No. It means the problem has to be dissected and solved from the inside out. It means behaviors occur in a context that teachers have helped to establish; therefore, teachers have to examine (and consider modifying) that context even at the risk of some discomfort to themselves. In short, if we want to help children grow into compassionate and responsible people, we have to change the way the classroom works and feels, not just the way each separate member of that class acts. Our emphasis should not be on forming individual characters so much as on transforming educational structures.

Happily, programs do exist whose promotion of children's social and moral development is grounded in a commitment to change the culture of schools. The best example of which I am aware is the Child Development Project (CDP), an elementary school program designed, implemented, and researched by the Developmental Studies Center in Oakland, California. The CDP's premise is that by meeting children's needs we increase the likelihood that they will care about others. Meeting their needs entails, among other things, turning schools into caring communities. The CDP offers the additional advantages of a constructivist vision of learning, a positive view of human nature, a balance of cognitive and affective concerns, and a program that is integrated into all aspects of school life (including the curriculum).[60]

Is the CDP an example of what character education ought to be—or of what ought to replace character education? The answer to that question will depend on tactical, and even semantic, considerations. Far more compelling is the need to reevaluate the practices and premises of contemporary character education. To realize a humane and progressive vision for children's development, we may need to look elsewhere.

Notes

1. See, for example, Linda Page, "A Conservative Christian View on Values," *School Administrator,* Sept. 1995, p. 22.
2. See, for example, Kevin Ryan, "The Ten Commandments of Character Education," *School Administrator,* Sept. 1995, p. 19; and program materials from the Character Education Institute and the Jefferson Center for Character Education.
3. See Alfie Kohn, *Punished by Rewards: The Trouble with Gold Stars, Incentive Plans, A's, Praise, and Other Bribes* (Boston: Houghton Mifflin, 1993); and Edward L. Deci and Richard M. Ryan, *Intrinsic Motivation and Self-Determination in Human Behavior* (New York: Plenum, 1985).
4. See C. Daniel Batson and others, "Buying Kindness: Effect of an Extrinsic Incentive for Helping on Perceived Altruism," *Personality and Social Psychology Bulletin,* vol. 4, 1978, p. 90; Cathleen L. Smith and others, "Children's Causal Attributions Regarding Help Giving," *Child Development,* vol. 50, 1979, pp. 203–210; and William Edward Upton III, "Altruism, Attribution, and Intrinsic Motivation in the Recruitment of Blood Donors," *Dissertation Abstracts International* 34B, vol. 12, 1974, p. 6260.
5. Richard A. Fabes and others, "Effects of Rewards on Children's Prosocial Motivation: A Socialization Study," *Developmental Psychology,* vol. 25, 1989,

pp. 509–515; and Joan Grusec, "Socializing Concern for Others in the Home," *Developmental Psychology,* vol. 27, 1991, pp. 338–342.

6. See Alfie Kohn, *No Contest: The Case Against Competition,* rev. ed. (Boston: Houghton Mifflin, 1992).

7. This statement is taken from an eight-page brochure produced by the "Character Counts!" Coalition, a project of the Josephson Institute of Ethics. Members of the coalition include the American Federation of Teachers, the National Association of Secondary School Principals, the American Red Cross, the YMCA, and many other organizations.

8. William Kilpatrick, *Why Johnny Can't Tell Right from Wrong* (New York: Simon & Schuster, 1992), pp. 96, 249.

9. For example, Kilpatrick was selected in 1995 to keynote the first in a series of summer institutes on character education sponsored by Thomas Lickona.

10. Edward Wynne, "Transmitting Traditional Values in Contemporary Schools," in Larry P. Nucci, ed., *Moral Development and Character Education: A Dialogue* (Berkeley, Calif.: McCutchan, 1989), p. 25.

11. Kevin Ryan, "In Defense of Character Education," in Nucci, p. 16.

12. Louis Goldman, "Mind, Character, and the Deferral of Gratification," *Educational Forum,* vol. 60, 1996, p. 136. As part of "educational reconstruction," he goes on to say, we must "connect the lower social classes to the middle classes who may provide role models for self-discipline" (p. 139).

13. Jarvis is quoted in Wray Herbert, "The Moral Child," *U.S. News & World Report,* June 3, 1996, p. 58.

14. Amitai Etzioni, *The Spirit of Community: The Reinvention of American Society* (New York: Simon & Schuster, 1993), p. 91.

15. See Alfie Kohn, *The Brighter Side of Human Nature: Altruism and Empathy in Everyday Life* (New York: Basic Books, 1990); and "Caring Kids: The Role of the Schools," *Phi Delta Kappan,* March 1991, pp. 496–506 (reprinted in this volume as Chapter Seventeen).

16. David E. Purpel, "Moral Education: An Idea Whose Time Has Gone," *The Clearing House,* vol. 64, 1991, p. 311.

17. This description of the character education movement is offered by Alan L. Lockwood in "Character Education: The Ten Percent Solution," *Social Education,* Apr./May 1991, p. 246. It is a particularly apt characterization of a book like *Why Johnny Can't Tell Right from Wrong,* which invokes an age of "chivalry" and sexual abstinence, a time when moral truths were uncomplicated and unchallenged. The author's tone, however, is not so much wistful about the past as angry about the present: he denounces everything from rock music (which occupies an entire chapter in a book about morality) and feminism to the "multiculturalists" who dare to remove "homosexuality from the universe of moral judgment" (p. 126).

18. Kevin Walsh of the University of Alabama is quoted in Eric N. Berg, "Argument Grows That Teaching of Values Should Rank with Lessons," *New York Times*, Jan. 1, 1992, p. 32.

19. I am reminded of a woman in a Houston audience who heatedly informed me that she doesn't send her child to school "to learn to be nice." That, she declared, would be "social engineering." But a moment later this woman added that her child ought to be "taught to respect authority." Since this would seem to be at least as apposite an example of social engineering, one is led to conclude that the woman's real objection was to the teaching of *particular* topics or values.

20. Kevin Ryan, "Mining the Values in the Curriculum," *Educational Leadership*, Nov. 1993, p. 16.

21. Telling students to "try hard" and "do their best" begs the important questions. *How*, exactly, do they do their best? Surely it is not just a matter of blind effort. And *why* should they do so, particularly if the task is not engaging or meaningful to them, or if it has simply been imposed on them? Research has found that the attitudes students take toward learning are heavily influenced by whether they have been led to attribute their success (or failure) to innate ability, to effort, or to other factors—and that traditional classroom practices such as grading and competition lead them to explain the results in terms of ability (or its absence) and to minimize effort whenever possible. What looks like "laziness" or insufficient perseverance, in other words, often turns out to be a rational decision to avoid challenge; it is rational because this route proves most expedient for performing well or maintaining an image of oneself as smart. These systemic factors, of course, are complex and often threatening for educators to address; it is much easier just to impress on children the importance of doing their best and then blame them for lacking perseverance if they seem not to do so.

22. Edward A. Wynne, "The Great Tradition in Education: Transmitting Moral Values," *Educational Leadership*, Dec. 1985/Jan. 1986, p. 6.

23. Mary Lord, "The Return of the 'Fourth R,'" *U.S. News & World Report*, Sept. 11, 1995, p. 58.

24. William Glasser, *Schools Without Failure* (New York: Harper & Row, 1969), p. 22.

25. Marc Desmond's letter appeared in the *New York Times Magazine*, May 21, 1995, p. 14. The same point was made by Robert Primack, "No Substitute for Critical Thinking: A Response to Wynne," *Educational Leadership*, Dec. 1985/Jan. 1986, p. 12.

26. Deborah Meier and Paul Schwarz, "Central Park East Secondary School," in Michael W. Apple and James A. Beane, eds., *Democratic Schools* (Alexandria, Va.: Association for Supervision and Curriculum Development, 1995), pp. 29–30.

27. See Richard de Charms, *Personal Causation: The Internal Affective Determinants of Behavior* (Hillsdale, N.J.: Erlbaum, 1983). See also the many publications of Edward Deci and Richard Ryan.

28. See, for example, Alfie Kohn, "Choices for Children: Why and How to Let Students Decide," *Phi Delta Kappan*, Sept. 1993, pp. 8–20 (reprinted in this volume as Chapter Eighteen); and Child Development Project, *Ways We Want Our Class to Be: Class Meetings That Build Commitment to Kindness and Learning* (Oakland, Calif.: Developmental Studies Center, 1996).

29. The quotations are from Wynne, "The Great Tradition," p. 9; and Edward A. Wynne and Herbert J. Walberg, "The Complementary Goals of Character Development and Academic Excellence," *Educational Leadership*, Dec. 1985/Jan. 1986, p. 17. William Kilpatrick is equally averse to including students in decision making; he speaks longingly of the days when "schools were unapologetically authoritarian," declaring that "schools can learn a lot from the Army," which is a "hierarchial [sic], authoritarian, and undemocratic institution" (see *Why Johnny Can't*, p. 228).

30. The sort of compassion I have in mind is akin to what the psychologist Ervin Staub described as a "prosocial orientation" (see his *Positive Social Behavior and Morality*, vols. 1 and 2 [New York: Academic Press, 1978 and 1979])—a generalized inclination to care, share, and help across different situations and with different people, including those we don't know, don't like, and don't look like. Loyally lending a hand to a close friend is one thing; going out of one's way for a stranger is something else.

31. John Dewey, *The School and Society* (Chicago: University of Chicago Press, 1900; reprint, 1990), p. 15.

32. Wynne and Walberg, p. 17. For another endorsement of competition among students, see Kevin Ryan, "In Defense," p. 15.

33. This passage is taken from page 21 of an undated twenty-eight–page "Character Education Curriculum" produced by the Character Education Institute. Emphasis in original.

34. Wynne, "Great Tradition," p. 9. Wynne and other figures in the character education movement acknowledge their debt to the French social scientist Emile Durkheim, who believed that "all education is a continuous effort to impose on the child ways of seeing, feeling, and acting which he could not have arrived at spontaneously. . . . We exert pressure upon him in order that he may learn proper consideration for others, respect for customs and conventions, the need for work, etc." (See Durkheim, *The Rules of Sociological Method* [New York: Free Press, 1938], p. 6.)

35. This is from Bennett's introduction to *The Book of Virtues* (New York: Simon & Schuster, 1993), pp. 12–13.

36. Constance Kamii, Faye B. Clark, and Ann Dominick, "The Six National Goals: A Road to Disappointment," *Phi Delta Kappan,* May 1994, p. 677.

37. Kevin Ryan, "Character and Coffee Mugs," *Education Week,* May 17, 1995, p. 48.

38. The second quotation is a reporter's paraphrase of Brooks. Both it and the direct quotation preceding it appear in Philip Cohen, "The Content of Their Character: Educators Find New Ways to Tackle Values and Morality," *ASCD Curriculum Update,* Spring 1995, p. 4.

39. See B. David Brooks, *Young People's Lessons in Character: Student Activity Workbook* (San Diego: Young People's Press, 1996), p. 12.

40. Kilpatrick, p. 231.

41. To advocate this sort of enterprise, he adds, is to "caricature the moral life." See Alan L. Lockwood, "Keeping Them in the Courtyard: A Response to Wynne," *Educational Leadership,* Dec. 1985/Jan. 1986, p. 10.

42. Kilpatrick, p. 97.

43. Personal communication with Ann Medlock, May 1996.

44. John Dewey, *Democracy and Education* (New York: Free Press, 1916; reprint, 1966), p. 11.

45. Bennett, p. 11.

46. Wynne, "Character and Academics," p. 142.

47. For a discussion of how traditional character education fails to offer guidance when values come into conflict, see Lockwood, "Character Education."

48. Rheta DeVries and Betty Zan, *Moral Classrooms, Moral Children: Creating a Constructivist Atmosphere in Early Education* (New York: Teachers College Press, 1994), p. 253.

49. For an argument that critics tend to misrepresent what Values Clarification was about, see James A. Beane, *Affect in the Curriculum* (New York: Teachers College Press, 1990), pp. 104–106.

50. Wynne, for example, refers to the developers of Values Clarification as "popularizers" of Kohlberg's research (see "Character and Academics," p. 141), while Amitai Etzioni, in the course of criticizing Piaget's and Kohlberg's work, asserts that "a typical course on moral reasoning starts with something called 'values clarification'" (see *The Spirit of Community,* p. 98).

51. Kohlberg's model, which holds that people across cultures progress predictably through six stages of successively more sophisticated styles of moral reasoning, is based on the decidedly nonrelativistic premise that the last stages are superior to the first ones. See his *Essays on Moral Development,* Vol. 1: *The Philosophy of Moral Development* (San Francisco: Harper & Row, 1981), especially the essays titled "Indoctrination Versus Relativity in Value Education" and "From *Is* to *Ought.*"

52. See, for example, James S. Fishkin, *Beyond Subjective Morality* (New Haven, Conn.: Yale University Press, 1984); and David B. Wong, *Moral Relativity* (Berkeley: University of California Press, 1984).

53. Researchers at the National Institute of Mental Health have summarized the available research as follows: "Even children as young as 2 years old have (a) the cognitive capacity to interpret the physical and psychological states of others, (b) the emotional capacity to effectively experience the other's state, and (c) the behavioral repertoire that permits the possibility of trying to alleviate discomfort in others. These are the capabilities that, we believe, underlie children's caring behavior in the presence of another person's distress. . . . Young children seem to show patterns of moral internalization that are not simply fear based or solely responsive to parental commands. Rather, there are signs that children feel responsible for (as well as connected to and dependent on) others at a very young age." (See Carolyn Zahn-Waxler and others, "Development of Concern for Others," *Developmental Psychology,* vol. 28, 1992, pp. 127, 135. For more on the adult's role in light of these facts, see Kohn, *The Brighter Side.*)

54. "Education Secretary Backs Teaching of Religious Values," *New York Times,* Nov. 12, 1985, p. B–4.

55. For more on class meetings, see Glasser, chaps. 10–12; Thomas Gordon, *T.E.T.: Teacher Effectiveness Training* (New York: David McKay, 1974), chaps. 8–9; Jane Nelsen, Lynn Lott, and H. Stephen Glenn, *Positive Discipline in the Classroom* (Rocklin, Calif.: Prima, 1993); and Child Development Project, *Ways We Want Our Class to Be.*

56. For more on the theory and research of perspective taking, see Kohn, *The Brighter Side,* chaps. 4–5; for practical classroom activities for promoting perspective-taking skills, see Norma Deitch Feshbach and others, *Learning to Care: Classroom Activities for Social and Affective Development* (Glenview, Ill.: Scott, Foresman, 1983). While specialists in the field distinguish between perspective taking (imagining what others see, think, or feel) and empathy (*feeling* what others feel), most educators who talk about the importance of helping children become empathic really seem to be talking about perspective taking.

57. Wynne, "Great Tradition," p. 9.

58. Kilpatrick, p. 141.

59. It is informative to discover whom the proponents of a hero-based approach to character education themselves regard as heroic. For example, William Bennett's nominee for "possibly our greatest living American" is Rush Limbaugh. (See Terry Eastland, "Rush Limbaugh: Talking Back," *American Spectator,* Sept. 1992, p. 23.)

60. See Victor Battistich and others, "The Child Development Project: A Comprehensive Program for the Development of Prosocial Character," in William M. Kurtines and Jacob L. Gewirtz, eds., *Moral Behavior and Development: Advances in Theory, Research, and Applications* (Hillsdale, N.J.: Erlbaum, 1989); and Daniel Solomon and others, "Creating a Caring Community: Educational Practices That Promote Children's Prosocial Development," in Fritz K. Oser, Andreas Dick, and Jean-Luc Patry, eds., *Effective and Responsible Teaching* (San Francisco: Jossey-Bass, 1992). For more information about the CDP program or about the research substantiating its effects, write to the Developmental Studies Center at 2000 Embarcadero, Suite 305, Oakland, CA 94606.

PART TWO

American Ideology Goes to School

CHAPTER FIVE

Resistance to Cooperative Learning

Making Sense of Its Deletion and Dilution

[My teacher is] always [going] on about help thy neighbour and [all] that [—but] you try and do that in his lessons and you're out.

*—Dave, a fourteen–year-old student
[quoted in Dunn, Rudduck, & Cowie, 1989, p. 186]*

In the 1960s educators were busy developing and introducing reforms. In the 1970s they were busy failing at putting them into practice." Those two sentences by Michael Fullan (1982, p. 5) will produce in many of us an unpleasant little twinge of recognition, particularly since this pattern of failing to implement reforms successfully did not end with the 1970s. New learning strategies, or perhaps the way these strategies are introduced, still lead some educators to react much as a body does to the implantation of foreign tissue. In each case, the task of figuring out the reason for this rejection, if it is undertaken at all, is conducted as a postmortem, by which time a new pedagogical transplant is already under way.

Those of us who do research, training, writing, or speaking about cooperative learning (CL) disagree on many issues, but we are united

---

Originally published in *The Journal of Education* in 1992.

in wanting to avoid this fate. Despite an enormous research literature supporting the value of having students work in pairs or small groups to help one another learn—and more interestingly, despite the growing *awareness* of CL on the part of educators—anecdotal evidence suggests that it might eventually meet the same fate as many other worthy educational innovations. It is impossible to specify the number of teachers who are rejecting CL, either before or after having attempted to use it, but one observer wrote recently, "Despite the academic vogue of cooperative learning and efforts at dissemination made by its proponents, it remains an instructional strategy seldom used in a systematic manner over the course of a school year or more" (Rich, 1990, p. 83). Even if this is an overstatement, enough rejection of CL is taking place to warrant a systematic analysis. Such an analysis, moreover, ought to take place while there is still time to address the problems we find. In the process, we may turn up deeper unsettling truths about the ideology of American education.

DELETING COOPERATIVE LEARNING

There are essentially two ways to account for educators' resistance to the idea of cooperative learning. The first set of explanations has to do with inferior presentation of the concept. I will describe these only briefly—not because they are unimportant but because there is nothing peculiar to CL about these criticisms; poor presentation sinks lots of educational reforms. The second set of explanations, to be treated in more detail, concerns the ways in which CL in particular is threatening to, or incongruent with, the beliefs that many teachers hold.

Misses and Myths

If administrators and teachers came to believe that installing a water fountain in every classroom might improve the quality of learning, educational consultants would instantly appear, claiming expertise as Liquid Delivery Systems Facilitators, to offer their services for a day or two of in-service training on how to install the fountains and how cold the water should be. In the real world, with CL in demand, consultants market themselves for a brief—and therefore seductively inexpensive—faculty training in the use of teamwork. But because CL, correctly understood, requires a radical reconceptualization of what learning involves and how the people who spend the day together in a classroom relate to one another, a host of problems and questions inexorably appear. What to do about children who resist being in the same group? ("I don't want to work with Michael; he's stupid.") How long until the groups should be shuffled? Is CL compatible with conventional curricula and systems of classroom management? What about students who seem put off by the very idea of helping each other to learn? Some children, after all, may be "threatened by group work . . . as a legitimate way of working and so give a powerful message to the teacher who experiments with a new method" (Cowie & Rudduck, 1990, p. 250). By the time teachers have enough experience to know what problems they need help with, however, the consultant is long gone.

> I have seen many teachers acquire cooperative learning methods and use them in their classes only to abandon them when the consultants left the scene. This occurs because cooperative learning had not become part of school-wide policy where teachers' needs and school goals were coordinated at the administrative level. . . . The *method* works, but if the *system* fails to support it, you cannot use the method [Sharan, 1986, p. 4].

It has been estimated, for example, that only 5 percent to 10 percent of participants in a CL workshop will continue to use the cooperative approach over time if ongoing coaching and support are absent (Male, 1989).

One consequence of inadequate training in CL, then, is its failure to address specific questions and problems that appear only after implementation. Another is its failure to include careful reflection on what cooperation means and does not mean. Consider three common misconceptions that may persist after one has been introduced to the concept in too perfunctory a fashion.

First, and most fundamentally, CL is sometimes regarded as a gimmick to perk up a classroom now and then, offering a break from serious instruction. ("OK, kids, it's the third Friday of the month. Remember, that means today we work in teams!") While teachers doubtless will want to continue making some use of whole-class discussion and individualized work, CL can—and, I would argue, ought to—become the "default" classroom arrangement.

Second, dividing a class into teams and announcing that students should work with their groupmates is not sufficient for, much less equivalent to, cooperative learning. Because of this, teachers who have merely put children in groups and are unimpressed with the results have not yet given CL a chance to prove itself. I have seen classrooms in which the teacher (1) presented a task that allowed children in groups to avoid interacting with one another, (2) offered no guidance regarding social skills, and (3) reminded them every so often to "be cooperative." Particularly in light of the values that are salient in our culture, the absence of a classroom norm of caring and the failure to build social skills will reduce the probability that extemporaneous work in groups can produce the psychological, interpersonal, or academic benefits reported in the literature. Moreover, children may not like it.

Finally, cooperation does not imply harmony. The relevant question is not whether conflict will occur when people are playing with ideas or struggling to make decisions together: it will and it should. The question, rather, is whether conflict will occur in the context of competition or cooperation. Teachers need not choose between creating a classroom in which students must arrive at a forced and artificial consensus, on the one hand, and one in which conflict is present but manifests itself as an adversarial exercise, such as debate, on the other. The former asks children to deny reality (because they know that disagreement exists) and deprives them of a real education; genuine learning does not smooth over or soothe. The latter shifts the lesson from whatever students are discussing to the goal of winning. Far preferable is a third alternative: inviting disagreement but nesting it in a framework of positive interdependence.

David and Roger Johnson, brothers who have spent two decades cooperating to research and refine the idea of cooperative learning, have referred to this optimal balance as "constructive controversy," "creative conflict," or more poetically, "friendly excursions into disequilibrium." Their research suggests that this approach is generally preferred by students to either "concurrence-seeking" or debate, and that it promotes both more effective learning and more interpersonal attraction than the other models (see, for example, Johnson, Johnson, & Smith, 1986). In short, people who are cooperating are working together to learn something—encouraging and depending on one another but not necessarily seeing eye-to-eye. Nothing about the concept of positive interdependence requires that members of the group avoid conflict, and there are good data to suggest that they should not do so.

If CL is presented as an infrequent respite from "real" teaching, a haphazard sort of groupwork, or an activity that precludes disagreement, the results will be predictable—and they will resemble the consequences of simply giving a teacher too little guidance (and follow-up support) on how to make cooperation work. Quick-and-dirty training sessions may help to explain both of these problems, and the very popularity of CL may in turn help to explain why such sessions take place.[1] There is a depressing logic to this process. A development that becomes sufficiently popular takes on the appearance of a fad. This means it is *treated* as a fad rather than with the necessary seriousness. Such treatment—by people who are either unmindful of what is required or else unable or unwilling to provide it—then virtually guarantees a parabolic trajectory. One day everyone is talking about cooperative learning; the next day it appears on a nostalgia list between CB radios and disco music.

Why Cooperative Learning Can Be Threatening

Workshops that cut corners were in existence long before most of us had heard of cooperative learning. Similarly, misconceptions about what is involved in a given pedagogical approach are nothing new. But there are obstacles to the successful adoption of CL that are peculiar to this way of structuring a classroom—features that would likely cause problems even if trainings were perfection itself. Advocates of CL need to grapple with these aspects of cooperation in the classroom and understand how they may be unsettling to many teachers.

1. CL reduces control and predictability. Someone—it may have been me—once said that the traditional model of teaching amounts to a rehearsed solo performance by the instructor (with students relegated to the role of audience), whereas CL not only offers instruments to everyone in the room but invites a jazz improvisation. The analogy has its limits, but it captures two features of CL: its demand that the teacher guide students in helping one another to learn (rather than being the only source of ideas and information in the room) and its introduction of uncertainty in place of a predictable progression through a prepared lesson plan. Some teachers have not bargained for either of these changes.

There is a certain pleasure to be taken from the role of king or queen, even if one's subjects are very short. To the extent that the process of schooling has been predicated on compelling students to follow directions (which a tenth grade teacher of mine once announced was "a sign of intelligence"), absorb information and regurgitate it on command, and work silently on whatever task is presented,[2] the profession may have attracted some people who thrive on autocracy. I regularly meet teachers who shine with generosity of spirit and an instinct for what children need to grow. But others, let us frankly admit, are disinclined to embrace an approach that has students look to one another for help and that treats them as beings who actively construct meaning instead of passively incorporating facts. CL is not simply a set of techniques. It is not simply the status quo except in groups. At its best, it is an entirely different way of approaching the act of learning.

Part of this shift is reflected in the movement toward Whole Language learning, about which much has been written. (For an engaging introduction intended for nonspecialists, see Gursky, 1991.) But CL introduces a new element: learning is no longer something that happens only as the individual child makes sense of a text or the world; it happens to some extent as children interact with one another. The teacher now has allies throughout the room—a scenario exciting and refreshing to some educators but highly disconcerting to those who, like trial attorneys during cross-examination, never ask a question to which they do not already know the answer.[3]

2. CL demands attention to social goals. When employers complain that the people they hire seem unable to work with others, we should not be surprised: through twelve or sixteen years of schooling they have had little encouragement for doing so—or even opportunity to do so. After all, when students in most American classrooms help each other to learn, this is called "cheating." Long before these students enter the workforce, a lack of social skills and concern for others can be worrisome to parents. Children sometimes seem indifferent to, or even amused by, suffering, unable to resolve conflicts fairly, and likely either to try to get their needs met by coercing others or, conversely, to be victimized by coercion.

Teachers can scarcely avoid noticing these patterns, but even those who recognize that the time spent together in the classroom *could* be used to attend to social goals may believe that this focus would be inappropriate. Because I have elsewhere argued that schools can and should play a role in helping children to become good people and not merely good learners (Kohn, 1990, 1991a), I will not attempt to reconstruct such a case here. Instead, I will simply observe that many educators assume that their charge is limited to providing instruction in the traditional academic subjects. Even when attention is given to the development of children's social skills and prosocial orientation, this enterprise is "frequently viewed through an instrumental prism of

how [these skills] affect academic achievement rather than as schooling goals with inherent legitimacy" (Rich, 1990, p. 83).

These attitudes constitute another explanation for resistance to CL
because many of the leading models explicitly call for attention to be
paid to the phenomenon of working together—what it means and
how it can be improved. The Johnsons, for example, emphasize that
"collaborative skills are directly taught in classrooms where teachers
are serious about using cooperative learning"—not only because these
skills are a prerequisite for realizing academic gains but also because
they are valuable in their own right (Johnson & Johnson, 1991, p. 146;
see also Graves & Graves, 1985). Models that call for the creation of a
caring classroom community, and not merely the teaching of discrete
social skills such as listening carefully or making eye contact (see, for
example, Solomon et al., 1990), would be even more disconcerting to
teachers who see such objectives as inappropriate.

> If cooperative learning is perceived by teachers as primarily promot-
> ing pupils' personal or social goals, we would not expect very many
> teachers to voluntarily participate. And if they are required to partic-
> ipate in the workshop, few of them will arrive at the decision to adopt
> the new method, assuming they are allowed some choice in the mat-
> ter, no matter how well the workshop is conducted. And if they are re-
> quired to adopt the new method, even fewer will implement it with a
> reasonable degree of fidelity [Rich, 1990, p. 89][4]

3. CL challenges our commitment to individualism. It would not
be an exaggeration to say that the watchword of the American classroom is "Keep your eyes on your own paper! I want to see what you
can do, not what your neighbor can do." This orientation, typically
taken for granted, is entirely compatible with—indeed, a reflection
of—the wholesale individualism of American culture. From our aversion to collective enterprises, which Tocqueville observed in the nineteenth century, to today's popular-culture celebration of personal
heroism, from an ethical orientation that begins and ends with non-
interference and personal choice, to schools of psychology that, however varied on other issues, all "reinforc[e] an individualistic,
self-contained perspective [and] play down the importance of inter-
dependent values"[5] (Sampson, 1977, p. 780), we are encouraged to emphasize and promote the accomplishments of separate selves.

Individualism has its costs. Any number of social critics have
pointed to the frantic mobility in American society, to the way we are

divided from one another, cast back upon ourselves to the point that it is profoundly unsettling to acknowledge our alienation. Instead, like lonely souls who noisily boast of being free from constricting attachments, we insist that this is not a predicament but a choice, indicative not of crisis but of an advanced set of values.

In the classroom in particular, our exclusive focus on individual accomplishments holds us back from doing even what we set out to do because

> learning is never the result of the efforts of isolated, competitive individuals alone. . . . [T]he evident weakness in American schools has much to do with the weakening of their community context. . . . Education can never merely be for the sake of individual self-enhancement. It pulls us into the common world or it fails altogether [Bellah et al., 1991, pp. 172, 176].

Arguably, it *has* failed altogether. But while there is no shortage of critics willing to charge American education with failure, often they miss the point about what has gone wrong and why. The problem is not that students cannot find Turkey on a map but that they do not find themselves part of a community of learners.

To understand CL properly may be to have exaggerated apprehensions about collectivism allayed. Children do not sacrifice their own psychological or academic development when they work with others; they do not lose their individual selves in an amorphous blob of a group. Indeed, because of the social support they receive and the intellectual successes facilitated by groupwork, conventional measures of self-esteem, for what they are worth, consistently reveal an advantage for cooperative as opposed to individualistic or competitive models of instruction (see, for example, Johnson & Johnson, 1989). Similarly, the positive interdependence at the heart of CL—the probability of one child's success being enhanced by another's success—is quite different from self-sacrifice. CL is not tantamount to unanimity, conformity, or the subjugation of the individual.

Nevertheless, there is no denying that teachers in CL classrooms are likely to have a new watchword—to wit, "I want to see what you and your neighbor can do together." They are likely to ask students to turn first to their partners to check out an idea or request an explanation. They may evaluate some projects as group efforts, which is what they are. They probably have arranged the room so that children are clustered around tables most of the day instead of seated at separate desks. They recognize that "socializing" is not something one relegates to recess and lunch, something that distracts from learning; rather, they know that learning proceeds not only from what transpires between student and teacher or between student and text but also from what happens between student and student. In short, CL challenges the extreme individualism of American education and may be viewed with suspicion for that reason.

4. CL challenges our commitment to the value of competition. When students in American schools are not separated from one another—and sometimes even when they are—they are set against one another, told in effect that their success comes at the price of someone else's failure and vice versa. Grading on a curve (which establishes an artificial scarcity of top grades), choosing only the best papers to be displayed on the wall, playing games such as spelling bees that sort children into winners and losers, forcing them to try to edge each other out for schoolwide awards—all of these explicit contests, along with the subtler competition for recognition and approval in the classroom, teach children one enduring, fundamental message: *other people are potential obstacles to my own success.* This message continues to be learned in classrooms around the nation despite literally hundreds of studies confirming that competition in the classroom not only sabotages relationships and undermines self-confidence but also impedes achievement and long-term interest in learning (Johnson & Johnson, 1989; Kohn, 1992b; Nicholls, 1989).

Competition signifies mutually exclusive goal attainment, an arrangement in which one person succeeds only if others fail—or in the stronger variety, only by actively making others fail. This is quite different from individualized achievement, in which the outcome of one person's efforts is unrelated to what others do. Still, both of these structures are supported by an ideological apparatus in our culture, and both are challenged by cooperative learning. If any antinomy could be more stark than "working alone versus working with others," it is "treating others as rivals versus treating others as collaborators." The pervasive rivalry sanctioned and socialized by our culture—in the workplace, on the playing field, in the family, and at the core of our political and economic system—is unsurprisingly manifested in the classroom as well. To that extent, any proposal that children should learn cooperatively will strike some teachers as unfamiliar or peculiar (and therefore will be dismissed as "unrealistic," "idealistic," or "utopian")—and even as un-American, radical, and subversive.

Strictly speaking, these last three adjectives are quite accurate: CL (1) offers an alternative to this country's confusion of excellence with victory, (2) by its very existence goes to the roots of established norms, and therefore (3) subverts efforts to teach children to accept competition as unavoidable and desirable. While not all teachers who use CL reject competition *tout court,* it is safe to assume that the more enthusiastic a teacher's endorsement of the value of setting children against one another in competitions, the greater the likelihood that he or she will be inclined to reject CL.

Before concluding these remarks on the rejection of CL, I should note that the extent and intensity of some educators' resistance cannot be predicted just by understanding CL's challenge to a teacher's control of the classroom, to an exclusively academic agenda, to individualism and competition, respectively. For predictive purposes, we would also want to know the teacher's subject matter, the grade level and achievement record of his or her students, and the model of CL to which that teacher had been exposed (Rich, 1990). But the point here is simply that CL explicitly or implicitly clashes with deeply held beliefs about school and society. It would be far more remarkable if it did *not* encounter resistance on a wide scale.

DILUTING COOPERATIVE LEARNING

From a distance, those who promote cooperation in the classroom seem distinguished principally by this commitment, particularly when contrasted with the rest of the education field. Up close, though, those who huddle together under this conceptual umbrella are sometimes strikingly different from one another in the way they conceive of cooperation and, for that matter, learning itself. The potentially threatening features of CL identified in the previous section may help to explain some of these differences. Just as some educators have decided to stay away from CL—or to back off very quickly once having tried it—others continue to use it but in a form intended to reduce its dissonance with their previous beliefs. In describing some of these variants, I mean to be prescriptive as well; I will argue against what I see as the dilution of CL's power.

Consider, first, the challenge that CL poses to a teacher's absolute power over the classroom. Like the conversation between a teacher and a pupil, a situation in which "teachers instruct pupils to talk to each other," specifying what and when and how they may talk leaves the teacher in control. "But when pupils talk to other pupils without the teacher's authority or without the teacher being able to hear the exchanges, then . . . an area of potential pupil power is exposed" (Dunn, Rudduck, & Cowie, 1989, pp. 186–187) and the classroom no longer belongs just to the teacher. When the nature of the interchange among group members is highly circumscribed—more than the students' age or the subject matter would seem to require—we might suspect that the teacher has compromised the process of cooperation more to maintain control than to maximize the heuristic value of the experience.

Interestingly, the versions of CL that seek to dictate to students each component of cooperation—thereby reducing their sense of autonomy as fellow meaning-creators and idea-explorers—are likely to be so structured and systematized that teachers, too, are deprived of authority. So-called teacher-proof curricula, we ought to have realized by now, are not only disrespectful but chimerical: they are the perpetual-motion machines of education. Cookbook approaches to CL similarly attempt to specify in advance what cannot be specified in advance, to reduce learning to a series of discrete steps that renders the process sterile and excludes both teachers and students from the real work (and joy) of what happens in the classroom.

The second feature of CL identified as potentially discordant with teachers' values is its emphasis on social goals. Here, the temptation for someone inclined to remake rather than repudiate cooperation is to take a narrowly academic approach to having students work in teams, letting the social interaction that must occur in these groups take care of itself. As noted previously, this approach is probably counterproductive on its own terms because children need to be helped to work together effectively in order to learn from one another. But the processes of coming to look upon one's peers as potential collaborators, of learning to accept those who are different from oneself, and of developing perspective-taking skills and a prosocial orientation more generally are valuable things in their own right. They may be lost if CL's social aspects are not given the appropriate weight and attention.

CL's third challenge—namely, to the ethic of individualism—unmistakably gives pause to the teacher who wants to bend the structure to fit his or her commitments. The fact of working together would seem an unavoidable affront to the principle that academic accomplishment is or should be a solitary phenomenon. Teachers who embrace this principle, however, could sharply limit the amount of class time spent in groups. Further, they might minimize interaction by employing versions of CL in which students learn on their own and are tested on their own but simply check one another's work in between.

Does the use of CL, per se, really serve to challenge an individualist worldview, though? David Hargreaves, an astringent English educational critic who argues that collaborative experiences are largely denied to teachers as well as students because of our ideological commitment to educating separate individuals, offers a startling observation in passing that has the effect of reframing the discussion about CL: "We tend to see collective experiences merely as means of giving students a range of social skills, the capacities to 'get along' with other people. This is the social dimension of the cult of individualism—the cult of 'chumminess'" (Hargreaves, 1980, p. 197). Hargreaves here calls our attention to the largely tacit doctrine that the only purpose of schooling is to offer each individual a set of skills. CL, paradoxically, may have the effect of legitimating that doctrine by virtue of the fact that it merely adds techniques of interpersonal engagement to the list of skills in each student's repertoire. At the very least, the practice of *marketing* CL in terms of how each student will benefit (such as teaching future employees how to deal more skillfully with their coworkers) does nothing to challenge the individualism at the core of American education or society. Although Hargreaves offers no specific alternative curricula, his implication is that schooling (and surely CL) would take on an entirely different coloration if its long-range goal was social transformation and not simply the education of a collection of discrete individuals.

Finally, there is the question of competition—a matter worth considering at some length. Teachers who continue to believe that there is value in having students try to defeat one another can keep competition alive in two ways even while making use of CL. The first is to turn cooperative activities into group competitions; the second is to have students compete individually when they are not engaged in cooperative activities. Neither, I will argue, is necessary for any conceivable academic or social goal. In fact, either version may defeat our best efforts to promote cooperation in the classroom, sending conflicting messages in the process and undoing much of what we have managed to achieve by the use of CL.

The predominant experience with cooperation in our society consists of having a group of people work together in order to defeat another group of people. The group may be a basketball team, a company, or in its most dangerous incarnation, an entire country. While some activities featuring a blend of intragroup cooperation and intergroup competition, such as sports, are widely acclaimed precisely on the basis of promoting teamwork, the most salient lesson they actually teach is that the ultimate reason to cooperate is to defeat a common enemy. Such a message is mixed at best and exceedingly damaging at worst.

Considerable evidence (reviewed in Kohn, 1992a) suggests that (1) nothing about the nature of group functioning presupposes the presence of a common enemy, (2) intergroup competition does not enhance, and may actually diminish, the achievement of a given group, and (3) intergroup competition also is unnecessary for promoting ingroup affiliation and other social benefits of cooperation. A comprehensive review of the classroom research supports the finding that "cooperation seems to promote better relationships when intergroup competition is absent" (Johnson & Johnson, 1989, p. 122).

This conclusion is particularly germane to the practice of CL. Individual teachers may sometimes decide to turn a cooperative learning experience into an intergroup competition, but the best-known packaged model requiring groups to compete against each other is Teams-Games-Tournament, devised by Robert Slavin and his colleagues. The third edition of a book describing this and another team learning activity (Slavin, 1986) begins with the announcement that "competition between teams is no longer recommended" (p. 1). This is particularly remarkable for two reasons. First, the reason given for this shift is not a change of heart or mind on the part of the author but a growing resistance to the technique on the part of educators themselves: "The same teachers who are attracted to cooperative learning are often repelled by moving competition up to the team level" (p. 1). Second, notwithstanding this comment in the introduction, the manual proceeds to set out the rules for how "students compete" in the tournaments (p. 24; see also Slavin, 1990, chap. 4).

Even teachers who avoid setting groups against each other in contests may establish competitive interactions alongside CL—that is, when students are not working in groups. Some do so deliberately, others inadvertently. Even a teacher who would never dream of grading on a curve may unwittingly create a classroom norm of competition by pitting students against one another for the teacher's attention and approval. This may occur through the use of manipulative behavior management strategies (such as, "I like the way Joanne is sitting so nicely and quietly") or through the conventional arrangement of asking a question of the whole class.

> The teacher asks the question, the students who think they know the answer raise their hands, and the teacher calls on one of them. We've all seen it many times: when one student is called on, the other students who have their hands up register their disappointment with a little "Oh." It's a structure that sets the kids against each other [Spencer Kagan in Brandt, 1989/1990, p. 8].

Anyone who doubts that competition is the subtext of most whole-class question-and-answer sessions need only continue watching the faces of the children who were not recognized. Are they rooting for Jeremy, who now has the floor, to succeed? Hardly. They are hoping he says something stupid because this will present them with another opportunity to triumph. The teacher's face is scanned for signs of dissatisfaction with Jeremy's answer; once found, their hands shoot up again, fingers reaching anxiously for the fluorescent lights. Some students participate energetically in this scramble to be the first one with the right response, while others stare dully and look beaten (which at some point they have been). Our attention, however, is properly focused not on the temperament of the individual participants but on the structure that has turned learning into a contest.

A teacher or trainer who deliberately employs competition in the classroom, whether among individuals or groups, may carefully limit the proportion of class time spent in such activities and take other steps to restrict its destructive impact, such as grouping or pairing students homogeneously, maximizing the number of winners, striving to minimize the importance of the result, and so on (see, for example, Johnson & Johnson, 1991, chap. 5). But the premise of this approach is the belief that the disadvantages of competition derive from its being overused or badly implemented. The contrary view, that *any* arrangement in which one person or group can succeed only at the price of another's failure is inherently destructive (Kohn, 1992b), will incline teachers to do their best to eliminate competition from the classroom.

Teachers who seek to turn a classroom into a caring community will be hard-pressed to justify any use of competitive activities. If the point is to promote concern and compassion for one another, then the last structure they would adopt, even temporarily, would be one in which students must work at cross-purposes. Competition typically reduces or retards perspective taking, empathy, and generosity (Barnett & Bryan, 1974; Barnett, Matthews, & Corbin, 1979; Feshbach, 1978; Lanzetta & Englis, 1989; Rutherford & Mussen, 1968; Tjosvold, 1983; Tjosvold, Johnson, & Johnson, 1984). In fact, "competition may serve to suppress generosity to others to a greater extent than cooperation serves to enhance it" (Barnett, Matthews, & Corbin, 1979, p. 93).

When this evidence is added to the enormous collection of data showing that competition can undermine both self-esteem and the quality of learning, the case for avoiding win/lose structures altogether—at least in the classroom—grows more compelling. Why, then, would a CL researcher or trainer continue to reserve a role for competition? Two justifications are frequently heard: first, children enjoy competing, and second, like it or not, they need to learn how to do so. Let us take each in turn.

The preference that some students express for competitive experiences may be confounded, to begin with, by the number and quality of their previous exposures to cooperation. While individual differences naturally play a part, it may be that those who say they enjoy competitive games, for example, have never had an opportunity to sample cooperative sorts of recreation. A student who seems glad for the chance to play a competitive game in the classroom, moreover, actually may be responding to its status as a game (and the break from ordinary studies this represents) more than to its competitive nature. In my experience, teachers who play games that do not create winners and losers find no less, and often a good deal more, enthusiasm for these activities.

For students who really seem to enjoy competitive experiences, it might behoove the teacher to ask what aspects of those contests they enjoy—and then to explore whether those features might not be attainable in noncompetitive activities. If some students—typically, those who win frequently—continue to insist that it is the irreducible pleasure of trying to beat other people that they seek, the teacher must attend to the consequences that these experiences have on the rest of the participants before deciding whether to retain them.

Some educators believe they are doing children a favor by having them compete because this will prepare them for the rivalry they will encounter when they leave school. To this we can respond that students in our society already are well acquainted with competition.

Even if some experience with it were useful, children have more than they could ever need. Imagine a school that studiously avoids having children compete against one another, in the classroom or on the playing field, from kindergarten through twelfth grade. We may be confident that not a single graduate of this school, upon entering college or the workforce, will suddenly exclaim, "Whoa! What's all this about 'competition'?" Our best efforts to promote cooperation notwithstanding, children are all too familiar with win/lose activities.

What students need is not more of the same but experience with alternative arrangements so they can achieve a sense of perspective about the competition that proliferates in our culture. While a case can be made that students would benefit from a curricular unit in which they explicitly consider the effects of competition, talking about it is quite different from immersing them in it.[6] (By way of analogy, consider the distinction between teaching children about religion and indoctrinating them to be religious.) Moreover, there is no reason to imagine that having children participate in competitive activities week after week after week would provide any incremental benefit.

Is competition justified because it teaches that we cannot always be successful in obtaining what we seek? In fact, the psychological benefits of failure are often overrated; the experience quickly becomes redundant and gratuitously punishing. Making children fail in order to teach them to cope—in fact, any use of competition—calls to mind an ironic notice I once saw tacked to a wall in a sixth grade classroom: THE BEATINGS WILL CONTINUE UNTIL MORALE IMPROVES. Perhaps another analogy will make the point: the notion that we best prepare children for unpleasant experiences by providing them with unpleasant experiences at a tender age is exactly as sensible as the proposition that because the environment is teeming with carcinogens, children ought to be exposed to as many cancer-causing agents as possible while they are young.

But even to the extent that some experience with failure is useful, let us remember that failure does not require losing. As far as I am aware, no evidence exists to suggest that the particularly toxic form of failure that comes from being defeated by someone else provides any psychological benefit at all. Conversely, while there is plenty of reason to arrange for children to have successful experiences with learning, interpersonal interaction, and so on, there is no reason for their success ever to occur in the context of triumphing over someone else. The fact that success and victory are conceptually—and often practically—

distinct experiences helps to explain why people typically perform better when they are not engaged in competition. The distinction proves relevant again here, belying the idea that competition provides students with a necessary or useful preparatory experience.

In short, there are no compelling reasons to have students try to beat one another—even for a small fraction of their total educational experience. There are, however, numerous reasons *not* to do so: competition's adverse effects on cognitive performance; its tendency, shared by other extrinsic motivators (Kohn, 1991b), to undermine a long-term commitment to learning; and the likelihood that it will inhibit both self-esteem and positive relationships with peers. For these reasons, CL trainers and teachers typically are skeptical of competition. It is disappointing when, instead of following their instincts, experience, and data to the logical conclusion, they continue to make use of competitive classroom activities—either alongside CL or as a framework in which to fit CL. Although completely eradicating any one structure may strike us as unpalatably extreme, we sometimes fail to appreciate a simple truth: not everything that is destructive in excess is desirable in moderation.

RISKING RESISTANCE, MAINTAINING THE CHALLENGE

If CL is falling victim to a series of generic problems concerning the implementation of pedagogical change—deficient trainings, the perpetuation of misconceptions, and so forth—it is only common sense to call for an effort to study and remedy those problems. Sociologists of education and other students of change (such as Berman & McLaughlin, 1976; Fullan, 1982; Fullan & Miles, 1992) have written detailed accounts of what can go wrong and, by extension, how to avoid these predictable pitfalls.

The more pressing question, however, is what to do with a specific reform that is discrepant with the values of some who are being asked to adopt it. The most obvious response is to water down the change in order to dilute its impact; in the case at hand, this process might be styled "co-opting cooperation." This option, as should be clear from the foregoing, I want to repudiate explicitly.

Some proponents take pride in the fact that CL is "easy to sell to teachers because it doesn't make them change that much of what they do." Unfortunately, this sales job "sells short both teachers and the process and potential of cooperative learning" (Sapon-Shevin & Schniedewind, 1989/1990, p. 65; also see Sapon-Shevin, 1991b). The question we might ask, in other words, is: What profit is there to gaining converts to a reform if we have lost the soul of that reform in the process?

This trade-off is particularly pronounced in the case of models of CL that are advertised as being appropriate to any curriculum. The soothing message here is not only that CL will work regardless of what is being taught, but that educators need not reflect on how challenging or valuable their material may be because students will benefit from learning whatever it is so long as they do it in groups. Sapon-Shevin (1991a) has mischievously referred to this approach as the "hamburger helper" model of cooperative learning. Sharan (1987/1988, p. 5) is no less blunt when he warns that if we reduce the potentially liberating principles of CL to "a set of prepackaged procedures for managing the movements of warm bodies in the classroom . . . to get them to study, with just a little less boredom, the same material that would bore them more if it were studied in some other way . . . [then CL] will soon be discarded as another fraud, as will so many other packaged methods now loudly touted in the educational marketplace."

We do not need to antagonize CL's skeptics gratuitously. Surely there is nothing objectionable in trying to show how CL, properly implemented, is likely to produce results in any number of areas that a skeptic values. In itself, there is nothing particularly controversial about wanting to enhance students' cognitive skills, their interest in intellectual exploration, their sense of personal competence and efficacy, and their ability and inclination to participate constructively in group efforts. In theory, there is no limit to the number of educators (as well as parents and students) who will respond positively to the promise that CL can bring these things about.

But teachers who expect to stay on center stage once children are in groups, teachers who scorn social goals as inappropriate to the classroom, and teachers who are firmly committed to individualistic or competitive arrangements might as well hear from the beginning that CL will rock these expectations and values. There is an enormous difference between emphasizing those aspects of teamwork that are likely to have wide appeal and effectively gutting cooperative learning in order to render it innocuous. CL, despite its literal replacement of desks with tables, is not merely a rearrangement of the furniture of the status quo, and it ought not to be billed as such.

In the long run, there is no substitute for constructive controversy—an ongoing dialogue in the fullest sense of that word—on the subject of the convictions that predispose some people to delete or dilute CL. If, for example, we encounter in someone an attachment—even a residual, half-hearted, heavily qualified attachment—to the value of competition, our response should not be to resign ourselves to stretching CL until it accommodates tournaments between cooperative groups. Rather, we should engage this individual in a continuing discussion on the nature of competition itself. The same is true for those wedded to a classroom configuration in which an omnipotent teacher imparts truth to passive student receptacles, and so forth.

This essay began by offering an account of what is impeding the successful implementation of CL. But it has proceeded, in idiosyncratic fashion, to draw one of many possible lines between acceptable and unacceptable varieties of CL, specifying compromises that may go too far in increasing its salability. The point of this is to stimulate discussion and reflection so that all those with an interest in promoting cooperation in the classroom can work together to address troubling questions about what that cooperation should look like and what its ultimate goal should be.

Notes

1. Limited budgets for in-service programs, as for other aspects of public education, also help to account for the reliance on inadequate—and in the long run, counterproductive—training sessions.

2. The extent of "on-task" behavior in a classroom tells us at least as much about the teacher as about the students. When a teacher complains that children are off task, our first response might be to ask, "What's the task?"

3. "Placing more emphasis on students' explanations necessarily requires teachers to relinquish some control over the direction the lesson will take. This can be a frightening prospect to a teacher who is unprepared to evaluate the validity of a novel idea that students inevitably propose" (Stigler & Stevenson, 1991, p. 44).

4. Rich's analysis not only draws out the implication of devaluing social goals, but also reminds us of a fundamental truth: policymakers, trainers, and theorists cannot change what goes on in classrooms. All they can do is invite teachers to change what goes on in classrooms.

5. For Freudians, humans are antisocial by instinct and driven principally by

intrapsychic forces; for behaviorists, the laws of learning pertain to the individual organism as it responds to the contingencies of its environment; for humanists, the summum bonum is self-actualization; for developmentalists, maturity and health are typically equated with autonomy and individuation; and so on.

6. For curriculum guides that not only suggest the use of CL but make cooperation and competition topics for study, see Schniedewind & Davidson (1987) and Hierta (1984).

References

Barnett, M. A., & Bryan, J. H. (1974). Effects of competition with outcome feedback on children's helping behavior. *Developmental Psychology, 10,* 838–842.

Barnett, M. A., Matthews, K. A., & Corbin, C. B. (1979). The effect of competitive and cooperative instructional sets on children's generosity. *Personality and Social Psychology Bulletin, 5,* 91–94.

Bellah, R. N., Madsen, R., Sullivan, W. M., Swidler, A., & Tipton, S. M. (1991). *The good society.* New York: Knopf.

Berman, P., & McLaughlin, M. W. (1976). Implementation of educational innovation. *Educational Forum, 40*(3), 345–370.

Brandt, R. (1989/1990, December/January). On cooperative learning: A conversation with Spencer Kagan. *Educational Leadership,* pp. 8–11.

Cowie, H., & Rudduck, J. (1990). Learning from one another: The challenge. In H. C. Foot, M. J. Morgan, & R. H. Shute (Eds.), *Children helping children* (pp. 235–255). Chichester, England: Wiley.

Dunn, K., Rudduck, J., & Cowie, H. (1989). Cooperation and the ideology of individualism in the schools. In C. Harber & R. Meighan (Eds.), *The democratic school* (pp. 183–193). Tickwell, England: Education NOW Books.

Feshbach, N. D. (1978). Studies of empathic behavior in children. In B. A. Maher (Ed.), *Progress in experimental personality research* (Vol. 8, pp. 1–47). New York: Academic Press.

Fullan, M. (1982). *The meaning of educational change.* New York: Teachers College Press.

Fullan, M. G., & Miles, M. B. (1992, June). Getting reform right: What works and what doesn't. *Phi Delta Kappan,* pp. 745–752.

Graves, N. B., & Graves, T. D. (1985). Creating a cooperative learning environment: An ecological approach. In R. Slavin et al. (Eds.), *Learning to co-operate, cooperating to learn* (pp. 403–436). New York: Plenum.

Gursky, D. (1991, August). After the reign of Dick and Jane. *Teacher Magazine,* pp. 22–29.

Hargreaves, D. H. (1980). A sociological critique of individualism in education. *British Journal of Educational Studies, 28*(3), 187–198.

Hierta, E. (1984). *Building cooperative societies: A curriculum guide for grades 6–9 on social and economic cooperation.* Ann Arbor: Michigan Alliance of Cooperatives.

Johnson, D. W., & Johnson, R. T. (1989). *Cooperation and competition: Theory and research.* Edina, MN: Interaction Book Co.

Johnson, D. W., & Johnson, R. T. (1991). *Learning together and alone: Cooperative, competitive, and individualistic learning* (3rd ed.). Englewood Cliffs, NJ: Prentice-Hall.

Johnson, D. W., Johnson, R. T., & Smith, K. A. (1986). Academic conflict among students: Controversy and learning. In R. Feldman (Ed.), *The social psychology of education* (pp. 199–231). Cambridge: Cambridge University Press.

Kohn, A. (1990). *The brighter side of human nature: Altruism and empathy in everyday life.* New York: Basic Books.

Kohn, A. (1991a, March). Caring kids: The role of the schools. *Phi Delta Kappan,* pp. 496–506. (Reprinted in this volume as Chapter Seventeen.)

Kohn, A. (1991b, February). Group grade grubbing versus cooperative learning. *Educational Leadership,* pp. 83–87.

Kohn, A. (1992a). Cooperation: What it means and doesn't mean. In A. Combs (Ed.), *Cooperation: Beyond the age of competition* (pp. 3–11). Philadelphia: Gordon and Breach.

Kohn, A. (1992b). *No contest: The case against competition* (rev. ed.). Boston: Houghton Mifflin.

Lanzetta, J. T., & Englis, B. G. (1989). Expectations of cooperation and competition and their effects on observers' vicarious emotional responses. *Journal of Personality and Social Psychology, 56*(4), 543–554.

Male, M. (1989). Cooperative learning and staff development. *Cooperation in Education* (newsletter of the International Association for the Study of Cooperation in Education), *5*(1), 4–5.

Nicholls, J. G. (1989). *The competitive ethos and democratic education.* Cambridge: Harvard University Press.

Rich, Y. (1990). Ideological impediments to instructional innovation: The case of cooperative learning. *Teaching and Teacher Education, 6*(1), 81–91.

Rutherford, E., & Mussen, P. (1968). Generosity in nursery school boys. *Child Development, 39,* 755–765.

Sampson, E. E. (1977). Psychology and the American ideal. *Journal of Personality and Social Psychology, 35,* 767–782.

Sapon-Shevin, M. (1991a). Cooperative learning: Liberatory praxis or Hamburger Helper? *Educational Foundations, 5,* 5–17.

Sapon-Shevin, M. (1991b, Winter). Cooperative learning, cooperative visions. *Holistic Education Review,* pp. 25–28.

Sapon-Shevin, M., & Schniedewind, N. (1989/1990, December/January). Selling cooperative learning without selling it short. *Educational Leadership,* pp. 63–65.

Schniedewind, N., & Davidson, E. (1987). *Cooperative learning, cooperative lives.* Dubuque, IA: W. C. Brown.

Sharan, S. (1986). Cooperative learning: Problems and promise. *International Association for the Study of Cooperation in Education Newsletter, 7*(5 & 6), 3–4.

Sharan, S. (1987/1988). Cooperative learning: New horizons, old threats. *International Association for the Study of Cooperation in Education Newsletter, 8*(5), 3–6.

Slavin, R. E. (1986). *Using student team learning* (3rd ed.). Baltimore: Johns Hopkins Team Learning Project.

Slavin, R. E. (1990). *Cooperative learning: Theory, research, and practice.* Englewood Cliffs, NJ: Prentice-Hall.

Solomon, D., et al. (1990). Cooperative learning as part of a comprehensive classroom program designed to promote prosocial development. In S. Sharan (Ed.), *Cooperative learning: Theory and research* (pp. 231–260). New York: Praeger.

Stigler, J. W., & Stevenson, H. W. (1991, Spring). How Asian teachers polish each lesson to perfection. *American Educator,* pp. 12–47.

Tjosvold, D. (1983). Effects of departments' interdependence on organizational decision making. *Psychological Reports, 53,* 851–857.

Tjosvold, D., Johnson, D. W., & Johnson, R. T. (1984). Influence strategy, perspective-taking, and relationships between high- and low-power individuals in cooperative and competitive contexts. *Journal of Psychology, 116,* 187–202.

CHAPTER SIX

"A Lot of Fat Kids Who Don't Like to Read"

The Effects of Pizza Hut's *Book It!* Program and Other Reading Incentives

Our culture is marinated in behaviorism. At work, at school, and at home, we take for granted that the way to get things done is to dangle goodies in front of people. Thus it seemed perfectly reasonable to observers across the political spectrum when Speaker of the House Newt Gingrich inaugurated a national campaign to pay children to read. The program, devised some time ago at West Georgia College, offers students $2 for each book they finish.

Politicians can be forgiven, perhaps, for a simpleminded faith in behavioral manipulation. But educators ought to know by now, in light of research and experience, that rewards are not merely ineffective over the long haul but actually counterproductive.

One study after another has demonstrated that the more someone is rewarded for doing something (or for doing it well), the less interest that person is likely to have in whatever he or she was rewarded for doing. Consider:

Originally published in *Education Week* in 1995.

- Children who are frequently rewarded by their parents are somewhat less generous than their peers. (They've learned that the only reason to help is that they will get something for doing so.)
- Students who are led to think about grades tend to be less interested in learning, less likely to think creatively, and less likely to choose difficult assignments than those who are encouraged to focus on the task itself. (The point is to do only what is necessary to snag an A, a mind-set that is, as one researcher put it, the "enemy of exploration." Small wonder that students come to ask, "Do we have to know this? Is this going to be on the test?")
- When children are offered tangible or verbal rewards for drinking an unfamiliar beverage, they are less apt to like that beverage later than are children who were never rewarded for drinking it in the first place. (They may have reasoned, "If this lady has to bribe me to try this, it must be something I won't like"—a thought process hardly limited to beverages.)

Consider the depressingly pervasive program called *Book It!*—Pizza Hut's edible precursor to Mr. Gingrich's plan. Since doggie biscuits can train the family pet, it was naturally assumed that pepperoni could get kids to open more books. And indeed, in some cases it does just that. After all, rewards, like punishments, often succeed in buying temporary compliance.

But what is the effect on these students' choice of reading (hint: look for a run on short books with large type), their comprehension of what they've read, and above all, their attitude toward reading when the program is over? The late educational psychologist John Nicholls speculated several years ago that the likely result of this program would be "a lot of fat kids who don't like to read."

Part of the problem is that many of us assume there exists a single entity called "motivation," such that students can have more or less of it. We want them to have more, so we offer stickers and stars, A's and praise, candy and cash. But what educational and social psychologists have learned is that there are qualitatively different kinds of motivation, and more of one kind often means less of another. Extrinsic motivators (inducements outside the task) are not only inferior to intrinsic motivation (an interest in the task itself): they actually tend to undermine such interest.

Thus, the question we need to ask is not "How motivated is this student?" but "*How* is this student motivated?" What matters is not the amount but the type of motivation involved—whether a child, for example, is encouraged to see reading as something gratifying in its own right, or as a tedious prerequisite to getting a reward.

The fact that interest in learning is typically undermined by offering rewards is not only a disturbing discovery in itself, but also a powerful explanation for another well-replicated finding: rewards usually reduce the quality of performance, particularly on challenging tasks. A quarter of a century ago, Professor Janet Spence, later to become the president of the American Psychological Association, wrote that rewards "have effects that interfere with performance in ways that we are only beginning to understand."

Of course, there is nothing wrong with pizza or money, per se. The problem comes when we offer such things contingently, and they become devices to manipulate behavior. Edward Deci and Richard Ryan at the University of Rochester have pointedly referred to the use of rewards as "control through seduction."

The most destructive arrangement of all, then, is to pile one reward on another—for example, by promising money or goodies to students who get good grades. A Minneapolis-based program called *Renaissance* (which might more accurately be termed *Dark Ages*) does exactly this. Not content merely to encourage students to see the point of school as collecting good grades, this program sets up a kind of caste system in which students are issued color-coded I.D. cards corresponding to their grade point average that entitle them to differential discounts from local merchants. If some foundation perversely commissioned me to develop a program whose aim was to utterly destroy children's interest in learning, I honestly don't think I could top this one.

Likewise, if a school institutes a "good citizenship" program, in which the aim is to "catch children doing something right" and offer them rewards for their good behavior, we can practically watch children's empathy evaporate before our eyes. Again, it isn't just that trying to control behavior fails to develop any commitment to that behavior; it's that rewards actively displace the motives and values that matter. Instead of helping children to ask, "What kind of person do I want to be?" or "What kind of community do we want to have?" a child in such a school is led to ask, "What do they want me to do, and what do I get for doing it?"

Here are three objections commonly offered to this sort of criticism:

1. *Why not use rewards at first to lure students into reading or helping and then fade them out later?* Unfortunately, this bait-and-switch

approach is naive in overlooking the fundamental difference in motives between what is created by rewards and what we ultimately want.
The introduction of an extrinsic motivator immediately changes the
whole Gestalt—the way a child looks at herself, the way she looks at
the person offering the reward, and the way she looks at the task.

2. *What if students aren't intrinsically motivated to do what we're
asking?* The trouble may be more with what we're asking than with
their lack of interest. If children are required to memorize a bunch of
facts or slog through sodden textbooks—things that few members of
our species would find interesting—then it is no wonder that adults
resort to offering bribes (and threats). But the challenge is to come up
with engaging tasks, and to bring students into the process of making
decisions about their learning, rather than coercing them into compliance. Kids' natural capacity to help others, meanwhile, is best
tapped by explaining, modeling, and transforming schools into caring communities.

3. *Adults are paid for working; why not pay children for learning?* To
begin with, this rather desperate rationalization ignores the crucial
difference between pay and pay-for-performance plans at work. Getting employees to see compensation as a reward (through bonuses and
such) is notably counterproductive if the objective is quality rather
than quantity, if the task requires any degree of creativity, and if the
time frame extends beyond what happens today.

Second, and more important, nothing in school is really analogous
to money, which adults must earn one way or another. Here our concern is with helping students not only to read but to want to read, to
become lifelong learners and decent people. Even if incentives were
effective with employees, this would offer no justification whatsoever
for using them to reach a different set of goals with a developmentally
different group of people.

We need to work *with* children to tap their natural desire to make
sense of the world and to play with words and numbers and ideas. Rewards, however well-intentioned, are basically ways of doing things to
someone. Educators need to help politicians understand that in the
long run, carrots and sticks are bound to backfire.

CHAPTER SEVEN

Grading

The Issue Is Not How But Why

W hy are we concerned with evaluating how well students are doing? The question of motive, as opposed to method, can lead us to rethink basic tenets of teaching and learning, and to evaluate what students have done in a manner more consistent with our ultimate educational objectives. But not all approaches to the topic result in this sort of thoughtful reflection. In fact, approaches to assessment may be classified according to their depth of analysis and their willingness to question fundamental assumptions about how and why we grade. Consider three possible levels of inquiry:

Level 1. These are the most superficial concerns, those limited to the practical issue of *how* to grade students' work. Here we find articles and books offering elaborate formulas for scoring assignments, computing points, and allocating final grades—thereby taking for granted that what students do must receive *some* grade and, by extension, that students ought to be avidly concerned about the ones they will get.

Originally published in *Educational Leadership* in 1994.

Level 2. Here educators call the above premises into question, asking whether traditional grading is really necessary or useful for assessing students' performance. Alternative assessments, often designated as "authentic," belong in this category. The idea here is to provide a richer, deeper description of students' achievement. (Portfolios of students' work are sometimes commended to us in this context, but when a portfolio is used merely as a means of arriving at a traditional grade, it might more accurately be grouped under Level 1.)

Level 3. Rather than challenging grades alone, discussions at this level challenge the whole enterprise of assessment—and specifically, why we are evaluating students as opposed to *how* we are doing so. No matter how elaborate or carefully designed an assessment strategy may be, the result will not be constructive if our reason for wanting to know how students are doing is itself objectionable.

GRADING RATIONALE I: SORTING

One reason for evaluating students is to be able to label them on the basis of their performance and thus to sort them like so many potatoes. Sorting, in turn, has been criticized at each of the three levels, but for very different reasons. At Level 1, the concern is merely that we are not correctly dumping individuals into the right piles. The major problem with our high schools and colleges, the argument goes, is that they don't keep enough students off the Excellent pile. (These critics don't put it quite this way, of course; they talk about "grade inflation.") Interestingly, most studies suggest that student performance does not improve when instructors grade more stringently and, conversely, that making it relatively easy to get a good grade does not lead students to do inferior work—even when performance is defined as the number of facts retained temporarily as measured by multiple-choice exams (Vasta and Sarmiento, 1979; Abrami et al., 1980).

At Level 2, questions are raised about whether grades are reliable enough to allow students to be sorted effectively. Indeed, studies show that any particular teacher may well give different grades to a single piece of work submitted at two different times. Naturally the variation is even greater when the work is evaluated by more than one teacher (Kirschenbaum et al., 1971). What grades offer is spurious precision, a subjective rating masquerading as an objective assessment.

From the perspective of Level 3, this criticism is far too tame. The trouble is not that we are sorting students badly—a problem that logically should be addressed by trying to do it better. The trouble is that we are sorting them at all. Are we doing so in order to segregate students by ability and teach them separately? The harms of this practice have been well established (Oakes, 1985). Are we turning schools into "bargain-basement personnel screening agencies for business" (Campbell, 1974, p. 145)? Whatever use we make of sorting, the process itself is very different from—and often incompatible with—the goal of helping students to learn.

GRADING RATIONALE II: MOTIVATION

A second rationale for grading—and indeed, one of the major motives behind assessment in general—is to motivate students to work harder so they will receive a favorable evaluation. Unfortunately, this rationale is just as problematic as sorting. Indeed, given the extent to which A's and F's function as rewards and punishments rather than as useful feedback, grades are counterproductive regardless of whether they are intentionally used for this purpose. The trouble lies with the implicit assumption that there exists a single entity called "motivation" that students have to a greater or lesser degree. In reality, a critical and qualitative difference exists between *intrinsic* and *extrinsic* motivation—between an interest in what one is learning for its own sake, and a mind-set in which learning is viewed as a means to an end, the end being to escape a punishment or snag a reward. Not only are these two orientations distinct, but they also often pull in opposite directions.

Scores of studies in social psychology and related fields have demonstrated that extrinsic motivators frequently undermine intrinsic motivation. This may not be particularly surprising in the case of sticks, but it is no less true of carrots. People who are promised rewards for doing something tend to lose interest in whatever they had to do to obtain the reward. Studies also show that, contrary to the conventional wisdom in our society, people who have been led to think about what they will receive for engaging in a task (or for doing it well) are apt to do lower quality work than those who are not expecting to get anything at all.

These findings are consistent across a variety of subject populations, rewards, and tasks, with the most destructive effects occurring in activities that require creativity or higher-order thinking. That this effect is produced by the extrinsic motivators known as grades has been documented with students of different ages and from different cultures. Yet the findings are rarely cited by educators.

Studies have shown that the more students are induced to think about what they will get on an assignment, the more their desire to learn evaporates, and ironically, the less well they do. Consider these findings:

- On tasks requiring varying degrees of creativity, Israeli educational psychologist Ruth Butler has repeatedly found that students perform less well and are less interested in what they are doing when being graded than when they are encouraged to focus on the task itself (Butler and Nissan, 1986; Butler, 1987, 1988).

- Even in the case of rote learning, students are more apt to forget what they have learned after a week or so—and are less apt to find it interesting—if they are initially advised that they will be graded on their performance (Grolnick and Ryan, 1987).

- When Japanese students were told that a history test would count toward their final grade, they were less interested in the subject—and less likely to prefer tackling difficult questions—than those who were told the test was just for monitoring their progress (Kage, 1991).

- Children told that they would be graded on their solution of anagrams chose easier ones to work on—and seemed to take less pleasure from solving them—than children who were not being graded (Harter, 1978).

As an article in the *Journal of Educational Psychology* concluded, "Grades may encourage an emphasis on quantitative aspects of learning, depress creativity, foster fear of failure, and undermine interest" (Butler and Nissan, 1986, p. 215). This is a particularly ironic result if the rationale for evaluating students in the first place is to encourage them to perform better.

GRADING RATIONALE III: FEEDBACK

Some educators insist that their purpose in evaluating students is neither to sort them nor to motivate them, but simply to provide feedback so they can learn more effectively tomorrow than they did today. From a Level 2 perspective, this is an entirely legitimate goal—and grades are an entirely inadequate means of reaching it. There is nothing wrong with helping students to internalize and work toward meeting high standards, but that is most likely to happen when they "experience success and failure not as reward and punishment, but as information" (Bruner, 1961, p. 26). Grades make it very difficult to do this. Besides, reducing someone's work to a letter or number simply is not helpful; a *B+* on top of a paper tells a student nothing about what was impressive about that paper or how it could be improved.

But from Level 3 comes the following challenge: *Why do we want students to improve?* This question at first seems as simple and bland as baby food; only after a moment does it reveal a jalapeño kick: it leads us into disconcerting questions about the purpose of education itself.

DEMAND VERSUS SUPPORT

Eric Schaps (1993), who directs the Developmental Studies Center in Oakland, California, has emphasized "a single powerful distinction: focusing on what students ought to be able to do, that is, what we will demand of them—as contrasted with focusing on what we can do to support students' development and help them learn." For lack of better labels, let us call these the "demand" and "support" models.

In the demand model, students are workers who are obligated to do a better job. Blame is leveled by saying students "chose" not to study or "earned" a certain grade—conveniently removing all responsibility from educators and deflecting attention from the curriculum and the context in which it is taught. In their evaluations, teachers report whether students did what they were supposed to do. This mind-set often lurks behind even relatively enlightened programs that emphasize performance assessment and—a common buzzword these days—*outcomes.* (It also manifests itself in the view of education as an investment, a way of preparing children to become future workers.)

The support model, by contrast, helps children take part in an "adventure in ideas" (Nicholls and Hazzard, 1993), guiding and stimulating their natural inclination to explore what is unfamiliar; to construct meaning; to develop a competence with and a passion for playing with words, numbers, and ideas. This approach meshes with what is sometimes called "learner-centered learning," in which the point is to help students act on their desire to make sense of the world. In this context, student evaluation is, in part, a way of deter-mining how effective *we* have been as educators. In sum, improve-ment is not something we require of students so much as something that follows when we provide them with engaging tasks and a sup-portive environment.

SUPPORTIVE ASSESSMENT

Here are five principles of assessment that follow from this support model:

1. Assessment of any kind should not be overdone. Getting stu-dents to become preoccupied with *how* they are doing can undermine their interest in *what* they are doing. An excessive concern with per-formance can erode curiosity—and, paradoxically, reduce the quality of performance. Performance-obsessed students also tend to avoid dif-ficult tasks so they can escape a negative evaluation.

2. The best evidence we have of whether we are succeeding as ed-ucators comes from observing children's behavior rather than from test scores or grades. It comes from watching to see whether they con-tinue arguing animatedly about an issue raised in class after the class is over, whether they come home chattering about something they dis-covered in school, whether they read on their own time. Where inter-est is sparked, skills are usually acquired. Of course, interest is difficult to quantify, but the solution is not to return to more conventional measuring methods; it is to acknowledge the limits of measurement.

3. We must transform schools into safe, caring communities. This is critical for helping students to become good learners and good people, but it is also relevant to assessment. Only in a safe place, where there is no fear of humiliation and punitive judgment, will students admit to being confused about what they have read and feel free to ac-knowledge their mistakes. Only by being able to ask for help will they be likely to improve.

Ironically, the climate created by an emphasis on grades, standard-ized testing, coercive mechanisms such as pop quizzes and compulsory recitation, and pressure on teachers to cover a prescribed curriculum makes it more difficult to know how well students understand—and thus to help them along.

4. Any responsible conversation about assessment must attend to the quality of the curriculum. The easy question is whether a stu-dent has learned something; the far more important—and unset-tling—question is whether the student has been given something worth learning. (The answer to the latter question is almost certainly no if the need to evaluate students has determined curriculum content.) Research corroborates what thoughtful teachers know from experience: when students have interesting things to do, artificial inducements to boost achievement are unnecessary (Moeller and Reschke, 1993).

5. Students must be invited to participate in determining the criteria by which their work will be judged, and then play a role in weighing their work against those criteria. Indeed, they should help make decisions about as many elements of their learning as possible (Kohn, 1993). This achieves several things: it gives them more control over their education, makes evaluation feel less punitive, and provides an important learning experience in itself. If there is a movement away from grades, teachers should explain the rationale and solicit students' suggestions for what to do instead and for how to manage the transitional period. That transition may be bumpy and slow, but the chance to engage in personal and collective reflection about these issues will be important in its own right.

AND IF YOU MUST GRADE . . .

Finally, **while conventional grades persist, teachers and parents ought to do everything in their power to help students forget about them.** Here are some practical suggestions for reducing the salience.

• *Refrain from giving a letter or number grade for individual assignments,* even if you are compelled to give one at the end of the term. The data suggest that substantive comments should replace, not supplement, grades (Butler, 1988). Make sure that the effect of doing this is not to create suspense about what students are going to get on their report cards, which would defeat the whole purpose. Some older students may experience, especially at first, a sense of existential vertigo: a steady supply of grades has defined them. Offer to discuss privately with any such student the grade he or she would probably receive if report cards were handed out that day. With luck and skill, the requests for ratings will decrease as students come to be involved in what is being taught.

• *Never grade students while they are still learning something and, even more important, do not reward them for their performance at that point.* Studies suggest that rewards are most destructive when given for skills still being honed (Condry and Chambers, 1978). If it is unclear whether students feel ready to demonstrate what they know, there is an easy way to find out: ask them.

• *Never grade on a curve.* The number of good grades should not be artificially limited so that one student's success makes another's less likely. Stipulating that only a few individuals can get top marks regardless of how well everyone does is egregiously unfair on its face. It also undermines collaboration and community. Of course, grades of any kind, even when they are not curved to create artificial scarcity— or deliberately publicized—tend to foster comparison and competition, an emphasis on relative standing. This is not only destructive to students' self-esteem and relationships but also counterproductive with respect to the quality of learning (Kohn, 1992).

As one book on the subject puts it: "It is not a symbol of rigor to have grades fall into a 'normal' distribution; rather, it is a symbol of failure—failure to teach well, to test well, and to have any influence at all on the intellectual lives of students" (Milton et al., 1986, p. 225).

• *Never give a separate grade for effort.* When students seem to be indifferent to what they are being asked to learn, educators sometimes respond with the very strategy that precipitated the problem in the first place—grading students' efforts to coerce them to try harder. The fatal paradox is that while coercion can sometimes elicit resentful obedience, it can never create desire. A low grade for effort is more likely to be read as "You're a failure even at trying." On the other hand, a high grade for effort combined with a low grade for achievement says "You're just too dumb to succeed." Most of all, rewarding or punishing children's efforts allows educators to ignore the possibility that the curriculum or learning environment may have something to do with students' lack of enthusiasm.

References

Abrami, P. C., W. J. Dickens, R. P. Perry, and L. Leventhal. (1980). "Do Teacher Standards for Assigning Grades Affect Student Evaluations of Instruction?" *Journal of Educational Psychology* 72: 107–118.

Bruner, J. S. (1961). "The Act of Discovery." *Harvard Educational Review* 31: 21–32.

Butler, R. (1987). "Task-Involving and Ego-Involving Properties of Evaluation." *Journal of Educational Psychology* 79: 474–482.

Butler, R. (1988). "Enhancing and Undermining Intrinsic Motivation." *British Journal of Educational Psychology* 58: 1–14.

Butler, R., and M. Nissan. (1986). "Effects of No Feedback, Task-Related Comments, and Grades on Intrinsic Motivation and Performance." *Journal of Educational Psychology* 78: 210–216.

Campbell, D. N. (October 1974). "On Being Number One: Competition in Education." *Phi Delta Kappan:* 143–146.

Condry, J., and J. Chambers. (1978). "Intrinsic Motivation and the Process of Learning." In *The Hidden Costs of Rewards: New Perspectives on the Psychology of Human Motivation,* edited by M. R. Lepper and D. Greene. Hillsdale, N.J.: Lawrence Erlbaum.

Grolnick, W. S., and R. M. Ryan. (1987). "Autonomy in Children's Learning: An Experimental and Individual Difference Investigation." *Journal of Personality and Social Psychology* 52: 890–898.

Harter, S. (1978). "Pleasure Derived from Challenge and the Effects of Receiving Grades on Children's Difficulty Level Choices." *Child Development* 49: 788–799.

Kage, M. (1991). "The Effects of Evaluation on Intrinsic Motivation." Paper presented at the meeting of the Japan Association of Educational Psychology, Joetsu, Japan.

Kirschenbaum, H., R. W. Napier, and S. B. Simon. (1971). *Wad-Ja-Get? The Grading Game in American Education.* New York: Hart.

Kohn, A. (1992). *No Contest: The Case Against Competition.* Rev. ed. Boston: Houghton Mifflin.

Kohn, A. (September 1993). "Choices for Children: Why and How to Let Students Decide." *Phi Delta Kappan:* 8–20. (Reprinted in this volume as Chapter Eighteen.)

Milton, O., H. R. Pollio, and J. A. Eison. (1986). *Making Sense of College Grades.* San Francisco: Jossey-Bass.

Moeller, A. J., and C. Reschke. (1993). "A Second Look at Grading and Classroom Performance." *Modern Language Journal* 77: 163–169.

Nicholls, J. G., and S. P. Hazzard. (1993). *Education as Adventure: Lessons from the Second Grade.* New York: Teachers College Press.

Oakes, J. (1985). *Keeping Track: How Schools Structure Inequality.* New Haven: Yale University Press.

Schaps, E. (October 1993). Personal communication.

Vasta, R., and R. F. Sarmiento. (1979). "Liberal Grading Improves Evaluations but Not Performance." *Journal of Educational Psychology* 71: 207–211.

CHAPTER EIGHT

Grade Inflation and Other Red Herrings

Higher tuition will not be the only topic of conversation on college campuses this fall. A number of universities seem even more concerned about the form of inflation that involves grades. News dispatches indicate that Stanford University is bringing back the F, Dartmouth College is "encouraging professors to grade more harshly," and other schools are scrambling to keep up in the race to bring grades down.

Unfortunately, this activity represents a noisy exercise in missing the point. The problem isn't grade inflation; it's grades.

First of all, lower marks are not necessarily more accurate: shifting A's to B's, or D's to F's, doesn't change the fact that grades are irreducibly subjective. Decades of research have found that there is often wide variation in the grade assigned to a single piece of work submitted at two different times—even to the same instructor.

Originally published in *The Boston Globe* in 1995.

But let's assume that curbing grade inflation really could help college deans meet the goal attributed to them in a *New York Times* article: "to provide graduate schools and employers with a way to compare students." The trouble is that sorting students more efficiently comes at the expense of another objective: learning.

Two decades later, I'm still delighted that I chose to attend Brown University, which realized its commitment to intellectual exploration, with no apparent sacrifice of rigor, precisely by deemphasizing grades. At most schools, however, students often seem less concerned about the content of the curriculum than about the requirements for snagging an A.

The problem isn't their attitude; it's a system that places disproportionate emphasis on grades, sometimes beginning in elementary school. Harsher grading will exacerbate that problem by making grades that much more salient.

The conclusion of perhaps the most comprehensive study of this subject, "Making Sense of College Grades," by Ohmer Milton and his colleagues, is worth taping to a professor's door:

> Faculty members have it within their power to reduce this pernicious and distorting aspect of educational practice that often seems to work against learning. If faculty would relax their emphasis on grades, this might serve not to lower standards but to encourage an orientation toward learning.

Along with most specialists in the field, Milton and his associates understand that it is not enough for a student to be "motivated" to study: what matters is the nature of that motivation. An extrinsically motivated student sees learning chiefly in terms of consequences outside the task itself. Research suggests that students led to think about extrinsic inducements (such as grades) tend to exhibit three predictable differences from those helped to become engaged with the subject matter: less creative thinking, less preference for challenging tasks, and less interest in learning per se.

The last of these findings corroborates scores of psychological studies demonstrating that the more people are rewarded for doing something, the less interest they typically have in whatever they were rewarded for doing. Extrinsic motivators are not just less effective than intrinsic motivation; they actually undermine it.

Thus, during his teaching career at New York University, the late guru of quality management, W. Edwards Deming, refused to be part of the grading game; he gave every student an A. At Harvard, biology professor Richard Lewontin announces at the beginning of each semester that all students who do the work will receive a B plus, the idea being to prevent a horde of grade-obsessed undergraduates from signing up but also to avoid seriously penalizing those who do.

The only reason to frown and cluck about too many high grades or devote precious time to recalibrating grading criteria is if we believe that schools exist to sort students for the convenience of business or other constituencies.

But what if we—as parents, educators and citizens—are more concerned about students' interest in ideas? What if we decided that a good school was one whose graduates continued to delight in playing with words and ideas? In that case, our obligation is clear: until we are able to dispense with them entirely, we have to do everything possible to help students forget that grades exist.

CHAPTER NINE

Only for *My* Kid

How Privileged Parents Undermine School Reform

*What the best and wisest parent wants for his own child,
that must the community want for all of its children. Any
other ideal for our schools is narrow and unlovely; acted
upon, it destroys our democracy.*

—*John Dewey,* School and Society

Mike McClaren, a superintendent in Oklahoma, was attracted to the idea of a "performance-based" curriculum: he believed in specifying his schools' learning outcomes in advance and shifting the emphasis from memorization to problem solving. This made sense to Mike King, principal of a nationally recognized middle school in McClaren's district, who wanted his teachers to have more autonomy and his students to have more opportunity to learn from one another. Neither man was pushing for anything too radical; they just thought that educators should be a little less concerned with deciding which students were better than others and a little more committed to helping all of them succeed.

As it turned out, both men felt obliged to find new jobs as a result of this agenda, with McClaren jumping before he was pushed. Key people in the community were unhappy, and three newly elected

---

Originally published in *Phi Delta Kappan* in 1998.

board members made sure that the changes—and the people responsible for them—didn't last. Predictably, the most vocal opponents were
affiliated with the Christian Coalition and other ultraconservative
groups. But here is the interesting part: even in small-town Oklahoma,
the usual suspects on the Right could not have done it on their own.
Their allies, who by all accounts gave them the margin of victory they
needed to roll back reform efforts, were individuals who were not particularly conservative or religious. King describes them as "your upper-
class, high-achieving parents who feel that education is competitive,
that there shouldn't be anyone else in the same class as my child, and
we shouldn't spend a whole lot of time with the have-nots."[1]

McClaren, who looks back on what happened from his new post
several states away, says he made "two fatal assumptions" when he
started: "I thought if it was good for kids, everyone would embrace it,
and I thought all adults wanted all kids to be successful. That's not
true. The people who receive status from their kids' performing well
in school didn't like that other kids' performance might be raised to
the level of their own kids.'"

It is common knowledge that the Christian Right has opposed all
manner of progressive reforms. They may act stealthily to get themselves installed on school boards, and they may read from identical
scripts in auditoriums across America about how outcome-based education and whole language will destroy our way of life. But they are
ultimately identifiable, and once their core beliefs are exposed and
their claims refuted, their impact (at least in many places) can be limited. Far less attention has been paid to the damage done by people
whose positions on other social issues are more varied and more
mainstream—specifically, the affluent parents of successful students,
those whose political power is substantial to begin with and whose
agenda was summarized by another educator in that same Oklahoma
town: "They are not concerned that all children learn; they are concerned that *their* children learn."

There is no national organization called Rich Parents Against
School Reform, in part because there doesn't have to be. But with
unaffiliated individuals working on different issues in different parts
of the country, the pattern is generally missed and the story is rarely
told. Take a step back, however, and you begin to grasp the import of
what is happening from Amherst, Massachusetts, where highly educated white parents have fought to preserve a tracking system that

keeps virtually every child of color out of advanced classes, to Palo Alto, California, where a similarly elite constituency demands a return to a "skill and drill" math curriculum and fiercely opposes the more conceptual learning outlined in the National Council of Teachers of Mathematics (NCTM) standards; from an affluent suburb of Buffalo, where parents of honors students quashed an attempt to replace letter grades with standards-based progress reports, to San Diego, where a program to provide underachieving students with support that will help them succeed in higher-level courses has run "head-on into vigorous opposition from some of the community's more outspoken, influential members—the predominantly white, middle-class parents of high-achieving students."[2]

Jeannie Oakes, author of *Keeping Track,* calls them "Volvo vigilantes," but that isn't quite accurate—first, because they work within, and skillfully use, the law; and second, because many of them drive Jeeps. They may be pro-choice and avid recyclers, with nothing good to say about the likes of Pat Robertson and Rush Limbaugh; yet on educational issues they are, perhaps unwittingly, making common cause with, and furthering the agenda of, the Far Right.

The controversies in which these parents involve themselves fall into three clusters, the first of which concerns the *type of instruction* that is offered. Here we find a tension between, on the one hand, traditional methods and practices, geared toward a classroom that is construed as a collection of discrete individuals, each of whom is supposed to absorb a body of knowledge and basic skills, and, on the other hand, an approach distinguished by active discovery and problem solving by a community of learners.

Second, there is the question of *placement,* or which students get what. This category includes debates over such issues as tracking, ability grouping, gifted-and-talented programs, and honors courses—as distinguished from efforts to create more heterogeneous and inclusive classrooms.

Finally, there are the practices that take place after (but undeniably affect) the instruction, in which the emphasis is on *selecting and sorting* students so only a few are recognized: awards, letter grades, weighted grades (which give an additional advantage to those in the selective courses), honor rolls, and class ranks—as opposed to the absence of these practices and, sometimes, the presence of an assessment system geared more to enhancing learning than to distinguishing one student from another. It is the difference between a bumper sticker that says, "My Child Is an Honors Student at . . ." (with the understood postscript: "And Yours Isn't") and one that says, "Every Child Is an Honored Student at. . . ."[3]

All affluent parents, of course, do not necessarily line up on the same side of every dispute. With respect to the type of instruction, anecdotal reports suggest that highly educated, middle-class parents sometimes support—or even demand—an emphasis on higher-order thinking, a literature-based approach to teaching reading, and the use of cooperative learning—at least within homogeneous groups. (After all, as Syracuse University's Mara Sapon-Shevin observes wryly, some parents figure, "My kid will have to learn to negotiate with the other Fortune 500 companies.") But just because most parents who support these innovations are middle-class doesn't mean that most middle-class parents support these innovations—just as the fact that a disproportionate number of truly progressive schools are private doesn't mean that a disproportionate number of private schools are progressive. The parents who prefer worksheets and lectures can use their clout to reverse or forestall a move to more learner-centered classrooms. Moreover, a tolerance for whole language or cooperative learning often does not extend to the newer approaches to teaching math, as reformers in Palo Alto and other California communities are discovering.[4]

By the same token, resistance to the elimination of letter grades and awards assemblies is not confined to those who live in large houses. Parents in some working-class neighborhoods have been particularly outraged by these proposals, banding together under such names as PURGE: Parents United to Restore Graded Evaluations.[5] Still, the experience of some educators matches that of Bob Gallagher, a staff development coordinator in the Buffalo area, who reports that the "parents of kids who were struggling" were pleased by a shift to rubrics and narrative assessments, while the parents of honors students "absolutely went crazy" at the prospect of losing traditional letter grades. Perhaps the reaction can more accurately be predicted by the status of the student than by the income level of the parent—although the significant correlation between these two is itself cause for concern.

If the position of a certain group of parents is not always clear-cut with respect to teaching and assessment, the battle lines are sharply drawn when it comes to placement and allocation issues, and the "gifted parents," as some observers like to call them, know what they want and how to get it. Sometimes their success is a function of being able to choose not only classes but schools—specifically, selective independent schools or well-funded public schools in affluent suburbs. American education is so segregated and stratified today that the elite mingle mostly with one another. Annette Lareau of Temple University wanted to study a school in Philadelphia whose student population cut across lines of race and class; she was unable to find a single example. "Who are the middle-class parents arguing against?" she asks. "I think that's why you don't see more of these conflicts. Poor kids are generally not in the same schools."

Pitched battles are more common in integrated schools, but even here they happen rarely, because in large measure the affluent white parents have already won. The plum classes and programs for their children already exist, as do the letter grades and awards to distinguish them from those other children. The system serves these parents well, and their influence is such—or the fear that they will yank their children out is sufficient—that few superintendents (and even fewer school boards) dare to rock this boat on which first-class cabins are so clearly delineated from steerage. The reformers eventually get tired—or fired.

As Amy Stuart Wells of UCLA sees it, even many liberal white parents may say, in effect, "We like the fact that our kids are in desegregated schools, but the fact that the white kids are in the top classes and the black kids are in the bottom is someone else's problem." Last fall, *U.S. News & World Report* published an article documenting how many "schools that appear integrated from the outside are highly segregated within. . . . Honors classes are dominated by whites, regular classes by blacks."[6] In response, a liberal *New Republic* columnist readily agreed that the honors program in his own daughter's school in Montgomery County, Maryland, amounted to "a school within a school" for the white and Asian students—and then announced that if this program were eliminated, he would pull his daughter out of that school "in a nanosecond."[7]

What is interesting about this exchange is that the *U.S. News* reporter had pretty much taken for granted the existence of tracking and seemed concerned only about the racial makeup of each track; the possibility of heterogeneous classrooms was not even raised until the very end of the article, and then it was immediately dismissed. Yet the liberal columnist served notice in a national magazine that any attempt to create a fairer system would be an invitation to white flight,

something in which he would unapologetically participate. Most affluent parents send this message more quietly and locally, of course,
but it reverberates through the offices of administrators and effectively
discourages meaningful change.

Or consider two essays published independently in 1996. The first,
in the *American Educational Research Journal,* describes a series of interviews with "educated, middle-class mothers, perceived by others as
well as themselves as liberals who believe in integrated and inclusive
education." In the course of conversation, these women pronounced
themselves committed to equity and tolerance, but then proceeded
(under questioning) to become far more passionate in dismissing
these very ideals when it came to the advantages they thought their
own children should receive. The self-described liberals tended to
"support segregated and stratified school structures that mainly benefit students of the middle class," the researchers discovered.[8]

The second article, published in the *Harvard Educational Review,*
contains a very serious charge leveled by Wells and her colleague Irene
Serna: tracking, advanced placement (AP) courses, and gifted programs do not provide differential instruction for legitimate pedagogical reasons—or allow for a system based on merit—so much as they
represent a naked grab for artificially scarce benefits by those who have
the power to get them.[9]

Think scientifically for a moment about how this disturbing hypothesis might be tested. If it were accurate, the beneficiaries of these
educational advantages would "be more concerned about the labels
placed on their children than about what actually goes on in the classroom."[10] And indeed, there is reason to think that this is frequently
true. To begin with, AP classes at the high school level are usually difficult but often poorly taught, with an emphasis on short-term memorization of facts presented in lectures and textbooks—in effect, one
long test-prep session. Yet many parents seem to care a lot more about
who is in these classes (namely, their own children and a few others
who look like them) than about how they are taught.

Granted, it is hard to deny the superiority of the instruction in
gifted-and-talented programs and some other honors or high-track
classes, what with hands-on learning, student-designed projects, computers, field trips, and other enrichments. But research generally shows
that it is precisely those enrichments that produce better results rather
than the fact that they are accorded only to a select few. What happens
in those classes is more decisive than the fact that they are homoge-

neous.[11] So if parents of those students were concerned about the quality of learning, they would have no reason to object to extending those benefits to everyone.

But object they do. Wells and Oakes have been studying the experience of ten schools across the country that are trying to ease away from tracking. Many of these schools have taken the advice of Anne Wheelock, who urged educators to help parents of top-tracked students understand that "inclusive schooling offers all students the type of education usually reserved for gifted and talented students."[12] The detracking in these ten schools was carefully planned to bring other students up to a high level, but not to take anything away from the privileged children. Yet the reaction from the parents of the latter students has been powerfully negative—often fatal for the reform efforts. These parents have pressured educators "to maintain separate and unequal classes for their children, . . . [demanding] to know *what their children will 'get' that other students will not have access to.*"[13]

This is essentially what happened in San Diego, where an attempt to give a leg up to lower-tracked students was, as Elizabeth Cohen of Stanford University puts it, "the kind of project that you'd think wouldn't bother upper-status parents at all. Wrong! They said, 'What are you going to do special for my kids?'" This posture, she adds, goes beyond a simple and commendable desire to do everything possible for one's own children. "When parents tell me they're terribly anxious about their kids getting ahead, I'm sympathetic. Everyone wants the best for their kids. But when it extends to sabotaging programs that are designed to help people, I have to draw the line."

Notice what is going on here. It isn't just that these parents are *ignoring* everyone else's children, focusing their efforts solely on giving their own children the most desirable education. Rather, they are in effect *sacrificing* other children to their own. It's not about success but victory, not about responding to a competitive environment but creating one. As Harvey Daniels of National Louis University sees it, "The psychology of those parents is that it's not enough for their kids to win: others must lose—and they must lose conspicuously."

This explains much of the frustration experienced by educators who insist that narratives or portfolios are far more informative about students' learning than letter grades are, or who cite evidence to show that focusing students' attention on getting A's tends to reduce their interest in the learning itself.[14] These arguments will only persuade someone who is looking for more information about his or her child's improvement or someone who is concerned about sustaining the child's interest. If, however, the point is not for assessment to be authentic but for it to serve as a sorting device, to show not how well the student is doing but how much better he or she is doing than others, then A's will always be necessary—and it will always be necessary for some people's children not to get them. It will be necessary not only to rate children but to rank them, to give out not only report cards but trophies and plaques and certificates and membership in elite societies, all of which are made artificially scarce.

This agenda is arguably antichild, but should that surprise us? We live in a culture that is remarkably unfriendly toward children in general; a "good" child is one who doesn't cause us any trouble. Even when politicians and businesspeople demand "world-class" schools, they usually mean those that produce high test scores, and their reasons evidently don't have much to do with meeting the children's own needs. As for material possessions, it is true that

> some parents—those who have enough income—spend lavishly on their children, generating the notion that we are a child-centered society. But public spending for children is often meager and always surrounded by contention, and it embodies the peculiar conception that children are not valuable as persons in their own right but only for the adults they will grow up to be. . . . The saccharine myth [that] . . . children are [America's] most precious natural resources has in practice been falsified by our hostility to other people's children and our unwillingness to support them.[15]

The problem does not rest solely with our attitude toward children, however, but also with our attenuated sense of community. Our culture is distinguished by an ethic of individualism as well as a tendency to collapse all human interaction and most matters of public policy into economic laws. Vouchers and school choice plans effectively say to parents, "Never mind about what's best for kids; just shop for the school that's best for *your* kids." It's not a community; it's a market—so why would we expect things to be any different inside the school? How much commitment to inclusive education can we expect in an exclusive society? Sadly, when parents (and shamefully some educators) go to great lengths to erect walls between the "gifted" and the ordinary, another generation is raised without a commitment to the values of community, and the vicious circle closes in.[16]

Beyond attitudes toward children and community, there is the question of how we view education itself. In a new book titled *How to Succeed in School Without Really Learning,* David Labaree of Michigan State University argues that schooling these days is not seen as a way to create democratic citizens or even capable workers, but serves more as a credentialing mechanism. "The purpose of education from this angle is not what it can do for democracy or the economy but what it can do for me," and this shift turns our school systems into "a vast public subsidy for private ambition." One implication of such a transformation is that education becomes "an arena for zero-sum competition filled with self-interested actors seeking opportunities or gaining educational distinctions at the expense of each other"—precisely what we've seen affluent parents doing so relentlessly and so well.

Labaree incisively demonstrates another implication of viewing education this way, which is that the quality of learning itself is likely to decline. "We have credentialism to thank for the aversion to learning that, to a great extent, lies at the heart of our educational system," he observes. While the pages of education journals are brimming with suggestions for how to make schools more effective, the impact of these ideas is perforce limited if making schools more effective is really beside the point for most Americans. The point is not to get an education but to get ahead—and therefore, from the student-consumer's point of view, "to gain the highest grade with the minimum amount of learning." In fact, efforts to help all students succeed, or to place more emphasis on teaching and less on sorting, would be not merely irrelevant but utterly contrary to the individualistic, competitive credentialing model of school—and so such efforts would be bitterly contested by those with the best chances of getting the shiniest credentials.

> It is elite parents [who] see the most to gain from the special distinctions offered by a stratified educational system, and they are therefore the ones who play the game of academic one-up-manship most aggressively. . . . They vigorously resist when educators (pursuing a more egalitarian vision) propose to eliminate some form of within-school distinction or another—by promoting multiability reading groups, for example, ending curriculum tracking, or dropping a program for the gifted.[17]

No wonder a somewhat disillusioned Anne Wheelock now muses that "all the research in the world" about the positive effects of detracking or abolishing letter grades "doesn't persuade these folks." No wonder such parents are more likely to ask, "How is my child doing compared to everyone else?" than to inquire about how effectively that child is learning. To paraphrase a popular song, What's learning got to do with it?

It is through this lens that we might regard the demand in some affluent communities for a transmission-based, "bunch o' facts" curriculum. Why, asks James Beane, an expert on the subject, would there be opposition to the contextual learning and cooperative inquiry entailed by a reform such as curriculum integration, which "seems to offer greater access to knowledge for more young people . . . [and] encourages multiple routes to knowledge and multiple ways of demonstrating it"? The question contains its own answer: if "young people who have traditionally monopolized 'success' in the classroom are likely to find themselves joined in success by more of their peers," this can be "profoundly upsetting to some of their parents whose ambitions for their children include being at the top of the class in school and getting into elite colleges." What's more, vocal concern about the effects of innovative teaching on standardized test scores may reflect "not a concern about their own children's continued success but about the possibility that their monopoly on success will be threatened."[18]

So, too, for the organized, sometimes virulent, opposition to the NCTM math standards among highly educated parents. In Stanford University's backyard, a group calling itself HOLD has lobbied since late 1994 for a continuation of (or return to) the kind of mathematics that stresses direct instruction, standard textbooks, and drills to teach basic computational skills. The highly educated and mostly well-to-do members of this group have used the Internet as well as their political connections and media savvy to persuade California officials to retreat from the state's new math standards, which had emphasized conceptual understanding, open-ended problems, and student communication about mathematical principles. Indeed, HOLD has gotten some of its members appointed to statewide commissions, and the implications are enormous for the adoption of curriculum materials in California and beyond.[19]

Of course, reasonable people can disagree about the best way to teach math and other subjects, but more than one observer of the "math wars" has wondered whether we are witnessing a debate over pedagogy or about something else entirely. Are parents really trying to deny that encouraging students to figure out together what lies behind an algebraic formula is more valuable than getting them to memorize algorithms or slog through endless problem sets? Do they seriously doubt that such an approach is better preparation for higher math in college? Or does parental opposition really just reflect the fear that more sophisticated math instruction might be less useful for boosting SAT scores and therefore for getting students *into* the most elite colleges? Math reformers who counterpose merely doing arithmetic with really understanding (and being able to apply) mathematical principles may be missing the more pertinent contrast, which is between doing what is best for learning and doing what is best for getting my child into the Ivy League.

This trade-off raises the intriguing possibility that the exertions of the moms and dads of top students may exact a price not only from other children but also from their own. Consider those parents who essentially mortgage their children's present to the future, sacrificing what might bring meaning or enjoyment—or even produce higher-quality learning—in a ceaseless effort to prepare the children for Harvard (a process I have come to call "Preparation H"). This bottom line is never far from the minds of such parents, who weigh every decision about what their children do in school, or even after school, against the yardstick of what it might contribute to future success. They are not raising a child so much as a living résumé. As repellent as we might find the corporate groups and politicians who regard education—and even children themselves—as little more than an "investment," these parents are doing the dirty work implied by this reductive worldview, and they are doing it to their own children.

Before long, the children internalize this quest and come to see their childhood as one long period of getting ready: they sign up for activities that might impress an admissions committee, ignoring (perhaps eventually losing sight of) what they personally find interesting in the here and now. They ask teachers, "Do we need to know this?" and grimly try to squeeze out another few points on the GPA or the SAT. What they don't know, for their parents surely will not tell them, is that this straining toward the future, this poisonous assumption that the value of everything is solely a function of its contribution to something that might come later, will continue right through college, right through professional school, right through the early stages of a career, until at last they wake up in a tastefully appointed bedroom to discover that their lives are mostly gone.

And those are just the successful students.

The parents, then, could be described as having sacrificed other children to their own, and also their own children's present to the imagined future. But there is a third sacrifice, too, and like the second it does their own children no favor: moral, social, artistic, emotional, and other forms of development are often jettisoned in favor of a narrow academic agenda. (Academics, of course, may simply be a stand-in for the ultimate goal of material success.) By ruling out a heterogeneous classroom on the grounds that it might slow down their precocious child's race to acquire more advanced math or reading skills, they ignore what he or she loses in other respects. By insisting that students be graded and then ranked against one another—or forced to compete for various awards—they deprive their children of the richer rewards to be gained from attending a school that feels like a caring community.

What Garrison Keillor said about school choice proposals could easily be applied to ability grouping and gifted programs: they seem to make sense "until you stop and think about the old idea of the public school, a place where you went to find out who inhabits this society other than people like you."[20] The experiences of students who have to struggle for what they have, who take so much less for granted, are not just valid but valuable for their privileged peers to hear. The latter get less than a full education, arguably become less than fully human, when they are segregated for the purposes of purely academic acceleration.[21]

Here, then, we have parents evincing what Nel Noddings calls a "mean-spirited attitude that they want their kids to have the best, and the heck with the other kids"—and in the process actually doing a disservice to their own children. How can we make sense of this? The reasons are multiple, some simple and some complex, some based on judgments most of us would regard as reasonable and some as simply abhorrent. The balance is different from one parent to the next and from one issue to the next, but clearly there are several identifiable factors at work.

For starters, it must be conceded that some parents are genuinely worried about the extent to which their children are learning, or would be learning, in a heterogeneous classroom. They are afraid that the curriculum might be "dumbed down," resulting in boredom and lack of appropriate challenge for their own children. In some places, there is legitimate reason for concern, but as a rule too much attention is paid to the difficulty level of what is being taught, the simplistic assumption being that harder is better.

The truth is that, if tests or homework assignments consist of factual recall questions, it doesn't make all that much difference whether there are twenty-five tough questions or ten easy ones. A basal does not become a more appropriate teaching tool just because it is intended for a higher grade level. Boredom may reflect a problem with the method of instruction (and the underlying theory of learning) rather than with the speed or difficulty with which a lesson is taught. To insist on homogeneity, then, would fail to address what is really wrong with many classrooms, which is not that certain students can complete the worksheets without breaking a sweat but that the teacher is relying on worksheets at all.

The flip side of this is that heterogeneity may be fairer but does not in itself constitute a prescription for effective teaching. In fact, heterogeneity is hard to do well. But the parents of high-scoring students ought to be providing support and respectful pressure for educators to do it better, rather than simply opting out of regular classrooms. "We remove the squeaky wheel, so we never repair the car," remarks Mara Sapon-Shevin. "We need fundamental changes in how we construct pedagogy and curriculum. If we continue to do segregation"— including segregation of the so-called gifted and talented, whom she prefers to designate as the rich and lucky—"we'll never get there."

Some parents are concerned less about the classroom than about their children's future, and this, too, cannot be written off. Yes, we live in a compulsively competitive culture; yes, the most selective colleges by definition accept only a small proportion of those who would like to attend; and yes, even the upper middle class has begun to grow uneasy now that they, too, may be the victims of mass firings (euphemistically called "downsizing"). "In a way you can't blame them," says Amy Stuart Wells of these parents. "It's a larger systemic issue in how we define intelligence and merit, how we push competition for the few spots at the top of the hierarchy."

And yet we find many people exaggerating the extent of competition around them, reproducing and exacerbating it by what they do to their children and their children's schools, overlooking the costs of pushing youngsters to become winners, and becoming part of the "them" to which other individuals will then point to justify their own unsavory behavior. Harvey Daniels suggests that we take a closer look at the explanations offered by people of privilege: "Do they really feel that unless their kid accumulates a bevy of awards, he or she is going to starve? Usually, these kids are going to be fine; they don't have anything to worry about"—except, perhaps, whether they attend a very elite college or only a somewhat elite college. Decades ago, Bertrand Russell pointed out that what is often meant by talk of "the struggle for life is really the struggle for [competitive] success. What people fear when they engage in the struggle is not that they"—or their children—"will fail to get their breakfast next morning, but that they will fail to outshine their neighbors."[22]

Alongside concern for the success of one's children we sometimes find a sticky attachment to the status quo. Larry Militello, a principal in Williamsville, New York, put it succinctly: "Parents say, 'Look, I live in this $600,000 house. I was successful with the system you currently have. Why do we have to look at anything different?'" The twin premises of this argument, of course, are equally ripe for challenge: that the most important kind of success in life can be measured in terms of real estate and that their own success occurred *because of* a system that includes letter grades, separate tracks, memorizing the multiplication table in third grade, and so on.

We find a different version of this same resistance when parents assert that the old system is *still* working—for their children. Why would someone whose daughter is in the top 5 percent of her class agree to stop ranking students? Here, says Deborah Meier, is the dilemma faced by the Coalition for Essential Schools: the elite students are getting a school-within-a-school with small classes and plenty of attention, so "why should you be for change when your kids are benefiting from exactly what we say is wrong with high schools?" More generally, Glenn Kleiman, a senior scientist at the Education Development Center in Newton, Massachusetts, reports that when educators from around the country are gathered at a seminar, those from "suburban districts have the hardest time making changes. They get the feedback that our kids are doing well; they're getting into the best colleges. . . . It ain't broke; why change it?"

The answer is that the system is quite clearly broken for most students—those who are not among the elect. And even with respect to those at the top, one has only to look past the infatuation with credentials to see the necessity for change: if students can read but don't, if they fail to think deeply or to take satisfaction from playing with ideas, if they are primarily concerned with what is going to be on the test, then something is drastically wrong with the status quo. Ignorance of those harms, obliviousness to the trade-off between credentials and learning, a simple lack of awareness about what (and who) is being sacrificed when a school is rigidly tracked and how even the winners ultimately lose as a result of competition[23]—these are probably the most charitable explanations for why some people fight reform. They just don't get it. But we cannot discount, at least in some instances, the presence of more malign motives. One is racism (or its twin, classism). This is no less a factor just because it is not splayed out on the surface with ugly, disparaging epithets, as Wells and Oakes explain:

> Unlike the more blatantly racist parents of an earlier generation, who resisted school desegregation policies because they did not want their children in schools with "colored" children, [today's] influential parents are more subtle and savvy in their resistance to detracking efforts that lead to desegregation within schools. They couch their opposition to detracking mainly in terms of the low-track students' "behavior"—lack of motivation to learn, lack of commitment to school or interest in higher education, tendency to act out, and so forth—without making the connection between these behaviors and the low-track students' "penetration" of an unequal and hierarchical system in which they are at the bottom.[24]

From personal experience, Hugh Mehan, a sociologist who has worked in the schools of San Diego, can tell you what racism sounds like in the nineties: "Bringing those lower-achieving students into the classroom is going to water down things for my children. They're not going to be able to keep up, and the teachers are going to have to slow things down." (Interestingly, a parent who dismisses the capabilities of "those" students may persist in the belief that white, middle-class children are smart—and therefore deserving of special treatment—even when their record of school achievement is not especially high.)[25]

Finally, our search for reasons must include simple selfishness, which sometimes accounts for both the callous disregard for other people's children and, in the final analysis, what many affluent parents are doing to their own. Social psychologists call it BIRG: basking

in reflected glory. "We didn't realize they had so much emotionally invested in the concept that they were the parents of the 'good' students,"
recalls Bob Gallagher from Buffalo. "Not to have the bumper sticker
to put on their car was more important to some parents than the
learning that was going on in the classroom."

Daniels has seen this, too: "When you meet these people for the
first time, they manage to insert into the conversation in the first two
minutes the fact that their kid is in some kind of gifted program. It's
not about the kid—it's about them, their egos, their bragging rights."
The child's needs and point of view often play little role in decisions
that are made by, as well as for, the parents. Indeed, "some of these
kids live in constant fear of letting their parents down," observes Lilian Katz, an authority on early childhood education—and that may
continue well after the high school valedictory address has been
delivered.

A list of explanations for the actions of these parents, then, would
include a simple desire to do what is best for one's children and a
preoccupation with what is most flattering to oneself, as well as anxiety about anything unfamiliar, prejudice about those children who
aren't like us, and simple lack of knowledge. It isn't clear which of
these is a deliberate rationale for fighting change, which is an uncon-
scious determinant, and which is simply a consequence of the others.
It's not even obvious whether the whole picture is getting brighter or
darker over time. Meier sees a disturbing trend: "Fifteen years ago people who were for tracking were on the defensive. Now it's right out in
the open in the middle of the West Side [of New York City]. There was
a certain *noblesse oblige* that these parents used to have. Now a green
light has been given to greed and self-centeredness."

Similarly discouraging is the fact that efforts to get rid of letter
grades have been going on for decades, with some of the most elo-
quent articles and persuasive research reports on the subject having
been published more than half a century ago.[26] Those districts that
have managed to replace letter and number ratings with narrative assessments, portfolios, and the like may find, as one assessment specialist in Kentucky describes it, that some parents "come to the
[parent-teacher] conferences and love everything they get. And then,
at the very end, they kind of lean over and *whisper,* 'But if you were
going to give a letter grade, what letter grade would you give my
child?'" Perhaps this is good news, though, she adds: "At least they

whisper now! . . . They are learning to do without grades, although they would still like them. Maybe in a few years they won't even whisper; they just won't ask."[27]

To get to that point—and to a comparable point with respect to other kinds of school reform—will require educators to understand the depth and strength of the resistance posed by affluent parents of high-achieving students. And it will require some or all of the following measures.

- **Appealing to fairness.** We need to invite people to live up to their own best ideals, to impress upon them the moral implications of these policies, and to help them understand that it's not just other children but the very prospects for a democratic society that are at risk from tracking and other practices.[28]

- **Focusing on broad, long-term goals for their children.** It's easy to get caught up with short-term issues such as grades, or to collapse all long-term discussions into such questions as college admission. But ask parents what they really want for their children over time, how they'd like their youngsters to turn out, and it's very rare, in my experience, to hear about Harvard or six-figure salaries. As I often do when speaking to such groups, I asked the parents of students at an elite independent school in Texas not long ago what their long-term goals were for their children. Here is the list that resulted: happy, balanced, independent, fulfilled, productive, self-reliant, responsible, functioning, kind, thoughtful, loving, inquisitive, and confident. A week later I asked the same question of another large audience of parents, this time in an affluent Minneapolis suburb. The answers were almost identical.

The reformer's job, then, is to help parents see that favored educational practices—from drill-and-skill teaching techniques to letter grades to awards assemblies—are actively impeding the realization of the very goals that they themselves say they want.[29] A number of parents (and educators, for that matter) may never have thought about the difference between seeing school as a place for learning and seeing it as a place for accumulating credentials. Provoking reflection about the ways these views pull in opposite directions may help parents reevaluate their positions.

- **Distinguishing between legitimate and illegitimate requests and then responding to the former.** If parents want to make sure their children are challenged and engaged by what they are learning, it is natural for them to be leery of any reform that might jeopardize that—an entirely legitimate concern. But wanting to make sure that *only* their children, or an arbitrarily limited group of similar children, receive the best possible education is not legitimate and should not be honored.

By the same token, if grades offer the only window through which parents can get a sense of how their children are doing at school, it is perfectly understandable that they would be nervous at the prospect of eliminating these grades. The educator's job is to show how various forms of authentic assessment can meet their legitimate need for information even more effectively than letter grades can. (In fact, it is hard to imagine something *less* informative about how well their children are learning than "B.")

But I believe that "How much better is my child doing than the other kids in class?" is not a legitimate question, and the educator's job is to explain why this is so rather than creating a system of ranking (or norm-referenced testing) designed to answer it, thereby doing a real disservice to all children. An elementary school teacher near Kansas City says she responds to this parental question by confiding, "You know, your child is the best in the class!" Then, after a pause, she muses, "Of course, this is the dumbest class I've ever had. . . ." Apart from its wit, her answer nicely points up just how useless norm-referenced evaluations really are.

• **Offering information.** Our job is not limited to educating students; sometimes we are called upon to educate parents and others in the community. Of course, we can also learn from them, and we must be respectful of their concerns and beliefs; finding a balance here is an art and sometimes an agony. But if we know from experience how children of different backgrounds (including the child whose parents brag that he was reading at age four) thrive when they can learn from one another in a cooperative classroom, if we have witnessed how children both understand and enjoy math better when they are tackling real-life problems than when they are staring at a ditto full of naked numbers, if we realize why it makes sense for children to write even before they can spell, then we need to share our experiences with parents.

Likewise, some parents will be relieved that detracking doesn't mean "teaching to the middle"—but they have to be made aware of this. Parents deserve to know that plenty of elementary schools give no letter or number grades at all without jeopardizing their students' eventual high school performance or chances for college admission. (Indeed, a few high schools, too, have done without grades—and even more have abolished class ranks—while continuing to place their graduates in the most selective universities.[30] For that matter, some children gain admission to these universities without ever having set foot in a school.)

In fact, rather than abandon reforms designed to make schools more equitable or learning more meaningful just because parents express concern about the impact on their children's future, educators can help these parents look more carefully at the chain of associations that are usually taken for granted. College admissions officers are not ninety-seven–year-old fuddy-duddies peering over their spectacles in horror at an unconventional application; they are more likely to be recent graduates praying to be saved from another earnest 3.7 GPA, student council vice president, flute-playing tennis star from the 'burbs. Apart from the flexibility about grades, at least 280 four-year colleges are now making the SAT and the ACT optional.[31]

Parents also might be invited to question the premise that admission to a top-ranked college is necessary or sufficient for success in life: people without the usual credentials (but possessed of determination and a genuine love for what they are doing) often flourish, and people *with* superlative credentials may be summarily sacked. Individuals representing each of these categories ought to be invited to speak to students and parents—possibly in place of the usual lecturers offering tips on how to polish a transcript. It might also be useful to hear from well-to-do, educated parents who have had an experience that changed their frame of reference: perhaps their children wound up in a heterogeneous classroom, or in a nearby school that feels like a caring community rather than a nonstop rat race, and they came to realize how much better off their children were there. (The real epiphanies, according to education consultant Willard Daggett, come to those parents who discover that one of their children is disabled.)

• **Organizing the less-powerful parents.** Rather than directly oppose the parents who demand the preservation of programs that benefit only their own children, Jeannie Oakes advises educators to reach out to all the other parents, to "build community advocacy for an equity agenda" so that school board members, administrators, and politicians hear from everyone with an interest in the issue, instead of just from the elite.

At the very least, people typically lacking in wealth, self-confidence, or political savvy can be provided with the skills to be more effective advocates for themselves and their children.[32] Ultimately, though, we want not only to have more parents demanding that their own children get more resources, but to build a constituency for a fairer, more effective sort of schooling for all children.

• **Respecting a moral bottom line.** Educators should do all they can to bring parents aboard, to persuade and inform and organize, but in the final analysis there are some principles that have to be affirmed and some practices that cannot be tolerated. As one Maryland educator put it, "We're not in the business of educating one group of students. As professionals we're responsible for educating everyone, and there are things that we must not do. That's a moral and professional issue."[33]

Notes

1. All unattributed quotations in this article are derived from personal communications.
2. Daniel Gursky, "On the Wrong Track," *Teacher Magazine*, May 1990, p. 43. The program, Advancement Via Individual Determination (AVID), continues to generate opposition from these quarters to this day.
3. Something similar to the latter slogan is actually used by the Friends School of Atlanta and other Friends schools around the country, as well as by the Drew Model School in Arlington, Virginia.
4. Joseph Kahne, assistant professor of educational policy at the University of Illinois, Chicago, attributes this disparity to several factors. First, there is a single right answer to most math problems, and parents may fear that their children won't know it, particularly when they sit down to take a standardized test. "They aren't nervous about whole language because they know their kids will be reading; their literacy skills aren't threatened." Moreover, these parents are already familiar with reading for understanding; in their own lives, they don't underline the topic sentence or circle the vowels. The more sophisticated approaches to mathematics, by contrast, are utterly alien to most adults, and few people will enthusiastically support—or even permit—a move from something comfortably familiar to something they don't really understand.
5. This particular group was formed in Silver Creek, New York.
6. Julian E. Barnes, "Segregation, Now," *U.S. News & World Report*, Sept. 22, 1997, p. 24.
7. John B. Judis, "Honor Code," *New Republic*, Oct. 20 1997, pp. 4, 45.

8. See Ellen Brantlinger, Massoumeh Majd-Jabbari, and Samuel L. Guskin, "Self-Interest and Liberal Educational Discourse: How Ideology Works for Middle-Class Mothers," *American Educational Research Journal,* vol. 33, 1996, pp. 571–97. The quotations appear on p. 590.

9. See Amy Stuart Wells and Irene Serna, "The Politics of Culture: Understanding Local Political Resistance to Detracking in Racially Mixed Schools," *Harvard Educational Review,* vol. 66, 1996, pp. 93–118.

10. Ibid., p. 103.

11. "When advantages to students in the high-ability tracks do accrue"—and even this result is not always found—"they do not seem to be primarily related to the fact that these tracks are homogeneously grouped. For example, controlled studies of students taking similar subjects in heterogeneous and homogeneous groups show that high-ability students (like other students) rarely benefit from these tracked settings." See Jeannie Oakes, "Tracking in Secondary Schools," in Robert E. Slavin, ed., *School and Classroom Organization* (Hillsdale, N.J.: Erlbaum, 1989). Slavin's own work, in addition to the research Oakes goes on to cite, is pertinent here.

12. Anne Wheelock, "Winning Over Gifted Parents," *School Administrator,* April 1995, p. 17. See also Wheelock's *Crossing the Tracks: How "Untracking" Can Save America's Schools* (New York: New Press, 1992).

13. Amy Stuart Wells and Jeannie Oakes, "Potential Pitfalls of Systemic Reform: Early Lessons from Research on Detracking," *Sociology of Education,* vol. 69, special issue, p. 138.

14. On the latter point, see Alfie Kohn, *Punished by Rewards: The Trouble with Gold Stars, Incentive Plans, A's, Praise, and Other Bribes* (Boston: Houghton Mifflin, 1993).

15. W. Norton Grubb and Marvin Lazerson, *Broken Promises: How Americans Fail Their Children* (New York: Basic Books, 1982), pp. 56, 85. *Kids These Days: What Americans Really Think About the Next Generation,* a report released by Public Agenda in June 1997, found "a stunning level of antagonism not just toward teenagers but toward young children as well," according to a story in the *New York Times,* June 26, 1997, p. A–25.

16. See, for example, Mara Sapon-Shevin, *Playing Favorites: Gifted Education and the Disruption of Community* (Albany: State University of New York Press, 1994).

17. See David F. Labaree, *How to Succeed in School Without Really Learning: The Credentials Race in American Education* (New Haven, Conn.: Yale University Press, 1997). The first chapter, which contains the heart of the argument, was also published as "Public Goods, Private Goods: The American Struggle

Over Educational Goals," *American Educational Research Journal,* vol. 34, 1997, pp. 39–81. The quotations used here are taken from pp. 30, 32, 258, and 259 of the book and, in one case, from Labaree's article "Are Students 'Consumers'? The Rise of Public Education as a Private Good," *Education Week,* Sept. 17, 1997, pp. 48, 38.

18. James A. Beane, *Curriculum Integration: Designing the Core of Democratic Education* (New York: Teachers College Press, 1997), p. 79.

19. See, for example, Allyn Jackson's two-part article "The Math Wars: California Battles It Out over Mathematics Education," *Notices of the AMS* [American Mathematics Society], June/July and Aug. 1997.

20. Garrison Keillor, "The Future of Nostalgia," *New York Times Magazine,* Sept. 29, 1996, p. 68.

21. Educational researchers, of course, tend to share this bias, evaluating the effects of ability grouping, class size, and any number of other variables mostly in terms of their impact on academic achievement—and indeed mostly in terms of their impact on standardized test scores.

22. Bertrand Russell, *The Conquest of Happiness* (New York: Horace Liveright, 1930), p. 45.

23. For more on the pervasive and inherent harms of competition, see Alfie Kohn, *No Contest: The Case Against Competition,* rev. ed. (Boston: Houghton Mifflin, 1992).

24. Wells and Oakes, pp. 138–139. Indeed, "advanced and gifted programs began to appear and proliferate at the same time that the schools in these districts were becoming more racially mixed," according to Wells and Serna, p. 108.

25. See Brantlinger, Majd-Jabbari, and Guskin, p. 585.

26. "If I were asked to enumerate ten educational stupidities, the giving of grades would head the list. . . . 'But it's a competitive world!' I am told again and again. Certainly it is, and a very messy one I should say. Look around. And I should add, 'It was also once a disease-ridden world and we are curing it.' . . . If I can't give a child a better reason for studying than a grade on a report card, I ought to lock my desk and go home and stay there." That was written by Dorothy De Zouche in "The Wound Is Mortal: Marks, Honors, Unsound Activities," *The Clearing House,* Feb. 1945. *Plus ça change, plus c'est la même merde.*

27. The comments of Merry Denny are quoted in Joan Gaustad, *Assessment and Evaluation in the Multiage Classroom,* a special issue of the *Oregon School Study Council Bulletin,* vol. 39, nos. 3 and 4, Feb. 1996, p. 51.

28. See Joseph Kahne, "Democratic Communities, Equity, and Excellence: A Deweyan Reframing of Educational Policy Analysis," *Educational Evaluation*

and Policy Analysis, vol. 16, 1994, pp. 233–48. Nel Noddings points out one difficulty with an appeal to fairness: many privileged parents insist that the present arrangement *is* fair, arguing that "if other parents would work as hard as I do, then their kids would do fine. They just have to pull up their socks and get with it."

29. I suppose it is possible that some of these parents are being dishonest, that they actually are less concerned about their children's ethics and happiness than about their wealth. But it is more respectful to take the parents at their word and more effective to hold them to their own rhetoric.

30. For example, the Carolina Friends School in Durham, North Carolina; the Poughkeepsie Day School in Poughkeepsie, New York; the Waring School in Beverly, Massachusetts; Saint Ann's School in Brooklyn, New York; and the Metropolitan Learning Center in Portland, Oregon, give no letter or number grades at all.

31. See "ACT/SAT Optional Colleges List Soars to 280," *FairTest Examiner,* Summer 1997, p. 5. For a copy of the list, send a self-addressed stamped envelope to FairTest, 342 Broadway, Cambridge, MA 02139, or download it from www.fairtest.org/optional.htm.

32. The Right Question Project, for example, trains facilitators to help parents ask four questions: What is my child learning? What does my child need to learn? Is the teacher teaching what my child needs to learn? If not, what can I do? For information, contact the Project at 218 Holland St., Somerville, MA 02144.

33. Jake Burks, quoted in Wheelock, *Crossing the Tracks,* p. 76.

PART THREE

Unquestioned Assumptions About Children

CHAPTER TEN

Suffer the Restless Children

Unsettling Questions About the ADHD Label

In March of 1902, Dr. George Still stood before the Royal College of Physicians in London and described some children he had observed—mostly boys—who seemed to him restless, passionate, and apt to get into trouble. The children were suffering, he declared, from "an abnormal defect of moral control."

Despite his invocation of morality, Still's lecture is often billed as the first recorded discussion of hyperactivity. Literally thousands of articles on the subject have been published in the journals since then, the great majority of them within the last two decades. A good proportion of these papers begin by citing the pervasiveness of the disorder. An opening sentence such as "Hyperactivity is the single most prevalent childhood behavioral problem" is usually regarded as sufficient because the readers of these journals are already convinced that, on average, at least one hyperactive child sits in every elementary school classroom across the United States.

Originally published (in abbreviated form) in *The Atlantic Monthly* in 1989.

The actual estimates vary, however, and not by a little. If a psychiatrist says that about 3 percent or 10 percent or between 1 and 5 percent of elementary school children are hyperactive, this is simply a rough average of studies whose findings differ dramatically from one another. One series of papers estimated the rate at between 10 and 20 percent. A California survey put it at precisely 1.19 percent. A nationally recognized expert says without hesitation that 6 percent of children qualify for the label. About all that the researchers can agree on is that hyperactive boys outnumber girls by at least four to one.

To some extent, the disparities can be explained by the varying stringency of the criteria that are applied, and by who is applying them. According to the latest guidelines for diagnosing what is now officially called Attention-Deficit Hyperactivity Disorder (ADHD), the problem must have been noticed before age seven, must persist for at least six months, and must include any eight of fourteen symptoms, among which are the following: the child is easily distracted by extraneous stimuli; has difficulty sustaining attention, following through on instructions, or waiting his or her turn in games; often does such things as talk excessively, fidget with hands or feet, squirm while sitting down, lose things, or fail to listen to what is being said to him or her.

In judging hyperactivity, most of the experts emphasize the importance of hearing from teachers, whose perspective is often quantified in the form of a rating scale developed by Keith Conners in the late 1960s. When that score is the sole basis for diagnosis, 10 percent or more of all elementary school children may be labeled hyperactive. If, however, a child must also score high on similar scales in other situations—as perceived by parents or pediatricians, for example—then the prevalence of the disorder is said to be closer to 1 percent.

The experience of two Canadian researchers, Nancy J. Cohen and Klaus Minde, is illustrative. They screened all 2900 kindergartners in one community and expected to find that between 4 and 10 percent would be hyperactive, based on the estimate offered by a widely used textbook. At first their procedure yielded sixty-three names. But when they looked more closely, they found that most of these children had altogether different psychological problems or else seemed to be suffering from poor nutrition or too little sleep. Only twenty-three children—less than eight-tenths of one percent—were left in the hyperactive category following their more rigorous screening.

Although the wildly divergent estimates of prevalence may seem disturbing given that each percentage point stands for hundreds of thousands of children, the situation becomes even more disconcerting when one realizes that different criteria for diagnosis produce different conclusions about whether *this particular child*—the one right over there, hunched over a spelling quiz—will carry the ADHD label and, as a consequence, be asked to swallow stimulants every day. Most unsettling of all is a flicker of doubt about the integrity of the diagnosis itself: Can we be confident that it is sensible to think of any child as having a disorder called hyperactivity or ADHD?

Overwhelmingly, child psychiatrists and psychologists answer in the affirmative. Just because it is difficult to pin down the prevalence of ADHD, or even to be sure that it accurately describes a particular child, doesn't mean the phenomenon isn't real, say most people in the field. Teachers, too, will testify that some students always seem to be blurting out answers, jumping from one activity to another, and bothering their peers until no one wants anything to do with them. They never seem to listen or think before they act, and they are generally hard to manage. Some parents seem perpetually at the end of their ropes because of their children's short attention spans and unusual intolerance of frustration. Everything must be done right this very minute. "If you'd ever seen a hyperactive kid, you'd know it," says psychologist Susan Campbell. "Something's there."

But it is a large conceptual leap from agreeing that some of these descriptions will ring true about certain children to deciding that there exists an identifiable syndrome—a distinctive disorder analogous to a disease. Indeed, a review of more than one hundred journal articles and book chapters, as well as conversations with many of the leading researchers in the field, raises troubling questions about the assumptions that pediatricians and psychiatrists, as well as parents and teachers, often make. And the trouble goes well beyond the fact that asking more people about a child makes it less likely that the child will be said to have ADHD.

To begin with, each of the constellations of symptoms that are supposed to lead to this diagnosis—hyperactivity, impulsiveness, and difficulty paying attention—occurs at least as often in children who have entirely different problems, as Cohen and Minde discovered. Similarly, there is no crisp set of symptoms in a toddler that can reliably be assumed to predict the appearance of ADHD a few years down the line. These facts raise questions about the existence of a distinctive disorder.

Second, the key symptoms often do not appear together. Douglas G. Ullman and his colleagues found that children said to be hyperactive did not turn out to be particularly likely to have trouble paying attention, and vice versa. One's ability to predict whether a child will be inattentive simply by knowing he is overactive—or the other way around—"is not much better than if one tossed a coin to decide the matter," the authors concluded.

Third, it is often forgotten just how arbitrary is the procedure for deciding exactly which behaviors make it onto that list of fourteen, or for determining that eight of them (rather than seven or ten) will suffice for a diagnosis of ADHD. These decisions are "made by committee," as Dennis Cantwell, a leading researcher in the field who was himself on those committees, admits.

Similarly, although there is no test to determine whether a child is hyperactive, a score on the Conners Teachers Rating Scale gives the appearance of scientific precision, as though it were, say, a white cell count. In reality, the score is nothing more than a numerical value that sums up a particular teacher's subjective judgments about whether Jason bounces around too much. A critic might argue that a more accurate label than ADHD would be NDEM: Not Docile Enough for Me.

Some theorists have attempted to get around these problems by arguing that the disorder is actually "heterogeneous"—that there is actually no single population of hyperactive children but several subgroups, each of which has its own etiology. This has a professional ring to it and seems plausible on its face, but on closer examination does not really say very much. It simply sets the problem back a step. What *are* the disorders mistakenly collected under the ADHD umbrella? How do we know *they* are valid diagnoses? One might say that using the word "heterogeneous" tells more about what we don't know than about what we do.

The history of the diagnosis does nothing to allay one's doubts. For many years, children with symptoms identical to those that now add up to ADHD were considered to have "Minimal Brain Damage." When it was eventually acknowledged that there was absolutely no proof that these children's brains were actually damaged, the label was changed to "Minimal Brain Dysfunction." This in turn gave way to the diagnosis of "hyperkinetic reaction," which became "Attention Deficit Disorder with (or without) Hyperactivity," which became "Attention Deficit Hyperactivity Disorder."

These changes—and it is a safe bet that the latest in the series will not be the last—reflect something more than quibbling over labels. They suggest a fundamental disagreement about what is behind the labels, if indeed anything is there. "The whole notion has gone through so many metamorphoses as to suggest a catastrophe in terms of conceptual integrity," says Gerald Coles, associate professor of clinical psychiatry at the Robert Wood Johnson (formerly Rutgers) Medical School, and author of *The Learning Mystique,* a critical analysis of what are commonly called learning disabilities. "Rather than moving toward ever-greater precision, they're constantly sweeping over the disasters of last year's conception."

These diagnoses appear in the successive revisions of the mental health clinician's bible, known as the *Diagnostic and Statistical Manual,* or *DSM.* Whereas *DSM II* talked about "hyperkinesis," the third edition, published in 1980, switched to Attention Deficit Disorder: now it seemed that difficulty paying attention was the core of the disorder, with excessive activity merely an optional feature caused by the attentional deficit. In 1987, with the publication of *DSM III-R,* the definers changed their minds again, deciding that no data existed to support the emphasis on attention, and that hyperactivity really was the center of the problem after all. As for children who have trouble paying attention but are not hyperactive, "they now have nowhere to go," says David Shaffer, professor of psychiatry at Columbia University— meaning that this category has been essentially defined out of existence.

Moreover, while up-to-date clinicians know they can simply check off any eight of the fourteen symptoms, someone still working with *DSM III* faces a Chinese menu: prior to 1987, the disorder didn't exist unless the clinician could vouch for three of four possible symptoms of inattention *and* three of six features related to impulsivity *and* two of five under hyperactivity. Leon Eisenberg, a psychiatrist at Harvard Medical School whose research in the 1960s helped pave the way for the widespread use of stimulants with hyperactive children, describes these revisions as "somewhere between chaos and progress"—a rather more charitable assessment than Coles's—but concedes that "the [latest] criteria remain vague and uncertain."

Some specialists, notably those who are British or Australian, think that the diagnostic category is not just vague but fatally flawed. "The term *attention* is so broad that it is impossible to know what it involves without substantial contextual information," Margot Prior and Ann Swanson argued in the *Journal of Child Psychology and Psychiatry.* The diagnosis "carries implications of a known, unitary, organically based and relatively invariant disorder, none of which is established to date."

In 1971, two investigators at the University of Iowa thought they had established something of the sort. They announced that parents of hyperactive children were disproportionately prone to various psychiatric disorders, including alcoholism. This, they concluded, might indicate the existence of a hereditary factor, but at the very least it proved that hyperactivity is a specific syndrome with a characteristic family background. Unfortunately they hadn't bothered to compare children rated as hyperactive with children receiving psychological services for other reasons. When one of the researchers, Mark Stewart, got around to checking this out in 1980, he and his associates found that all the differences evaporated. He was forced to admit that the original parental pattern "probably reflected a general characteristic of families attending a child psychiatry clinic rather than one specific to the families of hyperactive patients."

In light of all this, the disagreement about whether a given child "has" ADHD seems to signify something more than uncertainty about how best to apply a diagnosis. Consider the rather obvious point made by Kenneth D. Gadow, professor of special education at the State University of New York at Stony Brook: "What is diagnosed as hyperactivity by one physician may be considered emotional disturbance or 'spoiled child syndrome' by another." In passing, other researchers have acknowledged exactly the same thing with respect to both teachers and parents. Even within a single class of observers, that is, there is often no unanimity about whether a particular child is hyperactive.

When one compares that same child across *different* environments, there is even less consensus about his status. A number of studies by now have shown "relatively low levels of agreement among parents, teachers, and clinicians on which children should be regarded as hyperkinetic," psychiatrist Michael Rutter has written. Another researcher refers to "a striking discrepancy between reports of the child's behavior at home and/or school and his behavior while in the physician's office." This point is quantified by a careful reading of a study published in early 1989. Of about fifteen hundred children in Ontario between the ages of four and eleven, roughly 10 percent of the boys and 3 percent of the girls were rated as hyperactive by a teacher or a parent. But when the researchers counted the children who were so classified by *both* adults, they came up with a grand total of eleven boys and no girls, or about three-quarters of 1 percent of the total sample.

Why does the parent at home rate the child differently than the teacher at school? If it were only a matter of the inherent subjectivity of the ratings, the diagnostic category could conceivably be rescued—although with more qualifications and skepticism than one usually hears in the professional community. In fact, though, the reason that different observers come to different conclusions is due principally to the fact that *the child acts differently depending on where he is*. In light of this, the idea of a unified disorder threatens to slip away completely.

It is common knowledge among those in the field that all symptoms of hyperactivity often vanish when a child is watching TV, engaged in free play, or doing something else he likes. Similarly, the way a child's environment is organized and the way tasks are presented can mean the difference between perfectly normal behavior and behavior called hyperactive, a finding that has been replicated again and again. This is particularly true for the symptoms related to paying attention.

Since the early 1970s, for example, it has been known that hyperactive children do just fine on tasks that they can work on at their own pace as opposed to tasks controlled by someone else. Many of these children also seem virtually problem-free if they receive individual attention from a teacher or if the experimenter stays in the room with them. This suggests that the problem may have to do with the task or the setting rather than with a built-in deficit.

No less remarkable is the fact that the supposedly aberrant behavior depends in large part on the rigidity of the classroom. In his 1970 book *Crisis in the Classroom,* Charles E. Silberman offered glowing reports of a less structured style of learning. "There seem not to be any disruptive youngsters or even restless youngsters in informal classrooms," he wrote. "The formal classroom thus seems to produce its own discipline problems. . . . It is not the children who are disruptive, it is the formal classroom that is disruptive—of childhood itself."

This might be dismissed as fuzzy-headed hyperbole except for the fact that at least two studies have confirmed Silberman's perception. A small experiment published in 1976 compared a group of hyperactives after one year in a traditional classroom with a group in a classroom featuring individualized instruction, relatively free movement around the room, and teacher-child cooperation in planning lessons. After the year was up, teachers' ratings showed almost no change for the first group, but the hyperactivity scores of those in the open classroom had dropped so dramatically as to be in the normal range. A second study, which compared hyperactive children to a control group, found that the difference between them—as judged by the experimenters themselves rather than the teachers—remained significant in a formal classroom but had effectively disappeared in an open classroom.

These studies are not conclusive, partly because the hyperactive children were not randomly assigned to each kind of classroom and partly because the children may have benefited from more individual teacher attention rather than just from the informality of the setting. But it is interesting to observe how quick the researchers themselves were to dismiss the importance of their studies. After reviewing the "unexpected" findings, the authors of the first paper hastened to add that new approaches to teaching are "not intended to be any simple alternative to drug treatment." The second group of authors stated that arguments about what sort of classroom makes more sense are "moot . . . until academic achievement data are obtained"—as if the effect on hyperactivity itself no longer mattered. Moreover, it seems that virtually no one has taken the trouble to investigate the question further since those preliminary data were published.

"The degree to which hyperactives are viewed as deviant depends on the demands of the environment in which they function," veteran Canadian researchers Gabrielle Weiss and Lily Hechtman wrote in *Science*. One might even amend that to read: the degree to which children are viewed as hyperactive in the first place depends on the environment. But rather than seriously questioning the idea that there is a disease called ADHD, psychiatrists have responded by fashioning a subcategory of the disorder called "situational hyperactivity." Thus, says Keith Conners, "if data from parent and teacher conflict, there may be a true 'situational' hyperactivity, a pattern of behavior which only emerges, say, in the school setting but not the home setting. . . ."

Of course this approach can never be proved wrong, just as it would not be technically inaccurate to say that a child who cries when her friend moves away is suffering from "situational depression." The question is, What is to be gained from such labeling and what sorts of inquiry does it serve to encourage and discourage?

Some of us remember things more accurately if we see them rather than hear them; some of us learn better if abstract ideas are represented spatially. Similarly, some children learn better and jump around less if they receive personal attention or get to design their own tasks. In 1978, psychologists Charles E. Cunningham and Russell A. Barkley offered the heretical suggestion that "hyperactive behavior may be the *result* rather than the cause of the child's academic difficulties." (Two other psychologists found substantial evidence to support this conclusion ten years later.) This possibility raises the question of *why* these children fail—whether it may have more to do with how they are being taught than with the presence of a disorder within each of them.

If a good teacher finds relatively few ADHD children in her class, it may be because she designs appropriate tasks for students who might otherwise squirm, or it may be because she is less rigid in her demands and more tolerant of what educators refer to as "off-task behavior." (The use of this designation may, as a rule, say as much about the teacher as the student.) "Hyperactivity," says one researcher, "typically comes to professional attention . . . when the child cannot conform to classroom rules. . . ." This suggests questions about who is setting the rules and how reasonable they are.

Carol Whalen, a psychologist at the University of California at Irvine, once noted that "verbalization does not necessarily have to interfere with learning and performance. Academic activities could be designed in which interpersonal transactions were functional rather than disruptive . . . [but] some teachers function best in quiet, orderly classroom settings where all children follow a single, well-delineated routine." The implication here, though Whalen does not put it so impolitely, is that treating a child for ADHD is principally a response to what *teachers* need.

Similarly, in their highly regarded 1986 book, *Hyperactive Children Grown Up,* Weiss and Hechtman observe that children are typically diagnosed as hyperactive around the time they are first expected to pay "attention to tasks (which may be too difficult, too easy, boring, or repetitive). . . . Not only is the child expected to behave like the others in the class, but to learn at the normal rate in the normal way." Psychiatrists who design the research, shape the diagnostic categories, and prescribe the drugs rarely explore how children are being taught, except as an occasional perfunctory aside. In 1986, both the *Journal of Children in Contemporary Society* and *Psychiatric Annals* devoted special issues to the question of hyperactivity, and neither addressed so much as one paragraph to such matters as classroom organization or teacher attitudes. Or to take another sort of example, in a questionnaire sent to physicians who treat hyperactive children, 63 percent pronounced themselves undecided about whether anything could "be done in a child's classroom to accommodate his hyperactive behavior."

As Gerald Coles sees it, "You have [researchers] accepting the schools and their demands as a given. None of these people think about questions like 'What should an education be?' or look at the context in which children become noncompliant." Indeed, when I independently questioned two noted researchers about the value of stimulants, they both argued that pills provide an alternative to a "special ed" class assignment, and then asked me which one *I* would prefer.

Pressed as to whether these really are the only two alternatives, one expert agreeably replied that he was amenable to "talking about social philosophy"—implying that this was a digression from the topic of hyperactivity. Could the classroom be organized differently? "I don't know if there's a lot of research on that," he mused.

In addition to the possibility that symptoms ascribed to ADHD may result from classroom environments or academic failure, a number of studies have found that warped family patterns often go hand-in-hand with hyperactivity. As Weiss and Hechtman summarize the research, "[F]amilies of hyperactives tended to have more difficulties, mainly in the areas of mental health of family members, marital relationships, and, most particularly, the emotional climate of the home . . . [and they] tended to use more punitive, authoritative approaches in child rearing than [other] families."

These conclusions are based partly on the work of experimenters who watch children playing with their mothers and carefully code and tally the maternal responses. They tend to find that the mothers of hyperactives are less responsive to, and less positive with, their children. But these sorts of studies are corroborated by informal impressions that researchers often form while measuring something else. In one study of the effects of stimulants, the authors report parenthetically that "the homes of all hyperactives were judged as more tense" than other children's homes, and mothers talked and played less with their children than did the mothers of children who were not labeled hyperactive. It is possible, of course, that styles of discipline and interaction are not the cause but the consequence, the effect of a parent's frustration with a child who is already hyperactive for other reasons. This is the view of Russell Barkley, president of the American Psychological Association's section on clinical child psychology. His own research shows that parents' reliance on commands and punishments drops significantly when their hyperactive children are put on medication. "The majority of the problem is the effects of the child's behavior on the parents, not the other way around," he asserts.

But this may be too much of a leap. "Knowing that the behavior changes when the child is on Ritalin doesn't tell you how the behavior got started in the first place," says Susan Campbell, who goes on to emphasize that no one knows why some children are more fidgety or impulsive than others. L. Alan Sroufe, professor of child psychology at the University of Minnesota, thinks that early parent-child dynamics may play a key role. In a study with Deborah Jacobvitz, Sroufe followed children from birth until age eight and discovered that those who were eventually diagnosed as ADHD were more likely to have had mothers who were rated as "intrusive" during their infancy. Rather than responding to the baby's needs, such a mother might, for example, shove a bottle into its mouth even though it was trying to turn its head away.

Sroufe reasons that most of us, with our parents' help, learned quite early to regulate our arousal, to control ourselves when circumstances demanded. He suspects that some parents overstimulate their children precisely when the children are already too aroused. These children may well come to fit the ADHD pattern. The data to clinch this conclusion do not yet exist, Sroufe concedes, but then few people have gone looking for them. No one else has even bothered to try to predict hyperactivity from early caregiving, and no one has ever helped overstimulating parents to modify their behavior in order to see if the children have fewer problems later on.

What Sroufe and Jacobvitz did do, while they were investigating parent-child interactions, was look for biological differences between ADHD and other children in case those differences mattered more. They came up virtually empty-handed. Hyperactivity didn't seem connected to delivery complications or prematurity, to infant reflexes or distractibility, or to dozens of other measures. Indeed, reports Michael Rutter, "There is no indication of any biochemical feature that is specific to the hyperkinetic syndrome."

It is theoretically possible that the behavior of some tiny subset of those children called hyperactive really can be traced to neurotransmitters, the brain's chemical messengers, or to genetic factors or neurological damage. As of now, though, says David Shaffer, "Nobody's found anything" to demonstrate an organic, or biological, cause. This has not been for lack of trying. The medical journals are littered with the remains of discarded theories that purported to explain how restless children are actually suffering from a disease. For example, it was held for quite some time that stimulant drugs have a "paradoxical effect" on hyperactive children; the very fact that they—and only they—were quieted by this sort of medication was said to prove that their troubles were biochemical. But in 1978, Judith Rapoport and her colleagues published the results of an experiment showing that stimulants had precisely the same effects on the motor activity and attention of normal children. Later studies showed similar effects on normal adults and on children with entirely different problems.

The overwhelming majority of studies have shown that most hyperactive children have no discernible brain damage or neurological abnormalities; their EEG readings are not distinctive. For a while it was thought that the nervous systems of hyperactives were overaroused. Then it was thought that they were underaroused. No reliable differences have been found in either direction, however. And like Jacobvitz and Sroufe, other researchers find nothing amiss about hyperactive children when they look for signs of trouble before, during, and just after birth: there is no higher incidence of delivery complications, infections, hemorrhaging, or low birth weight.

What is remarkable here is not this series of failures to find a biological cause but the tenacity with which this line of investigation continues to be pursued. For every study investigating the families of hyperactive children there are hundreds searching for neurological abnormalities. This is the sort of research that gets funded, possibly because this is how the investigators (and the grantors themselves) were trained. The humanistic psychologist Abraham Maslow once observed that if people are given only hammers, they will treat everything they come across as if it's a nail.

"People who don't have a high tolerance for ambiguity aren't going to look at family factors," says Susan Campbell. "In the biological sphere, it seems as if one is on firmer ground." In any case, most physicians continue to assume that ADHD is biologically based, and when a researcher is asked whether there is any evidence to support this assumption, a typical response is, "Not yet."

This approach determines how the issue is framed and thereby manages to perpetuate itself, as Gerald Coles sees it: "The overwhelming majority of research is *not* a disinterested examination of a scientific question but a collection of tracts intent on making the child or the child's neurology responsible for his or her learning problems," he writes. The theory thus becomes "a research agenda . . . [that] carries with it a methodology in which brain structure and function are considered to be the primary, and usually the only, causal influences that need to be examined."

If the emphasis on drugs and biology among researchers crowds out work on prevention, environmental causes, and alternative forms of therapy, a similar pattern is played out among clinicians. The most striking consequence of assuming that an unusually distractible or impulsive child is suffering from a disease is the tendency to turn to medication to solve the problem.

"Assumptions of organicity have often been used, in practice, as a justification for prescribing drugs," write Jacobvitz and Sroufe. And in an interview, Sroufe adds: "The majority of [hyperactive] kids today are treated only with Ritalin. The *vast* majority."

Ritalin is the brand name for methylphenidate, which was approved for use with children in 1961. It, like Dexedrine (dextroamphetamine), another stimulant sometimes prescribed for hyperactivity, is classified as a Schedule II drug, meaning that it is regarded as having the highest abuse potential for a substance with legitimate medical use, and its manufacture is regulated by the Drug Enforcement Agency (DEA). (Other drugs in that class include morphine and the barbiturates.)

The best available figures on Ritalin use come from a careful annual survey of Baltimore County schools by psychiatrist Daniel Safer. In 1987, 5.9 percent of public elementary students in that county were taking Ritalin. Extrapolating to the United States, and correcting for the fact that Maryland doctors are a bit freer with their prescription pads than their counterparts elsewhere, Safer estimates that three quarters of a million children are receiving stimulants nationwide. "It's been increasing steadily since we first took a look in 1971 and it'll go over one million in the 1990s if the present rate continues," he says.

One way to confirm this increase is to look at the total amount of methylphenidate that the DEA allows to be manufactured each year—a ceiling based on expected demand. In 1982, the limit was 1,082 kilograms; in 1987, it was 2,682 kilograms. The figure dropped back slightly for 1988, but that reflects some leftover inventory in the warehouses rather than a real decline in prescriptions. About four out of every five children diagnosed as hyperactive are put on stimulants at some point, making it far and away the treatment of choice in the United States. (This does not seem to be true elsewhere; in most of Western Europe, for example, children rarely or never receive medication for hyperactivity.)

In the early 1970s, media coverage of Ritalin use seeded a storm of controversy, culminating in the publication of a widely read book by Peter Schrag and Diane Divoky: *The Myth of the Hyperactive Child*. This period also saw the publication of Benjamin Feingold's *Why Your Child Is Hyperactive*, which argued that drugs were unnecessary because hyperactivity could be cured by altering children's diet. (Subsequent studies have been unable to demonstrate that restricting sugar or food additives produces any significant improvement for the vast majority of children.)

Lately, the medication controversy has been heating up again, this time thanks largely to an arm of the Church of Scientology. Tirelessly arguing that "psychiatry is making drug addicts out of America's school children," the church group, calling itself the Citizens Commission on Human Rights, is picketing professional conferences and hitting the talk show circuit.

The church has also had a hand in a series of legal actions charging physicians with malpractice in Georgia, Massachusetts, California, Minnesota, Washington, and the District of Columbia. "We're giving kids a potentially dangerous drug based on a theory for which we have no proof," says D.C. attorney John P. Coale, who is handling several of the suits. Not surprisingly, virtually every psychiatrist and psychologist repudiates the tactics and ridicules the claims of the Scientologists. In an article in the *Journal of the American Medical Association* entitled "The Ritalin Controversy: What's Made This Drug's Opponents Hyperactive?" Gabrielle Weiss is quoted as regretting how the discussion has become so polarized. "It is seen as a cure or as the devil," she says. The truth is likely somewhere in between, with stimulants neither delivering the benefits some proponents claim nor proving to be as dangerous as detractors argue.

While it may seem peculiar that a stimulant can have a quieting effect, the fact is that these drugs don't so much slow down activity as redirect it. A child on Ritalin may move around just as much as a non-medicated child over the course of a day, but he will be better able to sit still for tasks that require concentration. His activity is more goal directed, less aimless, more likely to be "on-task."

Besides being less distractible and better able to sustain attention, the medicated child typically becomes less aggressive and less apt to get into trouble, less obnoxious to his peers, easier for his teachers to handle, and more compliant in general. It's not difficult to see why parents and teachers are often pleased with the change they see in a child who is put on Ritalin. The precise status of the ADHD label seems beside the point to many people; as David Shaffer sees it, "You don't have to have a diagnosis to know that drugs are effective."

That's the good news. The bad news has less to do with side effects—more about those in a moment—than with the qualifications about the drug's efficacy. The evidence shows, first, that drugs do absolutely nothing for between 25 and 40 percent of hyperactive children, depending on whose estimate you believe. Kenneth Gadow, in his book-length contribution to a series called *Children on Medica-*

tion, also reports, "Some youngsters even become worse on medication! Unfortunately, there is no way to tell whether medication is going to work other than to have the child take it."

Second, a large proportion of the children who do respond to Ritalin also improve on a placebo. After weeding out the nonresponders, Esther Sleator followed a group of medicated children for two years and began slipping some of them sugar pills instead. Of twenty-eight subjects for whom there were definite data, eleven continued to behave as if they were getting the real thing. Russell Barkley's review of several hundred studies indicates that about 40 percent of children are rated as improved when they're on a placebo, although the magnitude of the improvement generally isn't as high as it is for children receiving Ritalin.

Third, even for those children who respond well only to stimulants, the effect is more a temporary suppression of symptoms than anything like a cure. A child may have been taking Ritalin for years, but within hours of the last dose he is indistinguishable from a hyperactive child who has never taken a single pill. Or *almost* indistinguishable: in what is known as a rebound effect, the child will briefly become a little worse than before when the drug wears off.

Fourth, drugs do nothing to enhance academic achievement. Beneficial effects on concentration had long been assumed to translate into achievement, but an analysis of seventeen studies by Russell Barkley and Charles Cunningham in the late 1970s, and a subsequent analysis of another sixteen studies by Kenneth Gadow in 1985, were uniformly discouraging. "Behavioral interventions are clearly superior to stimulant medication in facilitating academic performance," Gadow concluded. On reflection, this doesn't seem so strange. Drugs do not address cognitive deficits or create skills. And if hyperactivity is the *result* of learning problems rather than the cause, two psychologists point out in a 1988 article, "interventions directed toward suppressing ADHD behaviors will have no long-term effects in reducing either the ADHD itself or learning difficulties unless the latter are specifically treated."

There is another wrinkle. Some children's behavior seems to improve only at relatively high dosages (around one milligram per kilogram of body weight). This much medication, however, tends to have a detrimental effect on thinking skills, thus forcing the careful physician to choose between reducing hyperactivity and enhancing cognitive performance. What's more, "the [dosage] where teachers perceive the most improved classroom behavior is also associated with side effects," Gadow reports.

These sorts of findings suggest hard questions about just exactly why children are put on Ritalin in the first place. Even assuming that it does make a difference, is it appropriate to prescribe drugs to help a third grader learn better? How about to reduce fidgeting, which Safer points out is "neither a disruptive influence nor highly unusual"? Or to create docility, so children will follow the rules and not annoy adults? At their best, the drugs "may have much greater relevance for stress reduction in caregivers than intrinsic value to the child," says Gadow. It may not be surprising, then, that Gabrielle Weiss and her colleagues found that "children on the whole preferred being without 'the pills.'" In a follow-up study with adults who had been medicated as children, Weiss's group reported that more listed medication as a hindrance than as a help.

Some of this reaction may be due to the social stigma of having to take pills every day, but part of it clearly has to do with side effects. The research on these effects, it should be said, does not support the extravagant claims of some critics, including the Church of Scientology. Children on Ritalin do not grow up to become drug addicts. There is the occasional report in the medical literature of a child who developed seizures or became psychotic—complete with hallucinations and paranoia—as a result of taking the drug, but these cases are very rare and crop up occasionally with other sorts of medications as well.

While there has been some concern that Ritalin stunts growth, this effect seems to be temporary. (It does seem possible that someone who continues taking medication straight into adulthood would be permanently affected, but no one knows for sure.) At higher doses, children's heart rate and blood pressure often increase, and some children have developed facial tics. Even more common are reports of children who have trouble sleeping and who lose their appetite, with some weight loss as a result.

Because of these and other risks, most specialists do not recommend using stimulants with younger children, such as those in preschool. For older children, most of these side effects turn out to be either uncommon or controllable by modifying the dosage or the medication schedule. It is less clear that these adjustments can eliminate all of the behavioral side effects, however. According to some (though not all) studies, children on Ritalin sometimes become withdrawn and stare off into space, which critics call the "zombie" effect.

Although stimulants make these children less likely to annoy their peers or pick fights, they are less likely to interact with others *at all,* according to Carol Whalen and others. And some investigators suspect that medications lead children to attribute their problems, as well as their improvement, to pills rather than to social causes or to factors within their control.

In any case, parents and other observers surely view a medicated child differently. Michael Schleifer and his colleagues came away from one study with the impression that "mothers preferred to attribute improvements to medication rather than to other variables." Barbara Henker and Carol Whalen found that when someone was told that a given child was on medication, he or she was more likely to believe that the child's problems were serious and due to "nervous system dysfunction" as compared with someone told that the child was in a behavioral treatment program. (Hence the circle is completed: assumptions of a biological cause lead to drugs, and drugs lead to assumptions of a biological cause.) Still other investigators, meanwhile, warn that medication may convince parents that the problem has been licked and that there is no need to bother with efforts to work on academic difficulties, poor self-image, and disturbed peer relationships.

So, far from prompting hesitation about prescribing stimulants, the number of prescriptions continues to rise. Further, more and more psychiatrists are talking seriously about keeping, or putting, adolescents and adults on stimulants, too. Ask the professionals to name the most important finding relevant to hyperactivity within the last decade and they will tell you it is the discovery that the disorder doesn't disappear at puberty. Some ADHD children continue to have problems with school and work as they get older, to be at risk for drug and alcohol use, for low self-esteem and depression. As adolescents and adults, they may seem impulsive, immature, and given to outbursts of temper. Most noticeably, those who were once diagnosed as hyperactive are more likely than the population at large to have poor peer relationships or even to be antisocial and otherwise troubled.

In an ongoing study described in print in 1985 and 1988, Rachel Gittleman Klein, Salvatore Mannuzza, and their colleagues reported that almost half of formerly hyperactive boys had one or another psychological disorder when they were between the ages of sixteen and twenty-three. The other half, however, were absolutely normal. A little less than a third of the young men continued to display symptoms of ADHD—a figure lower than in some other studies. As is often the case in the behavioral sciences, these data, which received prominent mention in the popular press, lend themselves to a variety of interpretations. Is it sobering that half of hyperactives will continue to be plagued with some sort of difficulties, or reassuring that half do seem to outgrow the problem? If it's bad news, does this reflect the tenacity of the disorder, or simply demonstrate the ultimate uselessness of medication?

A closer look at the data suggests that something else altogether is going on. One of the diagnoses that overlaps to a considerable extent with ADHD is "conduct disorder," which refers to aggressive, disobedient, troublemaking behavior; perhaps two thirds of all ADHD children also qualify for that diagnosis, which is one reason that some specialists doubt the value of the ADHD label. It turns out that the children who are at risk for delinquency in later life are primarily from the conduct-disorder group, rather than being a random sample of those who fidget and can't pay attention during a geography lesson. Some of the latter may, not surprisingly, have trouble finishing school and continue to be more distractible than most people when they grow up, but they apparently don't become mentally ill or get in trouble with the law any more than the rest of us. The major revelation in the field during the last ten years, then, turns out to be this: if you were aggressive and antisocial as a child, you may also be aggressive and antisocial as an adult.

E ven those researchers who are comfortable with both the ADHD diagnosis and the use of Ritalin have urged that care should be taken in prescribing the drug and deciding who gets it. Specifically, those who write in the professional journals have arrived at a consensus along these lines: (1) a physician cannot properly diagnose hyperactivity on the basis of an office visit; (2) drug use should be carefully monitored, with precise adjustment of dosage to minimize side effects; (3) teachers' observations are critical for both diagnosing and monitoring treatment; (4) "holidays" from drugs should be given periodically; and (5) drugs should be used only in combination with counseling, behavior therapy, and other nonmedical approaches to treatment—or should not be prescribed at all until it is clear that these other approaches aren't working.

The plain fact is that every one of these commonsense recommendations is routinely ignored by physicians throughout the country. Even if one is persuaded that ADHD is a real disorder, and that drugs are a safe and effective response to it, the gap between research-based guidelines and actual practice is enough to cause grave concern. There is, in Gadow's words, "a striking disparity between what are considered to be adequate standards for service delivery and what actually happens in everyday situations."

Consider each of the standards in turn. First, even though Esther Sleator's studies have shown that the child's behavior in the doctor's office "has no prognostic significance and . . . little diagnostic significance," a California survey of pediatricians revealed that how children acted in front of them "seemed to be the most important characteristic in physician judgments." If doctors seek further evidence to confirm their diagnosis, it may simply come from prescribing drugs and waiting to see whether they work. According to a national survey in 1987, three quarters of pediatricians continued to believe that a child's response to medication was helpful for purposes of diagnosis—despite proof that many hyperactive children do not respond to stimulants while many nonhyperactive children do.

Second, drug use is poorly monitored. In a survey of Washington state physicians who treated children for hyperactivity, more than half of the pediatricians evaluated their patients once a month at most, and nearly half of the family physicians and general practitioners saw the children once a year.

Third, teachers often play little or no role in the process. Studies in Illinois, New York, Massachusetts, and elsewhere have found that pediatricians and teachers exchange information directly in as few as 9 percent of the cases surveyed. Even observers who believe that this figure is atypical concede that such communication remains the exception almost everywhere.

The implications of excluding teachers from the process are not difficult to imagine. James Bosco, professor of education at Western Michigan University and a leading investigator of how hyperactivity is handled in the real world, recounts a typical exchange with a teacher: "They'd say, 'The kid's a zombie in my class [on Ritalin]. It's fine for me, but there's something wrong. I'm concerned about it.' 'Have you told anyone? Have you told the doctor?' 'Hell, no. It's none of my business. I'm not going to stick my neck out.'"

Fourth, Gadow and Safer have both found that drug holidays are not routinely scheduled. And fifth, many experts agree with Alan Sroufe that the typical child classified as hyperactive receives no treatment other than drugs. The Washington survey, published in 1983, painted a more hopeful picture, but psychiatrist Mina K. Dulcan reviews several studies and laments that "all too often stimulants are prescribed by a pediatrician or general practitioner without any other treatment."

And there is more. Ronald T. Brown, Dulcan's colleague at Emory University, and his coauthors wrote in 1986 that while research supports a daily Ritalin dose of 0.3 mg. per kg. of body weight—which works out to about 7 mg. for the average seven–year-old boy—"it is common clinical practice to use substantially higher doses."

The 1987 national survey found that only one of five general practitioners bothered to look at *DSM III* (which had been out for seven years) in deciding whether a child was hyperactive. Daniel Safer, in a recent spot check of Baltimore schools, was pleased to report that 75 percent of the children receiving stimulants met the accepted criteria for hyperactive behavior. But even assuming that a one-quarter failure rate is judged acceptable—most of the other children getting drugs were inattentive but not hyperactive—Safer's criterion was a high score on the Conners Teachers Rating Scale. Using that standard by itself, as already noted, permits 10 percent or more of American schoolchildren to be called hyperactive. Leon Eisenberg seems to incline toward understatement when he acknowledges that, as regards hyperactivity, "the record of general practitioners, pediatricians, and child psychiatrists is far from what it ought to be." And much as the public outcry over Ritalin in the 1970s may well have "spurred a wave of better designed studies," according to Dulcan, so Russell Barkley concedes that the newly filed malpractice suits may "motivate practitioners to bring their practices a little more up to date."

But Barkley makes a point of emphasizing that he believes that the practitioners being sued are not, strictly speaking, negligent. Negligence is judged according to customary practice in the field, not by the standards suggested by research. Put bluntly, this means that if most practitioners are diagnosing casually and prescribing irresponsibly, it is difficult to bring legal action against any one of them.

This, one might say, is analogous to the general assumptions made about hyperactivity. It could be argued that diagnoses of other psychological disorders are similarly arbitrary and subjective, made by committee and poorly defined, insensible of social factors and conducive to unfounded assumptions about biological causes. On the one hand, this may serve to excuse what goes on with ADHD or at least to place it in perspective. On the other hand, it may provoke larger, more disturbing questions about the theory and practice of mental health in the United States.

AUTHOR'S NOTE, 1998

I wish I could say that the article you have just read is now of only historical interest. Alas, in the decade since it was written we have witnessed an even greater tendency to throw around the ADHD label, to casually assume the existence of a biological disorder located within children's heads, and to give kids a pill to get them to sit still. ADHD has metamorphosed from a familiar diagnostic classification into a fad, and an entire industry has grown up around it. It's hard to go a week without running into a new book, magazine article, or talk show devoted to the topic, and nearly all seem oblivious to the sort of elementary questions raised here. (One welcome exception is a recent book by Thomas Armstrong, known to many educators for his work in multiple intelligences, called *The Myth of the A.D.D. Child.*)[1]

In 1987, a support group called Children with Attention Deficit Disorder (CHADD) was founded. Ten years later, the organization— now called Children and Adults with Attention Deficit Disorder—had 650 chapters around the country and had attracted some unwanted attention for the fact that part of its expenses are paid by Ciba-Geigy, the pharmaceutical giant that manufactures Ritalin. That company's interest in depicting jumpy kids as having a disease (which is how most Americans already see things) is as unsurprising as are its deep pockets. Based on surveys of pharmacists and doctors in 1995, *Forbes* magazine recently estimated that 8 million Ritalin prescriptions for children, and another 2.5 million for adults (sixteen and older), are written every year—although several prescriptions may be written for the same person. Measured by the number of daily doses, Ritalin use increased by an astonishing 400 percent in only five years, from 1989 to 1994, with Americans now spending more than a third of a *billion* dollars a year on the stuff.

The other major treatment for children diagnosed as "having" ADHD—the only alternative to drugs, as far as most people are concerned—is behavior modification. Some readers may be aware that a wealth of evidence shows that rewards are effective, at best, only superficially and temporarily, and at the cost of reducing interest in whatever had to be done to get the reward.[2] But several experiments have found that using reinforcement programs to deal with distractibility or hyperactivity in particular also doesn't make much sense. In one study, rewards given to hyperactive children made them respond *more* impulsively.[3] In another, any beneficial effects of rewards (on reaction times) disappeared as soon as the rewards stopped coming, and sometimes they had the consequence of undermining performance from the beginning.[4] In yet a third study, this one with children who had short attention spans but were not hyperactive, rewards did not improve reaction time as the experimenters had expected; rather, they caused the children to make more mistakes.[5]

Whatever the limits and risks of the treatments, however, the central question remains the status of the ADHD diagnosis itself. We live in a society where it is common to explain complicated phenomena by appealing to biological causes. On any given psychological issue, genetic factors get more attention than cultural factors do; emotional problems are likely to be investigated by looking at brains rather than at classrooms,[6] or even at families. This is the research that gets funded, this is the orientation that is favored by science reporters, this is the explanation that is accepted on faith by the general public.[7] (This is also the sensibility that helps to explain the current enthusiasm among educators for "brain-based learning"—a tacit assumption that explanations for human behavior are not really scientific, and that ideas for concrete practice are not truly justified, until they have been somehow grounded in biology.)[8]

Thus, it should not come as a surprise that the health columnist of the *New York Times* (to cite only one of hundreds of examples) declares without reservation—and without evidence—that ADHD "seems to be a neurological disorder that is often hereditary and that involves the brain mechanisms that regulate attention and impulse control."[9] (The last assertion is certainly true, in the same sense that the anxiety experienced upon being fired from one's job "involves" the brain mechanisms that regulate emotion, but the misleading and widely accepted implication here is that neurophysiological phenomena *cause* something called ADHD.)

As it was a decade ago, most of the current research on attention and hyperactivity is based on the premise that it is an organic disease. (To put this in perspective, at least three quarters of the research now conducted at the National Institute of Mental Health—that's *mental health*—is biological in nature.) When something is discovered, it is cited, sometimes in exaggerated fashion, to support the medical explanation that most people accepted going in. In 1993, for example, much was made of a report in the *New England Journal of Medicine* that of forty-nine people suffering from a rare, possibly genetic disease that involves resistance to thyroid hormone, thirty also satisfied the criteria for ADHD.[10] It was as predictable as it was foolish that this would be construed as evidence that ADHD per se (assuming there *is* an ADHD "per se") is genetic.

Two years later, a study was published in the journal *Child Development* showing that "maternal anxiety/aggression and intrusive caregiving"—as well as other family variables such as the level of emotional support that young children receive—were significantly "correlated with distractibility and/or hyperactivity."[11] The same year, a study appeared in a psychiatric journal demonstrating that children diagnosed as having ADHD "were found to be from families with higher conflict," thus emphasizing "the importance of adverse family-environment variables as risk factors in ADHD."[12] But neither of these studies made it into the popular press. Neither was publicized by the families in question or by other members of CHADD. And neither slowed the ADHD juggernaut or the demand for Ritalin.

Notes

1. Thomas Armstrong, *The Myth of the A.D.D. Child* (New York: Dutton, 1995).
2. Alfie Kohn, *Punished by Rewards* (Boston: Houghton Mifflin, 1993), especially chaps. 3–5.
3. Philip Firestone and Virginia Douglas, "The Effects of Reward and Punishment on Reaction Times and Autonomic Activity in Hyperactive and Normal Children," *Journal of Abnormal Child Psychology* 3 (1975): 201–215.
4. Virginia I. Douglas and Penny A. Parry, "Effects of Reward on Delayed Reaction Time Task Performance of Hyperactive Children," *Journal of Abnormal Child Psychology* 11 (1983): 313–326.
5. Janet A. Kistner, "Attentional Deficits of Learning-Disabled Children: Effects of Rewards and Practice," *Journal of Abnormal Child Psychology* 13 (1985): 19–31.
6. Although I have not made hyperactivity a primary area of study over the last ten years, I'm not aware of any attempts to replicate the two intriguing classroom studies mentioned in the article. Because the article was written for a popular magazine, it doesn't include footnotes, but readers of this book might appreciate the citations for those original studies: Nona M.

Flynn and Judith L. Rapoport, "Hyperactivity in Open and Traditional Classroom Environments," *Journal of Special Education* 10 (1976): 285–290; and Rolf G. Jacob, K. Daniel O'Leary, and Carl Rosenblad, "Formal and Informal Classroom Settings: Effects on Hyperactivity," *Journal of Abnormal Child Psychology* 6 (1978): 47–59.

7. Three books worth reading: Richard C. Lewontin, Steven Rose, and Leon Kamin, *Not in Our Genes* (New York: Pantheon, 1984); Dorothy Nelkin and M. Susan Lindee, *The D.N.A. Mystique: The Gene as a Cultural Icon* (New York: Freeman, 1995); and Ruth Hubbard and Elijah Wald, *Exploding the Gene Myth,* rev. ed. (Boston: Beacon Press, 1997). I've discussed this subject in *The Brighter Side of Human Nature* (New York: Basic Books, 1990), chap. 1; and in "Back to Nurture," *American Health,* April 1993, pp. 29–31.

8. For a critique of the tendency to make facile and unsubstantiated claims about neuroscientific "backing" for specific educational practices, see John T. Bruer, "Education and the Brain: A Bridge Too Far," *Educational Researcher,* November 1997: 4–16.

9. Jane E. Brody, "Attention-Deficit Hyperactivity Disorder: A Puzzling Childhood Syndrome," *New York Times,* 25 April 1991, p. B12.

10. Peter Hauser et al., "Attention Deficit-Hyperactivity Disorder in People with Generalized Resistance to Thyroid Hormone," *New England Journal of Medicine,* 8 April 1993: 997–1001.

11. Elizabeth A. Carlson, Deborah Jacobvitz, and L. Alan Sroufe, "A Developmental Investigation of Inattentiveness and Hyperactivity," *Child Development* 66 (1995): 37–54.

12. Joseph Biederman et al., "Family-Environment Risk Factors for Attention-Deficit Hyperactivity Disorder," *Archives of General Psychiatry* 52 (1995): 464–70.

CHAPTER ELEVEN

The Truth About Self-Esteem

The very act of "debating" a controversial issue tends to reduce the number of possible positions to two. This facilitates an adversarial encounter, which is embedded in the traditional notion of a debate.

Consider the question of whether schools should try to help students feel better about themselves. By now this topic has become sufficiently polarized that the vast majority of people who address themselves to it stand in one of two camps: the pro-self-esteemers, mostly educators, who can scarcely believe that anyone would question the importance of trying to improve children's perceptions of their own worth; and the critics, who dismiss such efforts as ineffective and nonsensical distractions from academics.

With no ax to grind on this matter, I embarked some time ago on a lengthy investigation of it—one that has finally led me to a posture of skepticism about *both* positions and, by extension, about the debate itself. In what follows, I try to show why most discussions of the

Originally published in *Phi Delta Kappan* in 1994.

theory and practice of self-esteem are unsatisfactory. Part I reviews the available research, which contains unwelcome news for anyone who sees self-esteem as a key causal variable. Part II continues the critique of self-esteem by calling into question the values implicit in the concept. Part III then turns the tables to look at the increasingly strident criticisms of self-esteem that are offered by conservative social critics and others. I argue that the view of education from which such attacks emerge is even more misconceived than the practices being challenged. This analysis leads me, finally, to a discussion of what might be more constructive than the usual arguments for and against self-esteem.

I. THE FACTS: What the Research Says (and Doesn't Say)

THE MEASUREMENT OF SELF-ESTEEM.   There is no getting around the fact that most educators who speak earnestly about the need to boost students' self-esteem are unfamiliar with the research that has been conducted on this question. At best, they may vaguely assert, as I confess I used to do, that "studies" suggest that self-esteem is terribly important. Very few people in the field seem to have any feel for the empirical literature as a whole—what the evidence really says and how meaningful it is.

Even before examining the results of studies cited to show the benefits of high self-esteem—or the problems associated with low self-esteem—it makes sense to ask just what the phrase signifies and how the concept has been measured. Typically, self-esteem is defined in terms of how we evaluate ourselves and our characteristics, the "personal judgment of worthiness that is expressed in the attitudes the individual holds toward himself," in the words of Stanley Coopersmith, a pioneering researcher in the field.[1]

But what does this mean in practice for people trying to assess differences in self-esteem? How have researchers operationalized the concept? The answer is that they have, in effect, simply asked experimental subjects how favorably they regard themselves. Researchers have subjects fill out a form on which they indicate how much they agree with such statements as "I feel that I have a number of good qualities."

Putting aside for a moment the questions of what statements are included and how they are scored, the point to be emphasized here is that self-esteem ratings are almost always based on what subjects say about themselves, and self-report measures are rather problematic. They may tell us more about how someone wishes to appear than about his or her "true" state (assuming this can ever be known). In fact, some of the most respected researchers in the area have argued that people designated as having high self-esteem are simply those who demonstrate a "willingness to endorse favorable statements about the self" as a result of "an ambitious, aggressive, self-aggrandizing style of presenting" themselves.[2]

As if this fact were not disturbing enough, something on the order of two hundred instruments for measuring self-esteem are now in use. Many of them haven't been properly validated (to use a popular self-esteem term in a different way) and are of questionable value. More important, even if every single test were top-notch, there is no reason to think that any two of them are comparable. It's difficult to generalize about research findings if self-esteem has been measured—and, indeed, conceptualized—differently in the various studies that have been cited.[3]

One result common to almost all measures, though, is that very few people who fill out self-esteem surveys wind up with scores near the bottom of the scale. When a researcher talks about subjects with "low" self-esteem, he or she means this only relative to other subjects; in absolute terms, the responses of these individuals put them somewhere in the middle range of possible scores. In other words, people classified as having low self-esteem are typically not so much down on themselves as simply "neutral in their self-descriptions."[4] This suggests that it may be necessary to reconsider all those sweeping conclusions about what distinguishes people who love themselves from people who hate themselves. Moreover, the very fact of defining low self-esteem in relative terms means that no intervention can ever make any headway; half of the population will, of course, always fall below the median on any scale.

But let us assume for the sake of the argument that we find none of these facts—or any other methodological criticisms that have been offered of the field[5]—particularly troubling. Let us assume that all the self-esteem studies to date, all ten thousand of them, can be taken at face value. Even so, the findings that emerge from this literature are not especially encouraging for those who would like to believe that feeling good about oneself brings about a variety of benefits. (I am ignoring here the vast number of studies that have treated self-esteem as a dependent rather than an independent variable—that is, those that have tried to figure out what causes self-esteem to go up or down rather than investigate whether such fluctuation affects other things.)

Although psychologists have been interested for decades in the way individuals think and feel about themselves, the most recent surge of interest in the concept, which has involved the formation of self-esteem councils around the country and the dissemination of classroom curricula, began in 1990 with the much-publicized report of a state-funded task force in California. In addition to issuing its own report, the task force commissioned a group of scholars at the University of California to review the available research; their monographs were published under the title *The Social Importance of Self-Esteem*. The point, presumably, was to reassure a skeptical public that claims about the value of self-esteem were based not on wishful thinking but on hard data. There is no question but that many of the researchers who contributed to this volume earnestly hoped to prove exactly that. Thus it is all the more significant—and perhaps even somewhat poignant—that the data refused to cooperate. In a passage understandably seized on by critics of the self-esteem movement, sociologist Neil Smelser conceded in his introduction to the book that his colleagues had come up virtually empty-handed:

> The associations between self-esteem and its expected consequences are mixed, insignificant, or absent. The nonrelationship holds between self-esteem and teenage pregnancy, self-esteem and child abuse, self-esteem and most cases of alcohol and drug abuse. . . . If the association between self-esteem and behavior is so often reported to be weak, even less can be said for the causal relationship between the two.[6]

Over the years, other reviewers have offered fairly similar readings of the available research, pointing to results that are unimpressive or characterized by "massive inconsistencies and contradictions."[7]

SELF-ESTEEM AND SOCIAL BEHAVIOR.   Consider the claim that feeling good about oneself is linked to a variety of constructive life choices—or at least to the absence of destructive behaviors. The metaphor preferred by the members of the California task force is that self-esteem offers a "social vaccine" against crime and violence, substance abuse, and other cultural diseases. Conversely (if we can press the metaphor a bit), low self-esteem is thought to weaken the immunity to these illnesses. It stands to reason that people who don't value themselves will be neither inclined nor able to value others.

But what do the data say? Some research, to be sure, has turned up an inverse relationship between self-esteem and delinquency or deviance (fighting, stealing, destroying property, and so on). But these studies either have found the relationship to be remarkably slight[8] or else have been designed so poorly as to raise questions about the validity of their findings. For example, one recent survey of teenagers discovered a moderate negative correlation between deviance and self-esteem, but the only teens who had been questioned were upper-middle-class students at a prep school. What's more, half of those surveyed failed to return the questionnaire, leaving a self-selected and potentially unrepresentative group from which to draw conclusions.[9] That the research would be unconvincing on this point, incidentally, makes perfect sense to many educators who specialize in teaching conflict resolution. Their strong intuition is that violent behavior does not typically result from low self-esteem, nor do people skilled at conflict resolution always seem to have high self-esteem.[10]

And here is a still more disconcerting possibility: even if low self-esteem were initially associated with delinquent behavior, this very behavior might then serve to *enhance* self-esteem. Some research has provided qualified support for this conclusion,[11] which, if borne out, would seem to caution against making the elevation of self-esteem our primary goal. If being part of an armed gang can help someone to feel better about himself, then feeling better about oneself is not the last word in social vaccines. On the other hand, a reanalysis of some older data found no support for the idea that delinquency has this effect, but neither did it support the premise that delinquency is caused by an absence of self-esteem in the first place.[12]

What about the positive end of the social spectrum? Are people who feel good about themselves more likely to help, share, and care? Ervin Staub of the University of Massachusetts looked at some of the early research conducted with children and concluded that while "a poor self-concept makes it more difficult to extend the boundaries of the self in benevolent ways," it also seemed to be true that "an extremely positive self-concept is less related to positive behavior . . . than a . . . more moderate self-concept" is.[13] Nancy Eisenberg of Arizona State University, like Staub a respected researcher of prosocial phenomena, has raised similar cautions about the simplistic assumption that high self-esteem means more helping. Depending on the circumstances, self-doubters may be just as likely as those who are pleased with themselves to come to someone else's aid, although perhaps for different reasons, Eisenberg believes.[14]

In looking for more recent research relevant to the question, I turned up nine studies (including three dissertations) published since 1980.[15] On prosocial measures that ranged from sharing among children to agreeing to donate one's organs after death, and from experiencing "feelings of benevolence" to rescuing Jews from the Nazis, the data offer more reason to doubt than to affirm the relevance of self-esteem. Most of the studies found the relationship between how people felt about themselves and how likely they were to reach out to others to be either weak or nonexistent. In other cases, the correlation was positive but dependent on other variables, such as gender or similarity between the helper and the helped. In sum, high self-esteem appears to offer no guarantee of inclining people toward prosocial behavior—or even of steering them away from antisocial behavior.

SELF-ESTEEM AND ACADEMIC ACHIEVEMENT.   Altruism aside, the idea that people who regard themselves favorably ought to be able to learn and work more effectively seems not so much a plausible hypothesis as a matter of plain common sense. Someone with high self-esteem would presumably expect to do well, thereby setting into motion an "auspicious circle"—as distinguished from the vicious one that traps individuals who are consumed by self-doubt. Theorists and therapists, to say nothing of teachers and parents, have been saying as much for decades.

Alas, the empirical evidence once again offers meager support for what seems intuitively indisputable. The problem does not stem from the relatively few studies that have found no significant correlation—or even a negative correlation—between self-esteem and academic achievement.[16] These results are exceptional; most research has indeed confirmed a positive association between self-esteem and achievement. The problem, rather, is that the qualifications to that association turn out to be more significant than the association itself.

First, as with social behavior, the size of the relationship is simply not very impressive. In a careful review of 128 studies on this topic, two Australian researchers, B. C. Hansford and J. A. Hattie, found that the average correlation was in the range of .21 to .26, which means that differences in self-esteem can account for only about 4 to 7 percent of variation in academic performance, or vice versa.[17]

Second, those same reviewers reported that the correlation was even lower in studies published more recently; in studies conducted with larger, representative national samples of students; and in studies that used standardized indicators of performance (as opposed to even less reliable measures such as grades).[18] The implication is that the better the research, the less significant the connection it will find between self-esteem and achievement.

Third, virtually all researchers seem to agree that in order to find any meaningful relationship with how well students perform it is necessary to look not at some "global" measure of self-esteem (how positively they feel about themselves in general) but at something more specific like academic self-esteem[19] or even self-esteem regarding the ability to succeed at a particular subject.[20] After all, "one can hardly expect an individual's general sense of self (such as, 'I am a pretty good person') to have very much to do with his or her success on a mathematics test."[21] The concept of self-esteem grows more empirically useful the more narrowly it is conceived. Unfortunately, what most of us have in mind when we use the term—and when we try to devise programs to enhance children's self-esteem—is the broadest version of the concept, which also appears to be the least valuable.

But take a step back and reflect for a moment on just what all this research really means—or doesn't mean. Even if good studies did find a significant correlation between global self-esteem and academic performance, this offers absolutely no reason to think that higher self-esteem *causes* academic performance to go up (or that lower self-esteem causes it to go down). Statistical concepts don't get much more elementary than this—correlation doesn't prove causation—but the number of people, including trained researchers, who fail to grasp this principle's relevance here fairly boggles the mind.

Over and over again, one encounters the assertion that (a) self-esteem and academic achievement are positively associated, followed by the conclusion that (b) it therefore makes sense to try to raise students' self-esteem if we want them to perform better. This is roughly comparable to noticing that absences from school are positively correlated with the appearance of winter coats—and then concluding that warm clothes make children sick.

Obviously, a causal relationship must be demonstrated. Unfortunately, it turns out to be even more difficult to defend the idea that self-esteem *produces* academic achievement than it is to defend a robust correlation between the two. The late Morris Rosenberg, for many years a leading figure in the self-esteem field, and his colleagues wrote in 1989 that "global self-esteem appears to have little or no effect in enhancing academic performance."[22] Other researchers have echoed

this conclusion: one huge study of high school students found "no significant causal relation," a review of the literature turned up "over-
whelmingly negative evidence . . . for a causal connection," and an
even more recent review concurred that there is "little if any evidence
that children's academic performance is causally determined by their
global self-concept."[23]

If self-esteem doesn't cause higher achievement and if there is some
kind of connection between the two, what exactly is the nature of the
relationship? The answer you get depends on the researchers you ask.
Some say that self-esteem and achievement are causally related, all
right, but the latter causes the former to a greater extent than the other
way around. That is, students feel good about themselves because they
do well rather than do well because they feel good about themselves.[24]
(I will have more to say later about the ideological uses to which this
argument is put.)

But are these two possibilities mutually exclusive? It would seem
not, and indeed some writers insist that the relationship is reciprocal,
with self-esteem and academic achievement each affecting the other.
Still others, however, argue that neither is truly an independent variable; something else is really driving both self-esteem and achievement, giving the appearance of an intimate connection between the
two (in much the same way that a third variable called winter is both
the reason that people dress warmly and the explanation for increased
absences from school). One group of researchers at the University of
Minnesota has made a strong case that two variables—social class and
academic ability—adequately account for most of the variance in self-
esteem *and* in performance. Thus self-esteem and academic achievement were "related only insofar as they shared the background
variables . . . as common causes."[25]

In "a somewhat ill-disciplined field," as the Australian researchers
politely put it, "it is possible to find support for all viewpoints"[26]—
which is not particularly encouraging for anyone looking for a defin-
itive answer, or even for reassurance that self-esteem matters at all.

SELF-ESTEEM PROGRAMS.   Again we coast on hypotheticals. Let us assume that self-esteem, despite all the research reviewed here, really is
an unequivocal producer of positive attitudes and behavior as well as
better academic performance. It remains an entirely separate question
whether self-esteem is enhanced by school programs intended for that
purpose. What we are looking for here is some indication that such

interventions can make a lasting difference in students' basic view of themselves.

Hard data to support the efficacy of such interventions are, as best as I can determine, virtually nil. A few unpublished doctoral dissertations have tested children's self-esteem in the fall, introduced some sort of program intended to raise those levels, and then tested again in the spring, revealing some gains. But the programs may be quite different from what most self-esteem-conscious teachers are actually using in their classrooms, the method for measuring self-esteem may be homegrown and of uncertain validity, and the duration of the effect is unknown.

If classroom interventions haven't proved successful in raising self-esteem over the long haul and if self-esteem hasn't been causally linked to achievement or positive social behavior, then the claim that classroom-based self-esteem programs will bring about these other benefits becomes even more dubious. The little research that addresses this question tends to be "somewhat contradictory, and the effects of the manipulation are typically short-lived," Martin Covington, one of the California task force scholars, regretfully concluded.[27] On such results does a national movement rest.

It isn't clear, at least to me, whether these disappointing findings mean that no classroom self-esteem intervention can ever produce lasting results. But even someone who remains determinedly sanguine about the idea itself must concede that a good number of the self-esteem programs currently in use are, to put it kindly, rather silly. Getting students to chant "I'm special!"—or to read a similar perfunctory message on cheerful posters or in prepackaged curricular materials—is pointless at best. Even Robert Reasoner, president of the International Council for Self-Esteem and a long-time champion of self-esteem programs in his days as a school superintendent in California, has remarked that "efforts limited to making students 'feel good' are apt to have little lasting effect because they fail to strengthen the internal sources of self-esteem related to integrity, responsibility, and achievement."[28]

THE MEANING OF DISAPPOINTING DATA. It is striking that even those investigators who would like to show that self-esteem is vital to social and academic development and who believe we ought to embark on a major effort to help students feel better about themselves have been largely unsuccessful in their attempts to demonstrate any of this through research. What is the significance of this failure? Consider several possible reactions to the evidence reviewed here.

• *No one has shown that self-esteem* doesn't *matter.* This is quite true, but it is generally impossible to prove the negative. Moreover, the burden of proof would seem to rest with those arguing that our education system ought to be attending to a given factor.

• *Self-esteem is related to things other than academic performance and social behavior.* This is very likely so. For example, depression and other psychological problems are highly correlated with low self-esteem. Once again, though, there is some disagreement about which causes which.[29]

• *Self-esteem may not be sufficient to produce achievement or to serve as a social vaccine, but it may be a necessary component.* True enough. It is entirely possible that children who feel very good about themselves are not necessarily high achievers or caring people—and yet, at the same time, it is possible that those who doubt their own worth are even less likely to be so. If high self-esteem failed to guarantee desirable outcomes but low self-esteem actively interfered with them, the overall correlation might be less than impressive (as indeed it is), but self-esteem could nevertheless be considered a relevant and important factor.

• *If the techniques for measurement are so problematic, how can we rely on studies using these measures to challenge the importance of self-esteem?* A reasonable question. But if we are going to dismiss the evidence against, we also have to write off the evidence in favor. That leaves us with no substantiation for the idea that self-esteem matters— at least until good data are found to show otherwise. Some researchers are convinced that these data will eventually appear. Neil Smelser admits (in his introduction to the California research anthology) that the available research fails to find much of an association between self-esteem and other variables. Yet he defiantly, or perhaps wistfully, continues to refer to this association as "the link that we all know exists." He then tries to figure out what methodological flaws have thus far prevented researchers from demonstrating it.[30] By contrast, another writer argues that limits inherent in the experimental method mean that traditional research will never produce more encouraging results. But he too remains convinced that self-esteem is a meaningful construct and an important reality, regardless of what the research shows.[31]

That, of course, is the central challenge for all of us: how to reconcile the powerful intuition that self-esteem is a significant causal variable with the studies that fail to support this notion. Are we entitled to dismiss inconvenient findings because they somehow fail to document what we strongly believe is true? Or must we—recalling other things that we think we "know" through intuition, personal experience, or clinical impressions, but which turn out to be false[32]—rethink our basic beliefs? What sort of research and how much of it would suffice to topple our intuitions? Conversely, what kind of nonexperimental evidence and how much of *it* should we demand before waving away the studies?

These are big, challenging questions that transcend the issue of self-esteem. But a thoughtful consideration of such issues is absolutely necessary when we find ourselves on the horns of an epistemological dilemma. Personally, I see no simple solution to this particularly vexing clash between research and common sense—or, from another perspective, between experimental and nonexperimental evidence. But in the meantime we have to contend with other objections to the notion of raising students' self-esteem, challenges rooted in basic values rather than in research.

II. THE VALUES: Why the Emphasis on Self-Esteem is Troubling

Apart from questions about the level of empirical support for self-esteem's significance, it is possible to challenge the *desirability* of focusing on this issue in the classroom. My concern here is not that children are encouraged to feel good about themselves so much as that their attention is trained primarily on themselves. *I'm* special, *I'm* important, here's how *I* feel about things. The whole enterprise could be said to encourage a self-absorption bordering on narcissism.

Of course, this focus is nothing new in American education—or more generally. If we exhort students to keep their eyes on their own papers; if we strand them in separate desks, as if on their own private islands; if we make the central lesson of school "how to be alone in a crowd,"[33] then this both reflects and contributes to our society's infatuation with individualism. Any number of commentators have pointed to our absence of commitment to shared values or to the value of what is shared.[34] We are taught that individual achievement and self-actualization are what matter. Any talk about generosity or caring is prefaced with the assertion that you must love yourself first in order to be able to love others—a belief that is decidedly debatable and also liable to result in people's failing to get past the first step. One can spend a lifetime trying to love oneself more fully, while other people fade into the background.

The self-esteem movement is hardly unique in fixing each child's attention on his or her separate self, but it is open to criticism for doing so just the same. Is it a coincidence that the man who helped make "self-esteem" a household phrase back in the 1970s was Nathaniel Branden, who emerged from the inner circle of Ayn Rand's ultra-individualists? Is it accidental that the rhetoric of self-esteem proponents often continues to recall the human potential movement's preoccupation with the self?

Lilian Katz, a past president of the National Association for the Education of Young Children, has sharply criticized elementary school self-esteem programs for just this reason.[35] She looks at sentence-starter exercises that begin with "I am special because . . ." and wonders why children's attention should "so insistently be turned inward." She notices assignments in which students produce booklets called "All About Me" and wonders why classes are not working on projects called "All About *Us*."

The criticism here derives from the value judgment that it is better to foster a sense of community among students than to produce (however unwittingly) a collection of self-absorbed individuals. But Katz goes on to offer an empirical argument as well, pointing out that self-esteem programs may not even succeed on their own terms, because merely being told (or asked to repeat) that one is worthwhile isn't likely to change anyone's underlying self-image.

Of course, the latter argument would seem to apply only to questionable versions of self-esteem programs that consist of chanting hollow phrases. But once the issue of individualism has been raised, the implications spill over into a more damning critique—one that calls into question all such programs and the focus on the self itself. That critique suggests that a self-oriented approach may fail to help students believe in themselves because it overlooks the political and economic realities that offer far more meaningful explanations of why some children doubt or even despise themselves. To put it bluntly, if children come to school hungry or bruised from beatings, no activity designed to promote self-esteem is going to help. These activities miss the point not because they have been designed poorly but because such activities by their very nature are concerned with the psychological states of individuals, which is not where the trouble lies. James Beane said it well:

A debilitating environment is likely to squash fledgling self-confidence no matter how much we exhort the individual to persist. . . . Moreover, suggesting that self-esteem can be preserved by developing "coping skills" endorses the status quo and, in so doing, ignores the fact that having positive self-esteem is almost impossible for many young people, given the deplorable conditions under which they are forced to live by the inequities in our society. . . . [F]ocusing on self-protection mechanisms . . . is, of course, "privatizing" at its extreme. It is a theory of alienation that pits the individual against the world.[36]

That theory, of course, reverberates with political implications, particularly for anyone whose agenda includes social change. As another critic has noticed, even if focusing on individual feelings is "not socially pernicious," it may, as a practical matter, divert energy and resources "from some socially useful approaches to social problems" that require the transformation of institutions instead of psyches.[37]

Indeed, the self-esteem movement is only the latest version of a familiar American emphasis on positive thinking and self-help—a tradition that has long served the interests of those who benefit from the status quo. Nothing maintains the current arrangement of power more effectively than an approach that ignores the current arrangement of power—and that focuses attention instead on how you feel about yourself.[38]

But if a concern with individual psychology distracts us from structural factors, it bears mentioning that those structures include the organization of our classrooms, not just of our society as a whole. The study of education has surely taken a step forward by recognizing the importance of internal variables (as opposed to mere behavior), but it is possible to become so preoccupied with what is going on inside a child's head that we lose sight of how such things as self-concept are influenced by how learning is conceived and designed.

A few years ago I spent some time in a California school district that was supposed to be a showcase for "self-esteeming." Sure enough, each classroom I visited was dedicated to the mission of pumping up every student's confidence. One teacher exclaimed, "You can do anything, can't you?" Another wore a button with a diagonal red slash running through the words "I Can't." Bulletin boards featured such slogans as "You are beautiful!" And classes were required to applaud after each student made a presentation or, in another case, to recite "I am somebody" each morning.

What struck me about these schools, though, was that this relentless cheerleading was grafted onto a profoundly disempowering dynamic. The rules displayed on the walls in these classrooms were devised by the adults and imposed on the children, and they included "When the teacher talks, everyone listens" and "Follow directions." Students were manipulated constantly with rewards and punishments to enforce compliance with the teachers' demands: stickers and lavish praise for conformity, punitive "consequences" for disobedience. Only the "Star Spellers" had their work displayed, turning learning into a quest for triumph. Children in the primary grades had to hold their hands over their mouths as they returned from recess in tightly formed lines.

In one sixth grade classroom, students were being led through a self-esteem exercise in which they were to reflect on their feelings by completing sentences started by the teacher. When I happened to walk in, she was reading, "I feel down and out when. . . ." My attention was drawn at that very moment to a boy sitting miserably apart from the rest of the class—his desk pulled over there by the teacher, I later learned, as a punishment for talking out of turn. The juxtaposition would have been funny if it weren't so appalling.

The climate and structures I am describing are, with the possible exception of the emphasis on praise,[39] not part of the self-esteem program—nor even, I assume, a direct result of adopting that program. Yet the self-esteem agenda may reflect a kind of myopia such that activities designed to help students attend to their own feelings can coexist comfortably with just such retrograde educational practices. Whether or not rampant individualism helps to explain the disappointing research results on self-esteem, I believe it stems from a value system that is disturbing in its own right.

III. THE CRITICS: Missing the Point

If teachers who are concerned about promoting self-esteem looked up from their lesson plans and if researchers put down their experimental protocols, they would find a growing interest in the topic on the part of people who are not professional educators. Over the last few years, quite a few essays, columns, and even comic strips have been devoted to the question of whether schools should help students to feel better about themselves. The tone of this coverage has generally ranged from harshly critical to downright snide.

The social commentators weighing in on the subject—most of them well toward the starboard side of the political spectrum—include Chester Finn in *Commentary;* the late Christopher Lasch in *The New Republic;* John Leo in *U.S. News & World Report;* Charles Krauthammer in *Time;* a *Newsweek* staff writer named Jerry Adler in a sneering 1992 cover story; Barbara Lerner in *American Educator;* Harold Stevenson in the *New York Times;* Albert Shanker, Mona Charen, and Judith Martin (Miss Manners) in their respective columns; Phyllis Schlafly (to any reporter who asks); any number of lesser-known local pundits; and the creators of *Doonesbury* and *Calvin & Hobbes.*

The extent of overlap among the arguments of these critics is so great that one sometimes suspects they share a single ghostwriter. But their attack on the enterprise of trying to boost children's self-esteem at school reflects a very different sensibility from the one that had led me to warn of an excess of individualism or a paucity of research. In fact, I believe not only that the critics base their attacks on faulty premises but also that the implications of their attacks are far more troubling than the self-esteem programs themselves.

The conservative case against trying to raise students' self-esteem relies principally on the creation of a sharp dichotomy in which worrying about how children feel about themselves is contrasted with spending time on academics. The former is depicted as a touchy-feely fad, the latter as old-fashioned honest toil. The former amounts to coddling students by pretending that everything they do is fine, while the latter means facing up to hard truths and insisting that students measure up to tough standards. When teachers join other commentators in parsing the issue this way, they typically do so with a tone of defiant self-congratulation for having chosen the latter option.[40]

The obvious response here, beyond questioning the loaded language with which these alternatives are usually described, is to expose the dichotomy itself as false. Concern about students' social and psychological needs hardly precludes attention to their intellectual development; in fact, the two enterprises may be mutually reinforcing. But this answer does not mollify the critics, many of whom proceed to make the following argument: if students are expected to work hard, if they are graded strictly and rewarded or praised only when they have earned it, they will come to develop a sense of self-respect, which is (depending on the critic) either better than self-esteem or a prerequisite for it.

Usually this point is made by emphasizing the harms of the opposite approach: easy A's, frequent praise, and a general emphasis on unconditional self-esteem (accepting children as they are and encouraging them to accept themselves) will lead to vulgar self-satisfaction. This in turn discourages students from making an effort. After all, why work hard to achieve if you are already perfect? Or to say it a bit differently, if your attention is focused on the value of who you are rather than on what you do, then you probably won't do very much.

Before responding directly to this position I want to make some observations about the context in which it is offered. To begin with, the attack on self-esteem must be understood as but one engagement in a much wider war to preserve what might be called the Old School of education. Critics who decry self-esteem programs typically slide into denunciations of any sort of affective education—and for that matter, any academic instruction that departs in content or method from a "basics" curriculum in which facts and skills in primary subject areas are transmitted from teacher to student. By and large these are the same critics who dismiss bilingual education, invented spelling, multicultural curricula, and cooperative learning as illegitimate. They reserve special scorn for anyone who challenges such favored traditional practices as tracking, competition, grades, or standardized testing. Sometimes they also speak up for punitive discipline, in which the point is to maintain control of the classroom and get students to obey.

Not every commentary includes all these elements, of course, but they coincide often enough to warrant thinking of them as forming a sort of ideological package. An attempt to help students feel better about themselves is thus viewed as just one more departure from the way things ought to be. And for rhetorical purposes critics prefer to describe their approach as being under siege—notwithstanding the pervasiveness of the practices they favor. For example, Finn insists with a straight face that the "prevailing wisdom" today is to renounce standardized testing, tracking, and competition,[41] while Lerner refers to the assignment of a dominant role to self-esteem as "the reigning orthodoxy" in education.[42]

It is also worth observing that the preferred method of justifying attacks on self-esteem (and on other challenges to the Old School) is the use of highly selective anecdotes: critics are apt to dredge up an example of silly classroom materials or a quotation about feeling good that would redden the cheeks of most self-esteem loyalists. Very rarely are real data provided to substantiate the criticism itself or its premises. (Of course, supporting evidence is also scarce in *defenses* of self-esteem programs.)

There is one exception to this tendency to ignore the data, however. It has lately become de rigueur for critics to cite, with a note of triumph, a single survey's finding that American students express more confidence about their knowledge of mathematics than do their counterparts in other countries, despite the fact that their test scores are actually lower. This contrast makes for arresting headlines, such as "Doing Bad and Feeling Good." But it proves to be a lot less meaningful on careful reflection. First, apart from the dubious validity of standardized test results, some researchers contend that the relative performance of U.S. students is not nearly as poor as is commonly believed.[43] Second, a misplaced optimism about one's math skills is quite different from high global self-esteem, which is what most classroom programs are intended to bolster. Third, as James Beane has pointed out, it is just as reasonable to summarize the results of that survey by saying that Asian youngsters were reluctant to pronounce themselves pleased with their own mathematical competence. This may say less about Americans' swelled heads than about the widely recognized Asian aversion to self-commendation.[44]

Beyond the dearth of evidence to buttress their position, critics offer what appears to be a curious conflation of fact and value. They typically insist on the point that self-esteem does not precede achievement but follows it, which suggests that educators should address themselves directly and exclusively to promoting academic performance. This is a plausible hypothesis, and it even enjoys some limited research support. But watch carefully: while the critics may offer a descriptive claim to the effect that trying to boost self-esteem *will* not work, the core of their argument is really that it *should* not be done. Lurking just below the surface of their polemics is the fear that somebody is going to get what might be called a "psychological free lunch." Children may end up being happy with themselves without having *earned* that right!

Here we have left the world of evidence and entered (through the back door) the realm of moralistic first principles. It is a place of puritanical fervor, where people should not be permitted to eat except by the sweat of their brows and where children must not think well of themselves until they can point to some tangible accomplishment. Like all worldviews, this one cannot be proved true or false, but it ought to be brought out into the open so we can decide whether it is reasonable and consistent with our most basic values.

The same could be said of another major premise of the conservative attack on self-esteem programs (and on all other forays into affective education): namely, that schools ought to be pursuing a narrowly defined academic agenda rather than trying to help children become happier and healthier. This position is typically asserted as if it were self-evident, overlooking vigorous defenses that have been offered in support of a wider mission for our schools. For example, Nel Noddings of Stanford University has gone so far as to challenge "the deadly notion that the schools' first priority should be intellectual development." She argues that "the main aim of education should be to produce competent, caring, loving, and lovable people."[45]

Others would like to see schools vigorously pursuing intellectual *and* sociomoral development, pointing out that the two are actually difficult to tease apart. (Note that intellectual development is quite different from a collection of discrete academic skills.) To the critics' complaint that activities intended to help children become good people just take time away from helping them to become good learners, it might be noted that any number of classroom practices can do double duty. When the members of a class meet to make decisions and solve problems, they get the self-esteem-building message that their voices count, they experience a sense of belonging to a community, *and* they hone their ability to reason and analyze. When students work together in well-designed cooperative learning groups, they are likely to feel more positively disposed toward themselves and one another—*and* to learn more effectively. When children are helped to develop the capacity (and inclination) to understand how other people see the world, they are more likely to act generously—and, given the focused use of imagination required, they also develop intellectual skills. Finally, conversations about carefully chosen works of literature can spark reflection on important values while they build a facility with and appreciation for the language.[46]

Next let us consider the criticism of self-esteem programs that assumes that children who are fundamentally happy with themselves will have no motivation to achieve. This proposition rests on several faulty premises, the first of which is a confusion between positive self-regard and arrogant self-satisfaction. Someone who has a core of faith in his or her own efficacy and an underlying conviction that he or she is a good person is no more likely than other people—and possibly a good deal less likely—to opt for stagnation. Slippery definitions have made empirical investigations of this point difficult, but if there is little evidence that high self-esteem promotes better learning, there is none to show that high self-esteem promotes laziness. The assumption that it does may be the product of careless thinking, or it may reflect the cryptoreligious beliefs that no one *deserves* to be satisfied and that nothing will get done without the anxious energy of perpetual self-doubt.

Closely aligned with the latter belief is the assumption that "human nature is to do as little as necessary," as one columnist remarked in the course of ridiculing self-esteem programs.[47] A thorough refutation of this prejudice would require a review of virtually the entire literature on personality theory and motivation.[48] But we can say this much: the desire to do as little as possible is an aberration, a sign that something is amiss. It may suggest that the individual feels threatened and has fallen back on a strategy of damage control, or that extrinsic motivators have undermined interest in the task by reframing it as a tedious prerequisite to obtaining a reward, or that the task itself is perceived as pointless and dull.

This last possibility suggests another hidden premise of the critics: that learning is bitter medicine, an inherently unpleasant experience that will naturally be avoided by happy, satisfied children. (Thus we had better make sure they aren't too happy or satisfied.) In the abstract, this is demonstrably false: it is almost impossible to *stop* happy, satisfied children from learning. But if learning is taken to mean multiplying naked numbers, or reading the sodden prose of a textbook and answering the even-numbered questions at the end of the chapter, or memorizing disconnected facts and definitions, then there is some truth to the charge. The problem, though, does not lie with the students or with "human nature" or with high self-esteem; it lies with a drill-and-skill curriculum. Ironically, this is the very pedagogical approach championed by many critics of affective education.

That is why we must be cautious about assenting to the reasonable-sounding thesis that what we need are tougher standards so students can achieve something of which they can be proud. Whose standards are we talking about? Achievement at what? "Real self-esteem is released when a child learns something," one columnist insists. To which we must immediately add, "if it's something worth learning." You will sift through those anti-self-esteem editorials and essays in vain looking for any attention to the differences between basals and real literature, between worksheets and discovery-based projects, between covering the curriculum and discovering ideas, between test-driven achievement and real learning. No "I Believe in Me!" self-esteem unit could possibly be more foolish than the expectation that students will feel good about themselves because they successfully filled in the blanks on a ditto.

The flip side of the fear that too much self-esteem will kill the desire to learn is the faith that the disappointment attendant on losing a contest or flunking a test motivates children to do better in the future. The logic here is that it is precisely the feeling that one is a failure that creates an incentive to improve, a redoubling of one's efforts to learn. (Premature or unearned self-esteem would therefore short-circuit that natural process.) Usually this dismal premise lurks in the shadows of diatribes about self-esteem, but occasionally it is spelled out explicitly:

> Once upon a time . . . you passed or you failed. You made the team or you didn't. If you fell short, if your ego was bruised by getting a D or by seeing your name on the cut list, then you buckled down and you made it next time and felt good about yourself. . . . Failure can be a terrific motivator.[49]

Again, it is difficult to imagine a point of view more at variance with everything we know about motivation and learning. We may *want* children to rebound from failure, but this does not mean that they will. While fortifying students' self-esteem may not guarantee academic success, the experience of screwing up is a poorer bet by orders of magnitude. When children fail at a task, the most likely result, all things being equal, is that they will expect to do poorly on similar tasks in the future, and this expectation can set in motion a self-fulfilling prophecy. In this highly qualified sense, self-esteem does indeed seem to matter; the chances of success are higher for students who feel competent. On the other hand, perceived competence comes to a large extent from experiencing success. Thus, because failure can engender a feeling of incompetence (if not helplessness), future levels of achievement are compromised.[50]

Beyond its detrimental effect on performance, an experience with failure can produce two other overlapping results: a desire to take the easy way out and a loss of interest in whatever one has been doing. Both of these are presumably troubling to educators across the ideological spectrum. Students who have failed at something are inclined to prefer less challenging tasks than students who have succeeded.[51]

(Many commentators on education seem to forget that trying to avoid failure and trying to succeed are two very different orientations.) Similarly, students who have come to feel incompetent are less likely than others to be interested in what they are working on.[52] This means that even those students who really do buckle down and try harder when they fail—the supposed success stories of the Old School methods—may be doing so out of an anxious, compulsive pressure to feel better about themselves rather than because they enjoy learning.[53] Even if they manage to understand what they are reading today, they may not *want* to read tomorrow.

The destructive impact of failure on intrinsic motivation shows up with startling consistency. Its effect on short-term performance, however, depends on a number of factors. "It is not so much the event of failure, or even its frequency, that disrupts performance as it is the *meaning* of failure," as Martin Covington has put it.[54] Did someone deliberately give me too tricky a task in the hope that I would somehow be a better person for failing at it—or did the task unexpectedly prove too challenging? Was failure defined on the basis of someone else's judgment—or something intrinsic to the task itself? Did I experience that uniquely toxic form of failure in which one person must lose to another in a public competition? Did the failure take place in the context of intense pressure to succeed—or in a relaxed climate of exploration? Do I fear ridicule or punishment (such as a poor grade) for having failed—or am I part of a supportive community where setbacks are no big deal?

Once again, the irony creeps up on us: the conditions *least* likely to make failure a "terrific motivator" (or even to prevent subsequent performance problems) are tough standards, grades, competition, rewards, and punishments—in short, the practices associated with the Old School, back-to-basics classrooms promoted by many of the same people who deride self-esteem and extol the motivational benefits of failure.

Of course, beyond situational factors, it is also true that individual differences help to account for the effects of failure: one child may redouble her efforts while another throws in the towel. But the most significant of these predictors may just be the extent to which a student is intrinsically or extrinsically motivated—that is, interested in the learning itself as opposed to being inclined to see success as a way of getting grades, approval, or other rewards. Studies indicate that it is children with the latter orientation who "showed performance impairment and less motivation . . . following failure."[55] And the latter orientation follows predictably from being in environments that *lead* students to focus on such artificial inducements.[56]

Of all the factors that determine how students will respond to failure, research has shown that the most important one of all is how they have come to *explain* that failure. If I fall short, do I think it is because I'm stupid (ability), because I didn't try hard enough (effort), because the questions were too hard (task difficulty), or because it just wasn't my day (luck)? Some of these things are internal and some are external; some are stable and some are variable; one of them (effort) is within my control and the rest are not. This framework, proposed a generation ago by Bernard Weiner, has inspired a small library of work by social and educational psychologists. The consensus is that "children who attribute their failures to invariant or uncontrollable factors, such as insufficient ability, tend to be debilitated by failure."[57]

Interestingly, even children who succeed are less likely to continue learning effectively if they explain their success in terms of how smart they are. Students who are encouraged to focus on their ability—or lack of it—typically become preoccupied with their performance. By contrast, those who explain their success or failure in terms of how hard they tried are more likely to become absorbed in the task itself. This in turn means that they are less likely to be thrown by failure and more likely to be intrinsically motivated and to keep working at something until they get it.[58] The key distinction here is not hard to grasp: success, persistence, and interest tend to follow when children are helped to think about *what* they are doing; the absence of these results suggests that children have been led to think about *how* they are doing and, by extension, how able they are. But what classroom practices create the latter, dysfunctional orientation?

> Generally, the available evidence suggests that a focus on ability is likely to develop when students are provided little choice concerning tasks, competition and social comparison are emphasized, ability grouping and tracking are used, public evaluations of performance and conduct are common, grading is based on relative ability, and cooperation and interaction among students are discouraged.[59]

To reflect on failure and success in the classroom is to return to the place we began—that is, to a discussion of self-esteem's relation to achievement. As we saw, the evidence doesn't support the claim that programs intended to help children feel good about themselves are likely to raise students' achievement. But now it seems clear that the Old School approach favored by many critics of these activities is even worse. So how *can* we help students to learn? If there is reason to be skeptical about what we hear from both boosters and bashers of self-esteem, where does that leave us?

The answer, once again, depends on our objectives. If we are genuinely concerned with students' intellectual development (as opposed to their scores on standardized tests), then it makes sense to do all we can to help them focus on effort rather than ability, to become absorbed with the learning itself rather than being preoccupied with their performance. This, in turn, can be facilitated by what I have elsewhere called the "three C's of motivation": collaboration, choice, and content (of the curriculum).[60]

Collaboration involves more than occasional cooperative learning activities; it means that students feel connected to their peers and that they experience the classroom as a safe, supportive community—not a place of isolation and certainly not a place where they must compete against one another. Choice means that students are brought into the process of making decisions about what (and how and why) they are learning—as well as other issues of classroom life. Finally, to raise the question of content is to challenge the assumption that students are indifferent about their schoolwork because they are not sufficiently "motivated" (or from another point of view, because they simply have low self-esteem). The real problem may be that the assignments themselves are not meaningful, engaging, or relevant.

Each of these considerations shows up again in slightly different form if our goals for children extend beyond academics to issues of psychological health. Given that many of the programs billed as self-esteem enhancers fail to have any appreciable effect on how children feel about themselves, what *does* make a difference? Edward Deci and Richard Ryan of the University of Rochester, drawing on the work of other psychologists before them, have proposed that human beings have three fundamental needs: first, to feel autonomous or self-determining—"to experience one's actions as emanating from the self"; second, to have a sense of oneself as competent and effective; and third, to be related to others and be part of a social world.[61]

It is not enough to meet these needs only when school is in session. But to the extent that we as educators want to help children feel good about themselves, we would do better to treat them with respect than to shower them with praise. We should embrace affective education, but in the context of building community rather than attending to each individual separately. We ought to work *with* students rather than doing things (Old School things or New Age things) *to* them. Contrary to what some in the self-esteem movement seem to hold, students do not come to believe they are important, valued, and capable just because they are told that this is so or made to recite it. On the other hand, they are even less likely to feel that way when they are compelled to follow directions all day. Students acquire a sense of significance from doing significant things, from being active participants in their own education.

In short, it is time we challenged the false dichotomy that has defined the debate about self-esteem. Whether our objective is to help children become good (that is, creative, self-directed, lifelong) learners, or good (that is, secure, responsible, caring) people—or both—we can do better than to concentrate our efforts on self-esteem. But let us be careful that in criticizing that approach we do not end up doing even more harm to students in the long run.

Notes

1. Stanley Coopersmith, *The Antecedents of Self-Esteem* (San Francisco: Freeman, 1967), p. 5.
2. Roy F. Baumeister, Dianne M. Tice, and Debra G. Hutton, "Self-Presentational Motivations and Personality Differences in Self-Esteem," *Journal of Personality*, vol. 57, 1989, pp. 556, 554.
3. See, for example, Thomas J. Scheff et al., "Crime, Violence, and Self-Esteem," in Andrew M. Mecca et al., eds., *The Social Importance of Self-Esteem* (Berkeley: University of California Press, 1989), pp. 175–177, which includes a mention of Morris Rosenberg's estimate of the number of instruments in use as of 1988. Ruth Wylie, a leading authority on the measurement of self-esteem, has made the same point about lack of comparability (personal communication, 1991). For corroboration of the sheer number of measures, see B. C. Hansford and J. A. Hattie, "The Relationship Between Self and Achievement/Performance Measures," *Review of Educational Research*, vol. 52, 1982, p. 135.
4. Dianne M. Tice, "The Social Motivations of People with Low Self-Esteem," in Roy F. Baumeister, ed., *Self-Esteem: The Puzzle of Low Self-Regard* (New York: Plenum, 1993), p. 41.

5. One more methodological criticism might be mentioned here: the tendency to confuse self-description with self-esteem. Researchers sometimes assume that subjects who rate themselves poorly must be suffering from low self-esteem. The truth is that the items dreamed up by the tester may not be particularly important to the subject; indeed, given the norms of his or her subculture a student may even attach a positive value to the inability to do something well. See James A. Beane and Richard P. Lipka, *Self-Concept, Self-Esteem, and the Curriculum* (New York: Teachers College Press, 1986).

6. Neil J. Smelser, "Self-Esteem and Social Problems," in Mecca et al., pp. 15, 17. A more recent review of studies investigating claims of a connection between low self-esteem and drug use confirmed that "no sizable relationship . . . has been found" and the results "strongly suggest no direct association" at all. See Debra S. Schroeder et al., "Is There a Relationship Between Self-Esteem and Drug Use?" *Journal of Drug Issues,* vol. 23, 1993, pp. 659, 658.

7. This phrase comes from Michael R. Jackson, *Self-Esteem and Meaning* (Albany: State University of New York Press, 1984), p. 3. Jackson mentions a frequently cited, if possibly dated, review of the literature: L. Edward Wells and Gerald Marwell, *Self-Esteem: Its Conceptualization and Measurement* (Beverly Hills, Calif.: Sage, 1976).

8. Florence R. Rosenberg and Morris Rosenberg, "Self-Esteem and Delinquency," *Journal of Youth and Adolescence,* vol. 7, 1978, pp. 279–291. The correlations never exceeded .19.

9. Xiaoru Liu, Howard B. Kaplan, and Will Risser, "Decomposing the Reciprocal Relationships Between Academic Achievement and General Self-Esteem," *Youth and Society,* vol. 24, 1992, pp. 123–148.

10. This is the view of Bill Kreidler, who conducts workshops on conflict resolution for Educators for Social Responsibility, and of Ron Slaby, an expert on the prevention of school violence with the Education Development Center in Newton, Massachusetts.

11. See Howard B. Kaplan, *Deviant Behavior in Defense of Self* (New York: Academic Press, 1980); and Morris Rosenberg, Carmi Schooler, and Carrie Schoenbach, "Self-Esteem and Adolescent Problems: Modeling Reciprocal Effects," *American Sociological Review,* vol. 54, 1989, pp. 1004–1018. However, Rosenberg's own analysis a decade earlier failed to find any increase in subsequent self-esteem as a result of earlier delinquent behavior. See Rosenberg and Rosenberg, pp. 284–287.

12. L. Edward Wells and Joseph H. Rankin, "Self-Concept as a Mediating Factor in Delinquency," *Social Psychology Quarterly,* vol. 46, 1983, pp. 11–22.

13. Ervin Staub, "A Conception of the Determinants and Development of Altruism and Aggression," in Carolyn Zahn-Waxler et al., eds., *Altruism and*

Aggression: Biological and Social Origins (Cambridge: Cambridge University Press, 1986), pp. 142, 145. References omitted from quotation.

14. For example, people with low self-esteem may be motivated to help "as a means of avoiding rejection or obtaining social approval," she speculates. See Nancy Eisenberg, *Altruistic Emotion, Cognition, and Behavior* (Hillsdale, N.J.: Erlbaum, 1986), p. 203.

15. References are omitted here for reasons of space, but they can be obtained from the author.

16. Reading achievement was found in one study to be completely unrelated to children's self-concept. See Jean H. Williams, "The Relationship of Self-Concept and Reading Achievement in First-Grade Children," *Journal of Educational Research*, vol. 66, 1973, pp. 378–380. A more recent study with Norwegian students found a "negative direct effect of global self-esteem on academic achievement over time" for a sample of sixth graders, but not for third graders. See Einar M. Skaalvik and Knut A. Hagtvet, "Academic Achievement and Self-Concept," *Journal of Personality and Social Psychology*, vol. 58, 1990, p. 305. As Martin Covington explains in his contribution to the research reviews for the California task force, "At times, lack of a sense of worth is a more powerful stimulant to achievement than self-confidence is, and, depending on its source, a sense of self-esteem may not always promote the continued will to learn." See "Self-Esteem and Failure in School," in Mecca et al., p. 98.

17. Hansford and Hattie, op. cit.; see also Covington, p. 79.

18. Hansford and Hattie, pp. 134–137. On the last point, another researcher argues that grades are more "responsive to motivational influences" than are standardized test scores and therefore might be more likely to show a relationship to self-esteem. See Herbert W. Marsh, "Causal Ordering of Academic Self-Concept and Academic Achievement," *Journal of Educational Psychology*, vol. 82, 1990, p. 648.

19. See, for example, Hansford and Hattie, p. 133; Mzobanzi M. Mboya, "The Relative Importance of Global Self-Concept and Self-Concept of Academic Ability in Predicting Academic Achievement," *Adolescence*, vol. 24, 1989, pp. 39–46; Marsh, p. 646; and Skaalvik and Hagtvet, p. 292.

20. See Barbara M. Byrne, "The General/Academic Self-Concept Nomological Network," *Review of Educational Research*, vol. 54, 1984, p. 450; and Herbert W. Marsh, Barbara M. Byrne, and Richard J. Shavelson, "A Multifaceted Academic Self-Concept," *Journal of Educational Psychology*, vol. 80, 1988, pp. 366–380.

21. Beane and Lipka, p. 173.

22. Rosenberg, Schooler, and Schoenbach, p. 1014.

23. The high school study: Sheila M. Pottebaum, Timothy Z. Keith, and Stewart W. Ehly, "Is There a Causal Relation Between Self-Concept and Academic Achievement?" *Journal of Educational Research,* vol. 79, 1986, p. 142; the first literature review: Mary Ann Scheirer and Robert E. Kraut, "Increasing Educational Achievement via Self-Concept Change," *Review of Educational Research,* vol. 49, 1979, p. 145; and the more recent literature review: Thomas G. Moeller, "What Research Says About Self-Esteem and Academic Performance," *Education Digest,* January 1994, p. 37.

24. See, for example, Robert J. Calsyn and David A. Kenny, "Self-Concept of Ability and Perceived Evaluation of Others," *Journal of Educational Psychology,* vol. 69, 1977, pp. 136–145; see also Marsh, p. 647, for an argument that this study suffers from "serious conceptual and methodological limitations."

25. Geoffrey Maruyama, Rosalyn A. Rubin, and G. Gage Kingsbury, "Self-Esteem and Educational Achievement," *Journal of Personality and Social Psychology,* vol. 40, 1981, p. 973. See also Pottebaum, Keith, and Ehly, op. cit.

26. Hansford and Hattie, pp. 123, 124.

27. Covington, p. 80. The same conclusion was offered as early as 1979, and with a hint of satisfaction, by Scheirer and Kraut, op. cit.

28. Robert W. Reasoner, "You Can Bring Hope to Failing Students," *School Administrator,* Apr. 1992, p. 24. Likewise, "there is an enormous amount of junk in the self-esteem world" is the assessment of Hanoch McCarty, a member of the National Council for Self-Esteem. See Jonathan Weisman, "Though Still a Target of Attacks, Self-Esteem Movement Advances," *Education Week,* Mar. 6, 1991, p. 17. And James Beane, a leading proponent of affective education, similarly insists that "direct instruction in separate courses alone is not enough to adequately address self-perceptions. . . . In a time when so many messages suggest that self-esteem is tied to what one buys (commodification of the self), it is perhaps not surprising that some schools would want to buy packages to improve self-esteem," in *Affect in the Curriculum* (New York: Teachers College Press, 1990), p. 103.

29. See, for example, Susan Harter, "Causes and Consequences of Low Self-Esteem in Children and Adolescents," in Baumeister, esp. pp. 105–106. Howard Tennen and Glenn Affleck ("The Puzzles of Self-Esteem," in Baumeister, ed.) caution that "although low self-esteem . . . may anticipate later depressed *mood* . . . there is little evidence that level of self-esteem predicts the onset of depressive *disorders*" (p. 245).

30. Smelser, p. 17. Similarly, he told an interviewer that, "while you don't have anything like scientific proof, there's no question there is some legitimacy." See Weisman, p. 15.

31. Jackson, pp. 4–7.

32. See, for example, Alfie Kohn, *You Know What They Say . . .: The Truth About Popular Beliefs* (New York: HarperCollins, 1990); and Thomas Gilovich, *How We Know What Isn't So: The Fallibility of Human Reason in Everyday Life* (New York: Free Press, 1991). Among the roughly eighty beliefs debunked in the former book are the significance of birth order and the effect of the full moon on human behavior.

33. The phrase is from Philip W. Jackson, *Life in Classrooms* (New York: Teachers College Press, 1968; reprinted 1990), p. 16.

34. For example, see Philip Slater, *The Pursuit of Loneliness* (Boston: Beacon, 1970); Robert N. Bellah et al., *Habits of the Heart* (Berkeley: University of California Press, 1985); Thomas C. Heller et al., eds., *Reconstructing Individualism* (Stanford, Calif.: Stanford University Press, 1986); and Alfie Kohn, *The Brighter Side of Human Nature: Altruism and Empathy in Everyday Life* (New York: Basic Books, 1990), chap. 9.

35. See Lilian G. Katz, "All About Me," *American Educator*, Summer 1993, pp. 18–23. An excerpt from this essay appeared in the *New York Times* on July 15, 1993. A similar point is made by Wesley R. Burr and Clark Christensen, "Undesirable Side Effects of Enhancing Self-Esteem," *Family Relations*, Oct. 1992, pp. 460–464. Katz criticizes self-esteem programs for other reasons, too, such as their failure to encourage creative thinking.

36. James A. Beane, "Sorting Out the Self-Esteem Controversy," *Educational Leadership*, Sept. 1991, pp. 27, 29.

37. Harry Specht, dean of the School of Social Welfare at the University of California at Berkeley, quoted in Weisman, p. 15. For a more detailed analysis along similar lines, see Ellen Herman, "Toward a Politics of Self-Esteem?" *Z Magazine*, July/Aug. 1991. Herman observes that "prophets of self-esteem are putting their faith in a new psychic order, certain that change will come, if at all, from the inside" (p. 46).

38. For an elaboration of this analysis, see Russell Jacoby, *Social Amnesia: A Critique of Contemporary Psychology from Adler to Laing* (Boston: Beacon, 1975); and some of the essays in Rollo May et al., *Politics and Innocence: A Humanistic Debate* (Dallas: Saybrook, 1986). While most of the criticism of the self-esteem movement has come from the political right (see below), it is interesting to note that the original California task force was enthusiastically supported by conservative Republicans. See John Vasconcellos, Preface to Mecca et al., pp. xvi–xvii.

39. For a critical discussion of praise, see Alfie Kohn, *Punished by Rewards* (Boston: Houghton Mifflin, 1993), chap. 6.

40. See, for example, Angie Ward Marsello, "Boosting Student Esteem All the Way—to Failure!," *English Journal*, vol. 80, no. 1, 1991, pp. 72–73; see also the letters generated by this essay in vol. 81, no. 3, 1992, pp. 74–81.

41. Chester E. Finn, Jr., "Narcissus Goes to School," *Commentary*, June 1990, p. 42.

42. Barbara Lerner, "Self-Esteem and Excellence: The Choice and the Paradox," *American Educator*, Winter 1985, p. 12.

43. See, for example, Gerald W. Bracey, "Why Can't They Be Like We Were?" *Phi Delta Kappan*, Oct. 1991, pp. 104–117.

44. Beane, "Sorting Out the Self-Esteem Controversy," p. 28.

45. Nel Noddings, *The Challenge to Care in Schools: An Alternative Approach to Education* (New York: Teachers College Press, 1992), pp. 12, 174.

46. The work of the California-based Child Development Project confirms each of these examples. See Catherine C. Lewis et al., "Beyond the Pendulum: Creating Challenging and Caring Schools," *Phi Delta Kappan*, in press.

47. John Powers, "Feeling Good (for Nothing)," *Boston Globe Magazine*, Jan. 24, 1993, p. 8.

48. Numerous studies have confirmed that children are naturally inclined to try to make sense of the world, to push themselves to do things just beyond their current level. More broadly, the idea that it is natural to do as little as possible is a relic of "tension-reduction" or homeostatic models, which hold that organisms always seek a state of rest. Few models have been so thoroughly repudiated in modern psychology. Interested readers might look up the work of Gordon Allport, as well as findings concerned with the fundamental human impetus to attain a sense of competence (Robert White), to be self-determining (Richard deCharms, Edward Deci, and others), to satisfy our curiosity (D. E. Berlyne), or to "actualize" our potential in various ways (Abraham Maslow).

49. Powers, pp. 7–8.

50. One of many studies showing that failing at something leads to an expectation of future failure is Jacquelynne E. Parsons and Diane N. Ruble, "The Development of Achievement-Related Expectancies," *Child Development*, vol. 48, 1977, pp. 1075–1079. For confirmation of the point that performance is undermined by feelings of incompetence, see Donald S. Hiroto and Martin E. P. Seligman, "Generality of Learned Helplessness in Man," *Journal of Personality and Social Psychology*, vol. 31, 1975, pp. 311–327.

51. See, for example, Allan Wigfield, "Children's Attributions for Success and Failure," *Journal of Educational Psychology*, vol. 80, 1988, p. 78; and Susan Harter, "The Relationship Between Perceived Competence, Affect, and

Motivational Orientation Within the Classroom," in Ann K. Boggiano and Thane S. Pittman, eds., *Achievement and Motivation: A Social-Developmental Perspective* (Cambridge: Cambridge University Press, 1992), p. 84.

52. See, for example, Harter, p. 83; and Edward L. Deci and Richard M. Ryan, *Intrinsic Motivation and Self-Determination in Human Behavior* (New York: Plenum, 1985), p. 61.

53. For empirical confirmation of this distinction, see Richard M. Ryan, Richard Koestner, and Edward L. Deci, "Ego-Involved Persistence," *Motivation and Emotion*, vol. 15, 1991, pp. 185–205.

54. Martin V. Covington, *Making the Grade: A Self-Worth Perspective on Motivation and School Reform* (Cambridge: Cambridge University Press, 1992), p. 62. The frequency of failure does matter, however. The more one's efforts have proved fruitless in the past, the more one comes to expect failure in the future. See Deborah J. Stipek and Joel M. Hoffman, "Children's Achievement-Related Expectancies as a Function of Academic Performance Histories and Sex," *Journal of Educational Psychology*, vol. 72, 1980, p. 861.

55. See Cheryl Flink et al., "Children's Achievement-Related Behaviors," in Boggiano and Pittman, p. 200.

56. See Edward L. Deci, John Nezlek, and Louise Sheinman, "Characteristics of the Rewarder and Intrinsic Motivation of the Rewardee," *Journal of Personality and Social Psychology*, vol. 40, 1981, pp. 1–10. This point, of course, raises deeply unsettling questions about assessment per se, not merely the particular assessment strategies being used. See Alfie Kohn, "Grading: The Issue Is Not How But Why," *Educational Leadership*, Oct. 1994, pp. 38–41. (Reprinted in this volume as Chapter Seven).

57. Barbara G. Licht and Carol S. Dweck, "Determinants of Academic Achievement," *Developmental Psychology*, vol. 20, 1984, p. 628.

58. See almost anything by Carol Dweck (for example, "Motivational Processes Affecting Learning," *American Psychologist*, vol. 41, 1986, pp. 1040–1048) or by Carole Ames (for example, "Classrooms: Goals, Structures, and Student Motivation," *Journal of Educational Psychology*, vol. 84, 1992, pp. 261–271). One recent study suggests that focusing on effort may not always promote motivation, but focusing on ability unquestionably undermines it. See Ellen A. Skinner et al., "What It Takes to Do Well in School and Whether I've Got It," *Journal of Educational Psychology*, vol. 82, 1990, pp. 22–32.

59. Martin L. Maehr and Carol Midgley, "Enhancing Student Motivation: A Schoolwide Approach," *Educational Psychologist*, vol. 26, 1991, p. 404.

60. See Kohn, *Punished by Rewards*, especially chap. 11. For more on the creation of caring communities in the classroom and the importance of allowing students to make decisions about their learning, see Alfie Kohn, "Caring

Kids: The Role of the Schools," *Phi Delta Kappan,* Mar. 1991, pp. 496–506 (reprinted in this volume as Chapter Seventeen); and "Choices for Children: Why and How to Let Students Decide," *Phi Delta Kappan,* Sept. 1993, pp. 8–20 (reprinted in this volume as Chapter Eighteen).

61. See Edward L. Deci and Richard M. Ryan, "A Motivational Approach to Self: Integration in Personality," in Richard Dienstbier, ed., *Nebraska Symposium on Motivation,* vol. 38 (Lincoln: University of Nebraska Press, 1990). The quotation appears on p. 243.

CHAPTER TWELVE

Television and Children

ReViewing the Evidence

W hen an extraordinary new technology is about to arrive, there is room for rapture or dread but nothing in between. Television, E. B. White declared shortly before regular national broadcasts began, "is going to be the test of the modern world. . . . We shall discover either a new and unbearable disturbance of the general peace or a saving radiance in the sky."

If this language seems hyperbolic now, remember that in 1938 there was still something miraculous about the idea that "a person sitting in one room could observe the nonsense taking place in another," as White put it. We grow used to miracles, though; this capability is rarely pondered by today's channel surfer. But if no one today speaks of TV as a saving radiance, an influential contingent of critics is still very comfortable with phrases like "unbearable disturbance of the general peace"—and worse.

Note: This chapter was written in 1990–1991 and is published here for the first time.

In fact, it is difficult to exaggerate the hysterical tone in which claims are routinely made about the medium—or the grip that these beliefs have on the educated sector of our society. No one blinked when a woman who stood up to ask a question after a recent panel discussion about television began with the observation that "watching [TV] makes people more dulled and hypnotized instead of thinking for themselves." Indeed, many academics share these assumptions. A few years ago, for example, a sports medicine journal inquired into a possible connection between watching television and gaining weight. The title of the article, "Is Childhood Obesity Related to TV Addiction?" implied that while such a relation may be open to question, the premise, that children may be meaningfully described as "addicted" to TV, is not.

An influential group of writers have practically built their careers on sweeping denigrations of television and italicized warnings of its effects on children in particular. Neil Postman, who teaches communications arts at New York University, asserted not long ago that when students see nothing wrong with contradicting themselves in their term papers, it is television that is to blame. Elsewhere he has written that TV "has the power to lead us to childhood's end," that it "brings ruin to any intelligent understanding of public affairs," and that viewing "requires no skills and develops no skills." In her best-selling book, *The Plug-In Drug,* the journalist Marie Winn declared that TV "distorts the sense of time . . . weakens relationships . . . [and causes] a serious diminution of verbal abilities," among other things. More recently, Jane Healy wrote in *Endangered Minds* that "brains of youngsters who spend lots of time in front of a TV set, for example, may be expected to develop differently from others . . ."—although she conceded much later in the book that there is virtually no evidence to support this. Even the influential pediatrician T. Berry Brazelton has warned about the "disintegration of ego mechanisms" and "screaming, thrashing, disorganized hyperactivity which ensues after a period of television watching in most [preschool-age] children."

What is interesting about such charges—apart from the fact that alarms of comparable volume were sounded in the early days of radio, movies, paperback novels, and other media—is that they go well beyond an indictment of the programs that network executives choose to put on the air. It is the medium itself that is said to be unhealthy for children and other living things; the prescription that follows from this view is not to watch selectively but, in the words of a bumper sticker now popular in college towns, to kill your television. Thus, parents who pressure the networks for better-quality children's programming are, in Winn's view, like people who deal with alcoholism "by striving to replace cheap whiskey with Chivas Regal."

The distinction between television and what is *on* television resonates with many people who agree with Newton Minow, whose famous phrase is still apt more than thirty years after he coined it: with respect to its content, TV is indeed a "vast wasteland." But there is no inconsistency in rolling one's eyes at, and deciding to shield one's children from, many of the programs beamed into our living rooms, on the one hand, and objecting to wild pronouncements about how television sucks in young viewers and sucks out their brains, on the other.

The distinction is meaningful for Peggy Charren, the founder of Action for Children's Television and no friend to the industry after two decades of lobbying against the Saturday morning "kid-vid" programming ghetto. "A lot of people think the act of watching television is a problem all by itself," she says. "I think that's just plain dumb. We tend to blame on television what are really other problems of society because it's a very easy scapegoat."

It is not merely the visceral reaction one has to parents who smile around a glass of chablis while confiding that "We don't let our children watch TV." It is that their assumptions, echoing those of self-assured critics and columnists, often cannot stand up to critical reflection or a careful review of the data. True, there is reason to think that watching certain kinds of programs may play a small role in making some children more aggressive, although research findings to this effect are shot through with qualifications. There is also reason to be concerned about a child who spends hour after hour in front of the television to the exclusion of other activities. (This, however, reflects "a problem in the family, not in the television," remarks Kathy Pezdek, a psychologist at Claremont Graduate School.)

Peter Miller, who directs the Institute for Modern Communication at Northwestern University, acknowledges that television "probably doesn't do a hell of a lot of good." But he adds that, "for most kids, [researchers are] not getting the kinds of deleterious impacts that are often attributed to television." This is precisely the conclusion that emerges from a review of more than a hundred empirical studies: there is very little about television viewing, per se, that is cause for alarm, according to the available evidence.

Such a finding is as significant as it is surprising. Even if TV is not generally beneficial, it matters that there is no good research to support the barrage of criticism insisting that the medium is *inherently* destructive. Moreover, it turns out that where good research on the topic does exist, its effect is typically to rebut the most frequently heard charges. That, in turn, forces us to rethink what has come to be common knowledge about children watching television.

Collecting evidence on the topic has provided researchers with a unique set of challenges. Even establishing how many hours children spend in front of the set isn't as easy as it might seem. The usual figure is between twenty-two and twenty-five hours a week (less time as children get older), but some critics think that those figures are inflated because unrepresentative families are surveyed or because networks lure viewers with special programs during the ratings periods. At least one TV-diary study found only half the expected amount of viewing by children.

Most of the research on television, in fact, has concentrated on children, and the bulk of it has been done since the mid–1970s. But that research has been handicapped by the fact that there is no natural comparison group to match with TV viewers; nonviewers are a tiny and otherwise peculiar group. Nor is there any way to get a baseline measure of behavior before viewing begins, because children typically come to consciousness with the TV on in the background. (Sometime between the ages of two and three a child starts to watch deliberately, developing preferences for particular programs.)

Except for the very few studies that managed to compare children's behavior before and after television came to their towns, most research consists of looking at heavy and light viewers to see whether they seem different from each other. The problem here is that such differences, even when they do show up, do not constitute proof that TV was responsible. One early study, for example, found that children who watched television were less likely to attend Sunday school—just the sort of fact that pundits love to pounce on and publish. Luckily, though, these researchers had questioned children before TV arrived, and it turned out that less religious families were especially likely to buy television sets and use them. This difference between viewers and nonviewers "already existed . . . before television came on the scene."

The very idea that TV is the cause and the child's behavior is the effect is a common way of approaching the subject. On reflection, however, it is not easy to defend. This model, derived from behavioral psychology, sees people as essentially inert and acted on, whereas communications researchers are coming to understand that viewers, even very young ones, are active choosers who shape their environment just as it shapes them. The question to ask, then, may not be "What does television do to a viewer?" but "To what uses does a viewer put television?"

The traditional model, implicitly employed by TV's least subtle critics, also ignores the fact that TV will affect any two children differently, depending on age, gender, race, personality, patterns of family interaction, who else is watching, what programs are being watched, and *why* they are being watched (because one identifies with a particular character? to be distracted from bickering parents? to learn about the world? to relax? to be able to participate in playground conversations the next day?). Context is all, which is why Wilbur Schramm and his colleagues began what has become one of the most influential academic books on the subject, *Television in the Lives of Our Children,* by declaring, "No informed person can say simply that television is bad or that it is good for children." Some pages later, they explained that "the relationship is always between a *kind* of television and a *kind* of child in a *kind* of situation."

With that in mind, let us consider what the research really says about the most frequent and (for parents) most frightening claims about watching TV—that it is a mindless activity, that it lowers school achievement by making children restless and by taking the place of pleasure reading, that it is addictive, that it engenders passivity, and that it inhibits the natural development of children's imaginations.

IS WATCHING TV A MINDLESS ACTIVITY?

Critics seem to be on very safe ground indeed when they argue that television is less intellectually challenging than books. After all, it seems indisputable that reading takes more effort, and it is precisely this ease of viewing that leads so many people, such as Postman, to mourn for a generation raised on images rather than words.

Immediately, though, we must put this argument into context. When the goal is to teach reading, giving children books obviously makes more sense than giving them a TV set. But when we are talking about recreation, why do we recoil from the prospect of a free-time activity that is relatively undemanding? Not very far below the fulminations against television rests the idea that even our play should be like work, that pure entertainment is somehow suspect.

For rhetorical purposes, it is much easier to dismiss television by contrasting very good books with very bad TV programs: No wonder this generation is in such trouble! Children spend their time with teenage mutant Ninja turtles instead of with the brothers Karamazov! But the comparison between the two media is not quite so neat when the choice is between an episode of *Nova* and a Danielle Steel novel, or when a Kurosawa film on cable is weighed against the sports section of the paper. Even if we are prepared to defend the idea that words are inherently superior to images—a belief rarely subjected to careful analysis—the functional relevance of this idea depends on *which* words and images we have in mind.

Whether TV is an inherently mindless or effortless medium, whether images "only require that your eyes be open . . . [because] the viewer is little more than a vessel of reception"—as Jerry Mander put it in *Four Arguments for the Elimination of Television*, a 1978 book that still commands something of a cult following—is an empirically testable question. The fact that people may work harder when they read than when they view does not answer that question because so many factors beyond the intrinsic features of the two media must be taken into account.

One factor, again, is *what* we watch: Thomas Hardy, even on TV, may take more concentration than the Hardy Boys. A second factor is *how* we watch, and specifically how much we anticipate having to think hard. Gavriel Salomon, professor of education at the University of Arizona at Tucson, likes to talk about the "perceived demand characteristics" of a task. "The way children treat TV strongly depends on their preconceptions rather than on any *necessary* limitations imposed by the medium on the processing of its material," he and a colleague have written. Someone who expects (or prefers) not to have to reflect while watching television probably won't. In fact, Salomon found, when high-ability children, who are especially likely to think of TV as "easy," are "faced with a somewhat demanding show, [they] learn *less* from it than their less able peers" do. Beliefs, in other words, may count for more than the medium itself.

What Salomon calls our "amount of invested mental effort" not only reflects the generalizations to which we subscribe ("TV is easy; reading is hard") but also varies by where we are and what we've been told. Children will probably concentrate harder on a TV show at school than at home—and harder yet if they think they will be tested on what they are watching. Altering the format of a show also leads children to watch more closely.

In fact, anyone can choose to approach any task, including television viewing, "mindfully," to use the favorite term of Harvard psychologist Ellen Langer. "Regardless of whether the material is good or not, one can watch it either mindlessly or mindfully, and parents can give their children either mind-set with which to watch," she says. Even the most formulaic sitcom can be an intellectual adventure for someone thinking about the social norms reinforced by the show, the characters' psychological motives, the way the writer has braided together and resolved the different subplots, how many cameras have been used to film it, and so forth.

The fact that TV *can* be watched mindlessly is not necessarily an indictment of the medium. "The minimum effort needed for the satisfactory processing of materials" may be low, but this "says nothing about the amount of additional effort one *could* expend" to get more out of it, Salomon points out. Likewise, the fact that TV *is* watched mindlessly by most Americans probably says more about the viewers than the viewed: "Who the hell wants to expend all that mental effort on 'Nova' after an eight-hour day at the office? People are entitled to mental laziness if they want." What they are not entitled to, Salomon implies, is to accuse TV of being mindless just because they have chosen to view it this way.

Some social scientists go on to argue that it is a fallacy to associate critical thought exclusively with the written word. To understand TV "requires mental elaboration, including perceiving information, drawing inferences, and generating hypotheses about what comes next," writes Susan B. Neuman, who teaches education at Temple University. A book tells a child outright that Madeline was sad when her Daddy left; a television show requires the viewer to infer this from her facial expression. A book tells a child that Madeline opened her front door and walked into the living room; a television program shows Madeline outside a house, then cuts to an interior sequence which the viewer, on the basis of having learned cinematic codes, must figure out is the inside of the same house.

This is not to make the reverse argument—that it is inherently more difficult to watch TV than to read. Until the skill of reading comes easily to a child, simply following a story at its most basic level undoubtedly is more demanding in text form. But in light of variations in content and perceived demand, in addition to the potential for mindfully attending to subtleties, the flat (not to say mindless) statement that television is unchallenging simply cannot be defended.

DOES WATCHING TV LOWER
SCHOOL ACHIEVEMENT?

It is an article of faith among many educators and parents that watching TV contributes mightily to a decline in cognitive skills and school achievement. Before reviewing the evidence on this question, however, we might consider the two leading explanations proposed for this effect. First, watching TV is thought to make children impulsive and restless, to reduce their attention span and capacity for deferring gratification. Presumably these effects would interfere with their ability to learn. Second, television is said to displace reading: an hour in front of the tube is an hour not spent in front of a book.

Researchers still aren't sure what to conclude about the first topic; the few available studies have yielded mixed results. Jerome and Dorothy Singer, cofounders of the Family Television Research and Consultation Center at Yale University, found a modest negative correlation between how long children were able to sit quietly on demand and how much TV their parents said they watched. In another of their studies, though, there was no relation between restlessness and viewing. Of course, even such correlations, where they do appear, don't establish that TV is the cause of this restlessness; some unknown third factor may lead children to watch more television *and* be unable to hold still.

At the University of Massachusetts, meanwhile, Daniel Anderson and his students found no connection between how much TV children were said to watch at home and how long they persevered at solving a puzzle, how impulsive they seemed, or how much they jumped around during free play in a laboratory setting. But other experiments hint that such a relationship may exist, at least on some measures and for some children. No one knows whether these effects, even if they are meaningful, are due to television per se, to violent television, to fast-paced television, or only to "excessive" amounts of television. Nor is it clear how long the effects might last. The question of television's contribution to impulsivity and perseverance, then, remains unresolved.

As for whether TV takes time away from other activities, the answer is obviously yes: those hours have to come from somewhere. But the more meaningful question, as Gary Gaddy, a communications researcher at the University of Wisconsin, puts it, is "whether or not the displaced activities were more educationally beneficial than the activity (TV) which displaced them." In fact, we want to know specifically whether children would read appreciably more if they watched less television. Surprisingly, the answer to both questions is, almost certainly not.

Several major studies have looked very carefully at the displacement hypothesis and, while the results are not identical from one to another, the consensus is that reading and watching TV serve very different needs. They are not, in the lingo of researchers, "functionally equivalent" activities; therefore, doing less of one will not necessarily lead to doing more of the other. Moreover, the majority of American children were not serious readers before TV was invented and they would not become serious readers if TV disappeared tomorrow.

Three major research projects have tracked children in areas that received television for the first time. In the first project, Hilde T. Himmelweit and her colleagues in England compared nearly two thousand children in areas with and without TV in the mid–1950s—including a city that started to receive broadcasts midway through the study, allowing the researchers to watch for changes in the children's behavior. They found that book reading fell off when TV arrived, but after three years or so the average number of books read by each child rebounded to original levels or, for some children, even slightly higher. Only comic book reading was permanently displaced; the effect on other books was due mostly to the novelty of television and therefore was temporary.

The second study, by Tannis MacBeth Williams and her colleagues, looked at a small Canadian town (referred to as "Notel") that for geographical reasons got television for the first time in the mid–1970s. Williams examined children's behavior before and after TV and also compared these subjects to those who lived in towns that received one channel ("Unitel") and four channels ("Multitel"). Overall, book reading and TV viewing were not statistically related. Library use was about the same in all three towns, and Multitel children actually did more reading than Unitel children. Multitel adults, however, reported reading fewer books than their counterparts in the other towns.

The third study was conducted in South Africa, which had no TV until 1976. More than two thousand children were followed from 1974 until 1980. Movie attendance and radio use were displaced by TV; time spent on homework declined at first but then returned to what it had been before television arrived—a confirmation of the novelty effect. (Of course, children sometimes do homework and watch TV at the same time. This raises questions about the very premise of the displacement model, which is that these activities are mutually exclusive.) Pleasure reading dropped by about three minutes a day on average from pre-TV levels.

So what *does* TV displace? Some investigators, including Williams, mention social activities, but Neuman's reading of the research is that "given a choice between viewing and playing with others, the majority of children still continued to prefer social interaction." Watching television more likely takes the place of entertainment activities like going to the movies (a process accelerated by the proliferation of VCRs) and time spent sitting around not doing much of anything.

"We want to hear that if it wasn't for TV, children would be going off to the library," says Neuman. But the most important influence on time spent with books is not time spent with TV but the time *parents* spend with books. "Targeting television as the source of children's lack of interest in leisure reading is simply too easy an answer to a much more complex issue."

Whether TV affects children's perseverance and personal reading habits are interesting questions in their own right, but for many people they are important principally with respect to the bottom-line issue—children's thinking and reading *skills*. The first problem with the argument that test scores are dropping because kids watch too much TV is that test scores are not dropping. According to the National Assessment of Educational Progress, the most widely cited data on student performance, reading scores for all three groups tested (ages 9, 13, and 17) were slightly higher in 1992 than they were in 1971. Needless to say, this cannot be explained by a decline in TV viewing.

These aggregate scores can tell us only so much, however, so it is worth looking at other measures. In 1986, when Gaddy of the University of Wisconsin sat down to analyze the standardized test scores of thousands of high schoolers, he expected to find that television viewing led to lower achievement. Once he controlled for other factors, though, he couldn't find any relationship. In fact, "the effects of achievement on the selection of television . . . are generally . . . larger than the effects from TV to achievement," he reported. It's not that staying away from television improves school performance, in other words, so much as that students who score high for other reasons choose to watch less TV.

A group of researchers at the Harvard School of Public Health published an extension of Gaddy's research in late 1990, looking at data from the 1960s in which the amount of television watched by a large, nationally representative sample of children (ages six to eleven) was compared to their standardized test scores. Then their TV habits were matched to their scores four years later. When other factors were taken into account, there was, once again, "no significant causal relationship."

If you look hard enough, you can find studies that show the expected negative effect on reading—effects on achievement in other subject areas having rarely been measured, for some reason—as well as a few that turn up a *positive* association between viewing and school performance. But most of the good research finds little or nothing.

Thus, a 1980 study of New Jersey middle-school students: "The primary finding is that IQ accounts for most observed relationships between viewing and achievement." A three-year study of California children: "The more sophisticated our analysis, the less conclusive the evidence" that TV lowers reading skills. An analysis of the state and national reading scores of more than two million students (by Neuman): at first glance, a curious effect in which children who said they watched a lot of television didn't do as well as those who watched less, but those who watched a little did better than those who watched none at all. And the final judgment: "Does television viewing affect reading achievement? Not meaningfully."

It may be that a genuine relationship does exist but only for some groups of children or only for viewing certain kinds of programs; most studies would have missed these correlations if they existed. But the better research to date seriously challenges the widely held belief that TV viewing by itself has a consistent impact on academic achievement.

IS TV-WATCHING ADDICTIVE?

Yale's Jerome Singer rose to deliver a lecture about the mass media at an academic conference. A mild man, then sixty-seven, Singer could never be accused of possessing mass media charisma. Yet he immediately endeared himself to his audience by confessing that he sometimes "flicks on the TV" rather than picking up a book when he gets home. "So . . . my name is Jerry Singer and I am a television addict," he announced, causing the room to erupt in laughter.

Singer went on to assert more soberly that "the television medium by its very nature, the ease of watching, is mildly addictive"—a belief held by so many people today that it nearly qualifies as folk wisdom. But this conviction may tell us less about television than about our culture's penchant for describing a range of popular activities—drinking liquor, eating chocolate, shopping, having sex, falling in love—as addictions. Our addiction to finding addictions, so to speak, may well invite suspicion that the word has been stretched beyond the point of usefulness. What does it really mean to say that someone who watches too many sitcoms is an addict? On the other hand, if so many activities really are addictive, we might ask whether television has any distinctive qualities that hook viewers or whether watching is simply one more pleasurable pursuit that can be overdone.

In either case, psychologists, social critics, and parents who claim that children are addicted to television almost never cite any supporting data—probably because such data do not exist. Only two researchers have investigated the subject directly, both focusing on adults, and neither offering much reason to accept such claims. For her doctoral dissertation, Robin Smith mailed questionnaires to nearly 1,000 residents of Springfield, Massachusetts. Of the 491 who returned them, two thirds thought that television is addictive—but apparently just for other people. Only 11 individuals called themselves addicts, and they, like the other respondents, said they almost never experienced Smith's specific descriptions of addiction, such as "When I'm watching TV, I feel like I can't stop."

Self-report data are of limited usefulness, of course, especially when those who dutifully filled out the form may not represent the population at large. The same problems compromise the findings of Robert McIlwraith, a psychologist at the University of Manitoba, who reported that 17 of 136 undergraduates described themselves as television addicts. Everything McIlwraith has seen on the subject, though, has made him cautious about using the word *addiction* to describe TV viewing. "People think they're addicted because they use the television as a relaxant," he says. But the concept "isn't justified in a syndrome sort of way." There's no evidence, for instance, that people develop a tolerance to viewing, that they "watch more and more and need a stronger fix to get a buzz."

As for going through withdrawal, another *sine qua non* of addiction, some parents report that their children become grumpy after the TV has been shut off, but no researcher has shown how widespread this really is. To whatever extent the phenomenon does occur, it may be simply a child's reaction to being told he must stop doing something he enjoys—or alternatively, it might be due to prolonged physical inactivity rather than to some ominous feature of TV itself. Some

Swedish researchers checked in with more than two hundred teenagers when a strike in 1980 shut down nearly all television broadcasts for two weeks. "Very few respondents expressed strongly felt deprivation in a situation of almost total television loss," they reported.

The fact that a child enjoys watching TV, and continues to do what he enjoys, does not justify invoking the word *addiction* (even though it may justify a parent's shutting off the set at some point). If we feel vaguely guilty about watching too much television or find it difficult to pull ourselves away, the first question to ask is whether this doesn't describe our behavior at other activities, too, such as reading mystery novels. The next question is whether this is truly comparable to the way heroin users regard their next fix.

Critics may fall back, at this point, to claiming that viewing is "habit-forming" even if not technically addictive. But this charge is no easier to support on closer inspection. After all, there is no reason to think that it is the act of watching TV last week that *caused* one to watch again this week. Rather, one watched both times because it was fun to do so. There is no evidence to support the charge that television has some uniquely ominous power over us; if tuning in is "habit-forming," it is only in the very weak sense that repeatedly eating a favorite food or doing anything else we enjoy qualifies for that label. The argument collapses into the question of whether watching TV is inherently less healthy than the other things we do, which is dealt with elsewhere in this article.

When Jerry Singer told his colleagues that TV was addictive, the only substantiation he offered was a reference to the writings of Robert Kubey, a psychologist at Rutgers University, who at the time was making such claims himself in the popular press. Kubey did his graduate work at the University of Chicago with Mihaly Csikszentmihalyi, who pioneered a clever experimental method in which subjects are given beepers and asked to fill out a form describing what they are doing and how they feel about doing it each time the beeper goes off.

In the mid–1970s, Kubey beeped 107 adults, all of whom were employed and most of whom were women, paying special attention to their self-reports while watching TV. In his 1990 book written with Csikszentmihalyi, *Television and the Quality of Life*, Kubey declared that "television viewing is unquestionably habit forming. It may even be addictive. . . ." Unfortunately, a close reading of his study turns up no evidence to support this belief and may even provide the basis for a partial refutation. Subjects were beeped about three thousand times when they weren't at home, for example, but in only five instances did someone report thinking about TV—not what one would expect of addicts.

Asked in an interview to justify his claims about dependence and addiction, Kubey pauses for a moment. "No," he says, "I don't think there is hard empirical data to support this." Instead, he appeals to anecdotes, common sense, and the finding that heavy viewers reported being slightly less happy than others when doing nothing (although they did not feel any worse than light viewers while talking or working).

While this is not much on which to build a case that TV is addictive, it does raise the possibility that television makes the average viewer depressed. But Kubey himself supplies the rejoinder to this: "Although there is some evidence that people may feel worse an hour or so after viewing than after other leisure activities, there is stronger evidence that negative affect precedes rather than follows heavy viewing. It is more appropriate to conclude, therefore, that television viewing is more a response to negative affect than a cause of it—at least in the short term."

DOES TV MAKE CHILDREN PASSIVE?

The phrase "glued to the TV set" has been used to refer not only to how long people watch but to *how* they watch. Critics like Winn have alleged that television makes children passive, putting them in something like a hypnotic trance (even though it is also supposed to make them hyperactive). The implication is that kids' brains shut off, that they are transfixed by, rather than truly attentive to, what they watch.

Now obviously this description does not apply to adults. Most of us wander in and out of the room while the TV is on and engage in various other activities even while sitting in front of the tube. (Nearly two thirds of the time that Kubey's subjects described themselves as watching TV, they were also doing something else.) This is hardly consistent with the idea that people are hopelessly mesmerized by the flickering images.

In fact, a growing body of evidence has also cast doubt on the validity of this idea where children are concerned. A child seated in front of the tube—or in front of a book, for that matter—clearly is not physically active at the moment. But no one has ever been able to show that TV makes children passive over the long haul. The two earliest and most famous studies of television and children examined this claim and were unable to support it. Himmelweit's English study found "no evidence whatever of increased passivity. . . . Viewers appeared to have as much initiative, imagination, and pleasure in active play as controls."

Schramm's North American study, meanwhile, reported that a normal, happy child "is not in danger of being made abnormally passive by television." So, too, noted Patricia Palmer, who observed and interviewed eight- to twelve-year-olds in a lesser-known Australian study in the early 1980s: "The still-popular view of passive children suffering from television's 'effects' lags well behind current research findings . . . [including those] described in this study."

Some critics retort that even if heavy viewers are no less physically active than their peers, TV has the effect of making them *mentally* passive—if not hypnotized while they watch. But research over the last two decades has established that children, like adults, often do other things while watching TV—half the time they are viewing, by one estimate—and that they typically look at and away from the set every few seconds. (Both of these findings also suggest another qualification to the usual claims about how many hours children watch television: a child is not actually attending to the TV every minute it is turned on.)

Perhaps most significant, it has been established that even toddlers think about what they are watching. "The popular notion of the 'zombie viewer,' sitting catatonic before the set, is not confirmed in real observations of children spending time with television," Susan Neuman writes in her book *Literacy in the Television Age*.

A good many of those real observations have been made by Daniel Anderson, a research psychologist at the University of Massachusetts at Amherst. Anderson is the sort of man who enjoys playing with data more than speaking in public and whose idea of a harsh epithet is "Oh, fooey!" In the early part of his career, never imagining that he might someday make his mark as an investigator of TV viewing, Anderson was grinding away on the sort of obscure behavioral research that fills the journals and brings its creators tenured obscurity. Then, one day, an undergraduate asked him a question he couldn't answer.

It was the fall of 1972, and he had just finished lecturing to an auditorium full of undergraduates. As most of them noisily collected their notebooks and shuffled out, a handful headed up to the podium to pepper him with more questions. The first student to reach Anderson on that particular morning was a young man he remembers as being intense, short, and athletic. During the lecture, Anderson had casually remarked that toddlers are much more distractible than older children. If that was so, this student demanded, how come a four-year-old can watch TV for hours?

"I gave a really glib answer," Anderson recalls. "'It's obvious. The TV's a distractor. It just *looks* like the kid is paying attention.'" Later, feeling both guilty and curious, he sent a graduate student to look up the existing research on how children attend to television. Nothing was there to be found. "So we sat around and watched kids watching TV. The more we watched, the more it seemed my glib answer was not correct."

Young children *do* pay attention to what they watch and control their own behavior while doing so, Anderson and his colleagues eventually found. At some point, any given child may seem transfixed by the TV, and some children will watch this way more than others will, but overall, children's attention is highly selective. "If they don't understand," Anderson says, "they don't watch. And even when they do get into it and you see"—he mimes an unblinking stare with jaw hanging open—"that sort of thing, the question is what does it mean. One interpretation is that the child's mind is a blank. Another interpretation is that the child is intensely concentrating. And now we have data to suggest the latter [is true]. Kids are cognitively engaged" with what is happening on the screen, he concludes, rather than passive victims of a "mesmerizing medium that exerts some kind of unique control."

In 1982, a state-of-the-science review of data on cognitive processing and television published by the National Institute of Mental Health vindicated this conclusion: "Viewing is more active and discriminating among even young children than is generally recognized." But that corroboration was nearly a decade in arriving. Anderson's first experiment on the topic, an analysis of how one- to four-year-olds watched a brand-new program called *Sesame Street,* was difficult to get published and was not the best strategy for securing tenure in the psychology department, his colleagues warned.

Those early studies were, in Anderson's words, "detailed, descriptive research" lacking any theoretical grounding or social agenda. He was one of the very first experimenters to videotape children watching TV so he could analyze their every glance. To make those sessions as realistic as possible, he set up a laboratory to resemble a comfortable living room, with toys and snacks for the children and coffee for their moms. Later, he convinced families in western Massachusetts to allow two video cameras in their homes—one to monitor the TV and the other to watch them (both rigged to work only when the television was turned on) so that people's attention to the set could be precisely correlated to what was being broadcast.

Pat Collins, a doctoral student of Anderson's, was in the lab one afternoon, painstakingly turning some of these videotapes into data. VCRs patched into humming computers were squeezed next to red LED number displays, time-code generators, shelves of tapes, and coils of cords on pegboards. Collins was watching a monitor on which a five-year-old girl, comic book on lap, sat in front of the TV. A small box in the lower right corner of the screen contained the image on the girl's set.

"OK, let's go back to where she entered the room," Collins mumbled as she hit first the rewind button and then play. "She goes back and forth between talking with her mother and sister and monitoring the set. . . . She really doesn't seem very interested in the commercial. . . . Now Batman has started. . . . That's where they do that 'dee dee dee dee.'" Collins imitated the theme song and looked up, suddenly self-conscious. "Hey, I grew up on this stuff," she laughed.

Every time her young subject looked at the TV, Collins stabbed a blue button marked "Attention" and held it down until the girl looked away. Earlier, she and the others in Anderson's lab had meticulously noted when each family member entered and left the room, then watched all the tapes again and recorded (by using a specially designed computer program) what the children were watching and what was happening on screen—whether it was live action or animation, whether there was violence, which character was on the screen, whether that character was male or female, and what else the viewer was doing. In all, she and the others in Anderson's lab would analyze 4,672 hours of videotape for this study.

"She's clearly splitting her time between the magazine in her lap and the television," Collins said, her eyes still fixed on the screen. "It's not clear how much her sister's pattern of attention influences *her* pattern." She punches a white button on the master panel. Anderson, standing behind her, watched the monitor as children zoomed in and out of the living room. He pointed to their mother, lying motionless on the couch. "*That's* your passive viewer," he said.

Back in his office, where a poster of Big Bird watched over the likes of *Imprinting and Cortical Plasticity* on his bookshelf, Anderson ticked off the information he hoped this research would reveal, such as the age at which kids start to leave the room during commercials and what time of day they watch TV most intensely. Mostly, though, "there doesn't exist a good description of TV viewing as a behavior. That's what we're trying to do here."

DOES TV IMPOVERISH CHILDREN'S IMAGINATIONS?

Whereas Dan Anderson's office bulletin board features Big Bird, Jerry Singer's is decorated with an autographed photo of Mister Rogers. In some respects, the two men are a study in contrasts, but not so much because Singer attacks television and Anderson defends it. For one thing, Singer acknowledges, when pressed, that the data don't support a simplistic emphasis on "the evils of television [to the point that] every family should throw it out." Anderson, meanwhile, protests, "In no sense am I trying to promote television. There's no way I'd defend much of the content of current programming."

Rather, what distinguishes the two are their styles of research and the way they use data—and herein lies a tale with implications beyond the study of television. Anderson is a man who hesitates to say that Thursday follows Wednesday until controlled studies have demonstrated this. But Jerry and Dorothy Singer give the impression that their minds were made up about the consequences of watching television long before they looked at the results of their studies. Unexpected evidence that television may have a positive effect (for example, heavy viewers' greater enthusiasm in school or more pronounced artistic orientations) are mentioned very quickly in their articles and books and then dismissed.

By contrast, any finding that supports an anti-TV view is enthusiastically repeated in the discussion section of their papers and then again in their subsequent publications. Take the question of whether television has an adverse impact on children's imagination—a claim for which the Singers' work is cited more often than anyone else's. In a 1984 study, they described several tests they had performed on seven- and eight-year-olds to determine whether the children's imaginativeness was related to TV viewing. Two of these tests showed a very weak negative relationship between viewing and imagination—so weak as to be practically meaningless until facts about the children's family life were entered into the equation. Another test showed that children who watched a lot of TV were *more* imaginative than their peers. Yet the Singers concluded their article by emphasizing the negative result and, in a later paper, declared unequivocally that "heavy television viewing preempts active play practice and the healthy use of the imagination." (Queried in person, however, Jerry Singer concedes that, "in terms of imagination, we don't have that dramatic a result.")

The Singers' contention that TV attenuates a child's fantasy life is exactly the opposite of Marshall McLuhan's warning that TV leads people to fantasize too much. But attempts to show *any* causal relation between TV and the imagination generally have not gotten very far. The Himmelweit study found that teachers' ratings of their students' imaginativeness were about the same for viewers and nonviewers. McIlwraith's research with first graders and adults found that those who watched a lot of television were no less likely to have positive, imaginative fantasies than those who watched less. "What we find again and again," he says, "is that there isn't an awful lot about media use that's related to imagination."

In general, a far more promising way to predict the richness of children's imagination, as several researchers have pointed out, is to look not at how much TV they watch but at how their parents live and what they value. But it is far more satisfying for critics—and more convenient for some parents, perhaps—to claim that if children today seem less imaginative than we were, well, television is to blame. This extends the practice of investing the medium with awesome, magical powers, including the capacity to hold children captive and turn them into addicts. Such claims have the effect, not so incidentally, of deflecting attention from the messier but far more critical issue of how families interact.

Some writers, including Neuman and Palmer, argue that, if anything, TV has the capacity to *stimulate* the imagination by supplying material that children later incorporate into their active play—exactly as books do. (We may wince at the content of this material, but that is very different from finding that the act of watching TV impoverishes the imagination.) In the view of George Gerbner, who for twenty-five years was the dean of the University of Pennsylvania's Annenberg School of Communications, "imagination comes from cultural participation." Television, while scorned by "upper-middle-class

intellectuals" who have other means for such participation at their dis-
posal, is "an enrichment to vast numbers of people, providing visions
from the whole world."

Given the amount of research that has been conducted by now on
how children are affected by watching TV, it is decidedly meaningful to keep encountering findings that imaginations are not attenuated, pleasure reading is not displaced, and minds are not emptied.
While one can never prove once and for all that viewing (or anything
else) has no effect, the data collectively should lay to rest many of the
fulminations about television that continue to be repeated.

On the other hand, none of these findings can be interpreted as offering a green light for the parental policy of using TV as a permanent
baby-sitter or otherwise allowing children unrestricted access. Many
researchers offer the commonsense suggestion that parents should
know what their children are watching, feel free to set limits on both
how much and what is viewed, and ideally, be present to explain, analyze, and filter the content, turning any program into an opportunity
to discuss ideas and values.

By the same token, it is worth repeating that the data about TV's
effects (or lack of effects) do not amount to an endorsement of the
mostly vapid programming that dominates American network television. (What about PBS? someone in the audience asked researcher
Michael Morgan after a talk he gave recently. The total audience for
public television, he replied, is less than the margin of error in national
viewing surveys.) News on television is "more television than news,"
says George Gerbner, Morgan's former mentor. "Its primary function
is to inherit the audience and pass it on" to the entertainment programs that follow. And aside from *Mister Rogers* and *Sesame Street,*
children's television in this country is by any measure a disgrace—
mostly animated, often violent, typically male-oriented, assembly-line-
quality shows that look like half-hour toy commercials.

There may be ultrachic critics who take self-conscious satisfaction
in defending the likes of *Doogie Howser* or *Wheel of Fortune,* but
they're hard to find and even harder to take seriously. Dan Anderson
is sometimes cast in the role of pro-TV professor and asked to debate
the medium's more voluble critics, but he will have none of it. "My
guess is that most of what's on commercial television for children is
no worse than a waste of time," but even if the arguments against
watching are not terribly compelling, that doesn't mean "that a parent

should have a child watch television." Current programming doesn't offer anything that a youngster "can't acquire in other ways."

But Anderson and other careful researchers have produced a body of data that force any responsible observer to reconsider all those middle-class truisms about the evil intrinsic to watching TV. Their work makes it more difficult for us to blame that activity for every problem involving children, and by extension, presses us to look just a little harder for real solutions.

PART FOUR

Business as Usual

CHAPTER THIRTEEN

The Five-Hundred–Pound Gorilla

The best reason to give a child a good school . . . is so that child will have a happy childhood, and not so that it will help IBM in competing with Sony. . . . There is something ethically embarrassing about resting a national agenda on the basis of sheer greed.

—Jonathan Kozol

Imagine that the nation's governors have been invited to a summit to discuss the future of American business: the proper role of technology in the workplace, what can be done to improve the way companies are managed—that sort of thing. Because politicians may have limited familiarity with such matters, however, each governor has been invited to bring along one adviser: a school teacher.

Originally published as the introduction to *Education, Inc.* in 1997.

The idea would strike most of us as absurd. In fact, it seems exactly as absurd as a summit on education in which each governor was accompanied by a corporate executive. The only difference between these two absurd scenarios is that the latter actually happened. In March 1996, a conservative Republican governor (Tommy Thompson of Wisconsin) joined IBM in hosting the National Education Summit at that company's suburban New York headquarters. There, various corporate chieftains joined most of the nation's governors in issuing proclamations about the need for "higher standards" and, to no one's surprise, the importance of technology in schools.

The first and most obvious problem with such a conference is that businesspeople are unlikely to be informed about the best theory, research, and practice on how children learn. But there is another reason to be concerned about the idea of letting corporate executives shape our country's educational agenda: it isn't just a lack of knowledge but a fundamental difference in objectives. Ultimately, the *goals* of business are not the same as those of educators. This simple truth is one that educators forget at their peril—or more precisely, at the peril of their students.

Corporations in our economic system exist to provide a financial return to the people who own them: they are in business to make a profit. As individuals, those who work in (or even run) these companies might have other goals, too, when they turn their attention to public policy or education or anything else. But business *qua* business is concerned principally about its own bottom line. Thus, when business thinks about schools, its agenda is driven by what will maximize its profitability, not necessarily by what is in the best interest of students. Any overlap between those two goals would be purely accidental—and in practice, as I will try to show, turns out to be minimal. What maximizes corporate profits often does not benefit children, and vice versa.

If corporations did indeed want to remake American education so as to promote their own interests, how would they set about doing that? Logically, their goal would be for schools to produce adequately skilled workers who will show up on time and obediently do their part to help these corporations triumph over their counterparts in other countries. Qualities such as a love of learning for its own sake, a penchant for asking challenging questions, or a commitment to democratic participation in decision making would be seen as nice but irrelevant—or perhaps even as impediments to the efficient realization of corporate goals.

Corporations might also want to see schools adopt managerial methods and metaphors, so that students would become accustomed to measuring everything in sight, or to following directions, or to seeing themselves as workers rather than as learners. These corporations might present high schools with a list of the qualities they would find it convenient for graduating students to possess, and ask that the curriculum be adjusted accordingly.[1] More broadly, businesses might push for privatizing the public schools or otherwise encourage the adoption of a profit-making sensibility when it comes to education. They might regard children not only as future workers but also as potential customers, attempting to insert corporate propaganda into the curriculum and advertising into the classroom.

Because each of these items follows naturally from the overriding purpose of business, it is not particularly shocking or scandalous that corporations would want all these things to happen. What is striking is that they are able to get so much of what they want. The disproportionate role that business has in fact been granted in determining the country's educational priorities is revealed by the guest list for the National Education Summit, among other recent developments. Many of our elected officials have in effect handed over the keys to our schools to corporate interests: "We must tell the business community that, if it wants better employees and higher profits, it must be involved in what the schools teach and how they teach it," announced James B. Hunt Jr., the Democratic governor of North Carolina.[2]

It doesn't take a degree in political science to figure out why politicians (and sometimes even educators) so often capitulate to business. For that matter, it isn't much of a mystery why a five-hundred–pound gorilla is invited to sleep anywhere it wishes. But that doesn't make the practice any less dangerous.

A s must be obvious by now, *Education, Inc.* (for which this chapter serves as an introduction) makes no pretense of offering a "balanced" treatment of the subject, with an equal number of pro- and antibusiness essays. Rather, as a collection of complementary critiques, it is itself meant to provide a small measure of balance, a tiny counterweight, to the overwhelming and underchallenged corporate point of view that surrounds us. In part because of its vast resources, the business community has no trouble disseminating its opinions on education. Corporate leaders give speeches around the country. Business magazines publish lengthy articles on the subject. And every few months another report on American schooling is released by the Business Coalition for Education Reform, the Business Roundtable, the Committee for Economic Development, or some other cluster of corporations.

These documents normally receive wide and largely uncritical press attention despite the fact that they all recycle the same buzzwords. Rather like a party game where players create sentences by randomly selecting an adjective from one list, then a noun from another, these dispatches from the business world seem to consist mostly of different combinations of terms like *world-class, measurable, accountability, standards,* and *competitiveness.* Also, almost all of them begin by solemnly announcing the arrival of the twenty-first century.

One's eyes may glaze over at the clichéd vocabulary, but the vision of education it bespeaks is worth considering carefully. Take the word *competitive,* which is always treated in these reports as something desirable. When business groups talk about education, they commonly characterize students as competitors—as people who do, or will, or should spend their lives trying to beat other people at something. Other nations are likewise depicted as rivals rather than as potential collaborators, and the Olympics is a favorite metaphor not only for schooling but for life itself. Over and over we are told that the principal objective for students and schools and the United States is to be Number One. Thus, to make our schools "world-class" means not that we should cooperate with other countries and learn but that we should compete against them and win.

Or consider the word *standards.* If businesspeople mean by this word that schools ought to be given what they need to help students learn more effectively, then no one can object. But read their reports and listen to their speeches carefully and it soon becomes clear that they have something more—or less—in mind. The references to "standards" suggest that (a) the main point of schooling is to raise students' performance with respect to (b) a very specific set of expectations for what is to be taught in (c) a few basic subjects, and that is best done by (d) efficiently transmitting a body of facts or skills to these students. The procedures for doing so should be (e) prescribed for, and imposed on, teachers, with (f) frequent measurement of results in the form of (g) standardized tests, whose scores will be the basis for (h) rewarding or punishing students, teachers, or administrators as a way of making sure that performance improves.

As with the assumptions about competition, each of these components is either presented as hardheaded common sense or else regarded as so obvious that it requires no discussion at all. In fact, though, every one of these precepts is debatable, and together they describe an educational philosophy based on dubious assumptions about human motivation, learning, and public policy. Whole books can be—and indeed have been—written on each of these eight propositions; here, a few pages about the lot will have to suffice.

PERFORMANCE

Even the least controversial of these ideas, that we ought to focus our efforts on raising students' performance, proves surprisingly complicated upon closer inspection. Research by Carol Dweck, Carole Ames, John Nicholls, and other educational psychologists has shown that there is a clear difference between students who are led to concentrate on their performance (that is, on how well they are doing) and students who are led to concentrate on the material being learned (that is, on *what* they are doing). These two orientations often pull in opposite directions so that an overemphasis on performance can undermine interest in the learning itself. While it does make sense at certain points in the learning process to help students think about how they can be more successful, this has to be done carefully and sparingly. Apart from reducing interest, too much emphasis on performance has been associated with three other disturbing results: students may come to attribute their success or failure to innate ability (as opposed to effort), they may become debilitated by failure (even if they are normally high achievers), and they may avoid challenge whenever possible (since the point is not to explore ideas or stretch themselves but to maximize their success).

Educators—and those who support them—therefore ought to make their top priority the creation of a school environment that preserves and enriches students' *desire* to learn. The academic skills we care about are likely to be acquired by a student who remains motivated to figure things out; conversely, a student who has come to regard learning as a chore is not likely to do well over the long haul. Performance, in other words, is properly regarded as a by-product of motivation. When we focus on performance to the exclusion of motivation—when we don't attend to how interested students are in what they are doing—we may wind up with students who don't particularly *want* to improve, and are thus less likely to become lifelong, self-directed learners.

The idea that short-term educational results may be less important than long-term motivation has never, to the best of my knowledge, been endorsed or even discussed by any business group. In fact, if we were looking for a way to make students *less* interested in learning, we could hardly do better than to adopt the other components of the corporate agenda for our schools. A good part of that agenda consists of calling for educators to make students work harder: We need to demand more from our children! Give them more homework! Keep them in school longer! Make their textbooks more challenging! Require them to jump through more hoops to get a good grade!

My argument is not that "easier" is actually better than "harder" but rather that such a discussion ignores most of what matters about schooling. To judge what goes on in a classroom on the basis of how difficult the tasks are is rather like judging an opera on the basis of how many notes it contains that are hard for the singers to hit. People who miss the many multifaceted criteria (other than level of challenge) by which the quality of schooling might be judged tend to be those who rely on the metaphor of "work" to talk about the process of learning (see Chapter 15, "Students Don't 'Work'—They Learn"). Particularly if we are sensitive to the importance of how students think and feel about what they are doing, it turns out that merely ratcheting up the standards may well be counterproductive over the long run.[3]

NARROW STANDARDS

The demand for higher performance is frequently accompanied by an insistence that the standards for that performance must be very specific. Yet, when asked for advice on the subject, former U.S. commissioner of education Harold Howe II summarized a lifetime's work with schools in four words: national (and, presumably, state) standards, he emphasized, should be "*as vague as possible*." Howe's point was that the more specific the requirement for what students must know or be able to do, the less responsive educators can be to what distinguishes one student—and one circumstance—from another. It makes matters worse when we demand that all students at a given grade level must be able to perform a certain task. This guarantees that some children will be branded as failures because they do not learn at the same pace as their peers.

Very specific, results-oriented standards do not suggest a commitment to excellence. They suggest a commitment to an outmoded, top-down approach to controlling production that is reminiscent of Frederick Taylor's "scientific management" model for factories. (Ironically, Taylor's assembly-line paradigm has been supplanted in many corporations by the work of W. Edwards Deming and others in the Quality movement, yet it continues to drive the corporate view of educational standards.) Elliot Eisner of Stanford University has seen the connection between Tayloresque thinking and rigid performance standards for students. He went on to observe:

> The language of standards is by and large a limiting rather than a liberating language. . . . It distracts us from paying attention to the importance of building a culture of schooling that is genuinely intellectual in character, that values questions and ideas at least as much as getting right answers. . . . The challenge in teaching is to provide the conditions that will foster the growth of those personal characteristics that are socially important and, at the same time, personally satisfying to the student. The aim of education is not to train an army that marches to the same drummer, at the same pace, toward the same destination. Such an aim may be appropriate for totalitarian societies, but it is incompatible with democratic ideals.

Thoughtful opponents of specific standards would rather guide than dictate; they are motivated by respect for teachers as professional educators and respect for differences among learners. Unhappily, the most visible challenge to the business-led emphasis on detailed academic standards has come from fundamentalist Christians and ultraconservatives fearful of the role of the federal government in setting those standards. This has led to a skewed debate about education in which the nature of teaching and learning is often overlooked entirely.[4]

BASIC SUBJECTS

Just as the standards for a given subject may be too narrow or specific, so the number of subjects to which students are exposed may be too few. The fewer subjects we teach, the fewer capabilities we value, and the more students who are likely to feel excluded and uninterested. Consider a classroom in which only certain talents (such as those needed for verbal-analytical tasks) count for anything. The most likely feature of such a classroom is an informal but entrenched status hierarchy, where students are sorted from excellent to poor. By contrast, the use of tasks that call for many different kinds of skills helps more students to feel competent—and ultimately to become competent.

This doesn't mean that reading and math don't matter: the evidence suggests that when these subjects are taught effectively (more about that later), other subjects can be included in the curriculum without reducing competence in the basics. The answer, in other words, is to teach more effectively rather than to teach fewer things. But if we do choose to focus relatively more energy on the three R's, that decision ought to be made on the basis of the kind of people we want children to be—not on the basis of which skills corporations demand of their employees.

It might also be noted that the back-to-basics doctrine tends to exclude—and sometimes to dismiss explicitly—the importance of social skills, moral development, and affective learning. Not only can we make a case that schools should be used to help students become good people, but we can also point to empirical evidence that intellectual development is more likely to take place when schools are transformed into caring communities. That transformation requires time, resources, and above all, an inclusive view of learning. The bottom line is that a relentless focus on, say, multiplication not only deprives students of the chance to become socially skilled or artistically enriched—it also may perpetuate an environment that isn't even optimal for learning multiplication.[5]

TRANSMISSION

Listing a bunch of facts and skills that every *n*th grader must know has been described quite aptly as a "curriculum of superficiality." But the problem with this model goes beyond the particular content that appears on the list—or even the specificity of the content. The real trouble is with the tacit theory of learning on which such an approach is based. That theory, which holds that we can transmit knowledge or skills *to* students, is out of step with the best thinking in the field. Children are not empty vessels to be filled with information; they are active meaning makers, testing out theories and trying to make sense of themselves and the world around them. Learning comes from discovering surprising things—perhaps from grappling with a peer's different perspective—and feeling the need to reformulate one's own approach. It entails playing with words and numbers and ideas, coming to understand these things from the inside out and making them one's own. Skills are acquired in the course of arriving at that deep and personal understanding, and in the context of seeking answers to one's own questions.

When children are instead required to accept or memorize ready-made truths, they do not really "learn" in any meaningful sense of the word. This is what we witness when students have to do problem sets in math, multiplying rows of naked numbers; or make their way through worksheets until they can identify vowels or verbs; or slog through textbook lessons about scientific laws or historical events; or spend most of the day listening to somebody lecture. This "transmission of right answers" approach characterized the schooling to which most of us were subjected, and despite exciting demonstrations that things could be better, it also characterizes the schooling that businesspeople, among other constituencies, seem determined to foist on another generation.

In their calls for specific standards, more testing, basic skills, and so on, corporate-style educational "reform" tacitly accepts—and sometimes explicitly endorses—the transmission model.[6] The irony here is palpable: corporate reports vibrate with alarm over how much students today don't know when they get out of school—yet it is the transmission model that contributes mightily to this problem. The educational crisis we are allegedly facing has occurred under a "drill-and-skill," test-driven system in which students are treated as passive receptacles rather than as active learners. Yet the business prescription is: more of the same.[7]

CONTROL

The performance standards set out for schools are frequently offered not as guidelines (along with the help necessary to meet them) but as requirements to be imposed on educators. The operative word in such discussions is *accountability,* which almost always turns out to mean tighter control over what happens in classrooms by people who are not in classrooms. The effect on learning is comparable to the effect a noose has on breathing.

When teachers are required to prove that their students can meet very specific standards, or to work their way through a prescribed curriculum, or to spend their time preparing students for standardized tests, the people imposing these requirements are doing things *to* teachers rather than working *with* them. They are relying on power to try to compel certain results. This is a tendency that can be witnessed in many arenas: people higher up in a hierarchy often attempt to maximize efficiency by tightly directing the actions of those down below. Unfortunately, when people's basic need for autonomy is violated, the costs are usually high—in psychological terms, and ultimately with respect to effectiveness.

This is as true in classrooms as it is in countries. When teachers are held strictly "accountable" for their students' performance on tests— when they feel pressured to produce results—they in turn tend to pressure their students and remove opportunities for the students to direct their own learning. Research has shown that these students are less likely to learn successfully than are their counterparts in classrooms where the teachers had simply been invited to "facilitate the children's learning." The more we pressure teachers to *make* their students perform, in other words, the less well the students actually perform.

Much the same is true of our posture toward the students themselves. Rather than trying to figure out how we can *support* students' desire to explore what is unfamiliar, to develop a competence at (and a passion for) learning, the prescription offered by the business world has more to do with *demand:* students are seen as "workers" who have an obligation to do a better job. One corporate executive, for example, declared that children must be "made to understand the importance of learning." If, to paraphrase a famous critical report, an unfriendly foreign power had attempted to impose on America a mediocre educational system, it could have devised no better plan than to establish mechanisms for tightly controlling what students and teachers do.[8]

QUANTIFICATION

We have to go back several centuries to find the origin of what one writer has called "the prosaic mentality": a preoccupation with that which can be seen and measured. Any aspect of learning or life that resists being reduced to numbers is regarded as vaguely suspicious. By contrast, anything that appears in numerical form seems reassuringly scientific: if the numbers are getting larger over time, we must be making progress. Concepts like intrinsic motivation and intellectual exploration are hard for the prosaic mind to grasp, whereas test scores, like sales figures, can be calculated and charted and used to define success and failure.

In a broad sense, it is easier to measure efficiency than effectiveness, easier to assign a number to how well we are doing something than to whether what we are doing makes sense. But the heirs of Descartes and Bacon, Skinner and Taylor, rarely make such distinctions. More to the point, they fail to see how the process of coming to understand things is not always linear or quantifiable. Contrary to virtually every business discussion of education, meaningful learning does not proceed along a single dimension such that we can nail down the extent of improvement. In fact, what matters most about learning may well be impossible to measure—and attempts to do so anyway may distort that which is quantified.

If, moreover, we are interested in students' *motivation* to learn, it becomes clear that more motivation—even assuming we could reduce this to numbers—is not always better than less motivation for the simple reason that the amount is less important than the kind. (A lot of extrinsic motivation is not particularly desirable.) To talk about what happens in schools as moving forward or backward in specifiable degrees is not only simplistic, in the sense that it fails to capture what is actually going on; it is destructive, because it can change what is going on for the worse. Once teachers and students are compelled to focus only on what lends itself to quantification, such as the number of grammatical errors on a composition, or the number of state capitals memorized, the process of intellectual development has been severely compromised.[9]

STANDARDIZED TESTS

The sort of quantification of educational performance that is most commonly used—and once again, accepted unreflectively by those in the business world—is the traditional machine-scored, norm-referenced, multiple-choice, fill-in-the-bubble exam. The goal of all that control, the product of all that transmission, indeed the very definition of performance comes down to better scores on standardized tests. The limits of those tests, along with their pernicious effect on creative teaching and learning, are well-known to educators. Rote recall of facts and algorithms is typically emphasized above deep understanding—and *interest* in learning is, of course, ignored altogether. But those in the corporate world typically avoid all discussion of what these tests really measure and of what happens when educators must become preoccupied with the results of these tests.

A respected middle-school teacher in northern Wisconsin stood up at a community meeting not long ago and announced that he "used to be a good teacher." His use of the past tense surprised and disturbed those sitting in the auditorium, and he explained that he had lately begun to rely on a textbook for his lessons, having abandoned the innovative learning projects that his students had loved (and from which they had benefited). The reason, he explained, was that he was increasingly being held accountable for raising students' standardized test scores: that was what administrators in his district were using as the indicator of success. Now he was giving them what they demanded, and his students were the losers.

Multiply this teacher's experience by the tens of thousands, and then add the frustrated struggle of thousands more who haven't given up yet—those who persist in being innovative educators despite the growing emphasis on these tests. While educators around the country understand the deadening effect of having to turn over more and more of their time in the classroom to test preparation, the people who are much less likely to understand this are those with the power to demand ever more frequent administration of these tests: school board members, state legislators, and business leaders. Moreover, a bad thing is made even worse when newspapers report the scores of particular schools or districts—making the results of the tests that much more salient and setting these schools or districts against each other in a competition. Apart from the meaninglessness of comparing one school's performance to another's—that is, of emphasizing relative rather than absolute scores—educators who are defined as rivals are far less likely to engage in the kind of exchange and collaboration that leads to excellence.[10]

CARROTS AND STICKS

Not surprisingly, when corporate leaders talk about getting educators to do this or that, they fall back on devices described as incentives and disincentives—in plainer words, bribes and threats. Their premise, if it were spelled out, is that the way to make change is either to dangle something desirable in front of people if you get the results you want or to threaten something unpleasant if you don't. Rather than providing more resources to the schools that are struggling, this approach would therefore use budgets as an instrument to get compliance: give or withhold money on the basis of test scores. By the same token, business groups often recommend making it easier to fire teachers and making more of their salaries contingent on how well their students perform.

Apart from the inherent problems of control, there are specific problems with each of these methods of imposing control. The use of punitive sanctions creates a climate of fear, and fear generates anger and resentment. It also leads people to switch into damage-control mode and act more cautiously. Human beings simply do not think creatively and reach for excellence when they perceive themselves to be under threat. The tendency, rather, is to avoid risks and play it safe. One might say that those who are forced to cover their rear ends don't have their hands free for more important tasks. When teachers are deprived of job security or pay raises in an effort to compel them to teach better, the usual result is that they become demoralized rather than motivated.

What is true of sticks is ultimately true of carrots as well. The simplistic call to reward excellence (or what passes for excellence in the minds of many observers) overlooks an enormous body of research and experience demonstrating that rewards are just "control through seduction." One of the most thoroughly documented findings in social psychology is that people tend to lose interest in whatever they had to do to receive a reward: the intrinsic motivation that is so vital to quality (to say nothing of quality of life) often evaporates in the face of extrinsic incentives. More specifically, researchers have found that people's interest in a task ordinarily plummets when they are acutely aware of being evaluated on their performance—even if the evaluations they receive are positive. "When subjects expect rewards for attaining a specified level of competence, the anticipation of performance evaluation interferes with intrinsic interest," one group of investigators has concluded.

Nor does this exhaust the problems with the behaviorist tactic of using artificial inducements, such as money, to buy results. Rewarding "good" teachers—even assuming we can find criteria more reasonable than students' test scores—is likely to generate rivalry and resentment. And it is also apt to undermine innovative teaching, since innovation by definition isn't certain and a reward-driven individual is inclined to minimize risk. Likewise, tell a student that she should learn something in order to pass a test, satisfy an instructor, or win a prize, and the student will quickly come to look upon the process as a chore rather than as a source of intellectual excitement. To use rewards with teachers *and* students is a recipe for precisely the sort of problems that we already find in schools—which, come to think of it, are already marinated in behaviorism.[11]

Of course, businesspeople are not alone in endorsing the approach to education that these separate tenets constitute. From Congress to local school boards, politicians also uncritically call for higher standards, incentives, and all the rest of it.[12] So, shamefully, does the head of one of the nation's teachers' unions; Albert Shanker's opinions are usually indistinguishable from those of corporate executives, so business groups happily cite publications of the American Federation of Teachers in their own reports.

Still, this model is particularly consistent with a marketplace mentality, and so it is no coincidence that business generally takes the lead in formulating and promoting it. It is at least possible to imagine that a state legislator presented with the case against standardized testing, or against the transmission approach to teaching, would reconsider. This is harder to imagine in the case of corporate executives, which brings us back to the question of ultimate goals. For business, the point is not to promote active participation in democratic institutions, or social justice, or even the well-being or enrichment of the students themselves. The point is sales, revenues, profits.

Some people in the business world have complained that this characterization is unfair and out-of-date. They insist that today's executives want students who are skilled at teamwork and can cooperate with those who have different talents and interests. Today's companies need people who are critical thinkers and problem solvers. Their goals, therefore, are not so different from our own. But if this were really true, we would see cutting-edge corporations taking the lead in demanding a constructivist approach to instruction, where students' questions drive the curriculum, as well as a "whole language" model for teaching literacy. They would be demanding that we throw out the worksheets and the textbooks, the decontextualized skills and rote memorization. They would demand greater emphasis on cooperative learning and complain loudly about the practices that undermine collaboration (and ultimately quality)—practices like awards assemblies and spelling bees and honor rolls. They would insist on heterogeneous, inclusive classrooms in place of programs that segregate and stratify and stigmatize. They would stop talking about "school choice" (referring to programs that treat education as a commodity for sale) and start talking about the importance of giving *students* more choice about what happens in their classrooms. They would publish reports on the importance of turning schools into caring communities where mutual problem solving replaces traditional obedience-based discipline.

The sad truth, of course, is that when business leaders do address these issues, their approach tends to be precisely the opposite: they write off innovative, progressive educational reforms as mere fads that distract us from raising test scores. While there may be more talk in boardrooms these days about teamwork, it is usually situated in the context of competitiveness—that is, working together so we can defeat another group of people working together. While "social skills" are often listed as desirable attributes, business publications never seem to mention such qualities as generosity or compassion. While it is fashionable to talk about the need for future employees who can think critically, there is reason to doubt that corporate executives want people with the critical skills to ask why they (the executives) just received multimillion-dollar stock option packages even as several thousand employees have been thrown out of work. (More concretely, corporations may encourage high school English teachers to assign students the task of writing "a sample personnel evaluation,"[13] but they seem less keen on inviting students to critically analyze whether such evaluations make sense, or who gets to evaluate whom.) What business wants from its workers in the twenty-first century—and, by extension, from our schools—may not be so different after all from what it wanted in the nineteenth and twentieth centuries.

This is why it is so important for educators to be wary of innocuous-sounding "business-school partnerships" even though it can be difficult for a public school starved of resources to turn down funds from anyone. This is why it is so important for a democratic society to limit the power that corporations have in determining what happens in, and to, our schools. Note I do not say that corporations should be silenced. Ideally, we would say to business leaders something like the following:

Thank you for your latest list of what you would like schools to do, which skills you would like graduating students to have, and so forth. We appreciate your advice. As educators working with parents and

with the students themselves, we will be happy to consider your opinions . . . right alongside the opinions of labor unions, college admissions officers, philosophers, social scientists, journalists, elected
officials, and other interest groups. Your recommendations will carry
particular weight when they comport with those of other parties—for
example, in emphasizing the importance of making sure that students
know how to think logically. When they seem out of step with what
others are saying, and ultimately of benefit only to you, then those suggestions will be viewed with the appropriate skepticism. We recognize,
of course, that as the leaders of giant corporations, you represent financial resources far beyond those of other interest groups. We are sure that
you realize, however, that to give your recommendations any greater
weight because of that fact would violate core democratic principles.

Not long ago, as Joel Spring pointed out, one would have been
branded a radical for suggesting that our schools were geared to meeting the needs of corporations. Today, corporations freely complain
when our "educational system . . . fails the business sector,"[14] and they
openly try to make over the schools in their own image. It's up to the
rest of us to tell them firmly to mind their own businesses.

Notes

1. The Business Coalition for Educational Reform frankly asserts that "workplace performance requirements of industry and commerce must be integrated into subject-matter standards and learning environments." (See that
coalition's booklet "The Challenge of Change: Standards to Make Education Work for All Our Children," published in Jan. 1995 by the National
Alliance of Business.)

2. James B. Hunt Jr., "Education for Economic Growth," *Phi Delta Kappan*,
Apr. 1984.

3. Some references to the work of Dweck, Ames, and Nicholls are included in
Chapter Sixteen of this book, "The Littlest Customers." Also see Martin V.
Covington, *Making the Grade* (Cambridge, England: Cambridge University
Press, 1992); and Martin L. Maehr and Carol Midgley, "Enhancing Student
Motivation: A Schoolwide Approach," *Educational Psychologist* 26 (1991):
399–427.

4. See Harold Howe II, "Uncle Sam Is In the Classroom!" *Phi Delta Kappan*,
Jan. 1995: 374–77; and Elliot W. Eisner, "Standards for American Schools:
Help or Hindrance," *Phi Delta Kappan*, June 1995: 758–764.

5. For an intriguing argument in favor of a wider vision of schooling, see Nel Noddings, *The Challenge to Care in Schools* (New York: Teachers College Press, 1992). Howard Gardner's well-known theory of multiple intelligences is certainly relevant to this general discussion; less well-known is Elizabeth Cohen's contribution to the literature on cooperative learning, which emphasizes a curriculum requiring a range of skills so as to minimize status distinctions among students. (See, for example, her book *Designing Groupwork: Strategies for the Heterogeneous Classroom,* 2nd ed. [New York: Teachers College Press, 1994].) That students' interest in academic learning may depend on the extent to which classrooms are experienced as caring communities—and thus the extent to which time is spent on affective issues—has been demonstrated in Victor Battistich et al., "Schools as Communities, Poverty Levels of Student Populations, and Students' Attitudes, Motives, and Performance: A Multilevel Analysis," *American Educational Research Journal* 32 (1995): 627–658.

6. A 1996 publication by the Business Roundtable approvingly describes how one state was convinced to eliminate the phrase "construct meaning" from its standards for reading instruction, substituting the blander and more traditional word "understand." (See *A Business Leader's Guide to Setting Academic Standards,* p. 22.)

7. Writers from John Dewey to Paulo Freire to John Holt have identified and criticized what I am calling the transmission model of instruction, while any of a number of writings in the constructivist tradition offer an alternative. A very readable introduction to the subject is provided by Jacqueline Grennon Brooks and Martin G. Brooks, *In Search of Understanding: The Case for Constructivist Classrooms* (Alexandria, Va.: ASCD, 1993), and a more detailed summary of the most effective strategies for teaching reading, writing, math, science, and social studies is contained in Steven Zemelman, Harvey Daniels, and Arthur Hyde, *Best Practice: New Standards for Teaching and Learning in America's Schools* (Portsmouth, N.H.: Heinemann, 1993). It is in this book that the phrase "curriculum of superficiality" is used to describe the approach popularized by E. D. Hirsch Jr.

8. For a brief discussion of the support versus demand models, see Alfie Kohn, "Grading: The Issue Is Not How But Why," *Educational Leadership,* Oct. 1994: 38–41 (reprinted in this volume as Chapter Seven). On the counterproductive effects of trying to control what teachers do, see Cheryl Flink, Ann K. Boggiano, and Marty Barrett, "Controlling Teaching Strategies: Undermining Children's Self-Determination and Performance," *Journal of Personality and Social Psychology* 59 (1990): 916–924; and Edward L. Deci et al., "Effects of Performance Standards on Teaching Styles: Behavior of

Controlling Teachers," *Journal of Educational Psychology* 74 (1982): 852–859. The quotation about making students understand the importance of learning comes from a speech given by Owen B. Butler at the second Fortune Education Summit in Washington, D.C., Oct. 1989.

9. On the prosaic mentality, see chap. 6 of George W. Morgan, *The Human Predicament: Dissolution and Wholeness* (New York: Delta, 1970). Linda McNeil's quotation is taken from her book *Contradictions of Control* (New York: Routledge & Kegan Paul, 1986), p. xviii.

10. See D. Monty Neill and Noe J. Medina, "Standardized Testing: Harmful to Educational Health," *Phi Delta Kappan,* May 1989: 688–697; a report by the Center for the Study of Testing entitled "The Influence of Testing on Teaching Math and Science in Grades 4–12" (available from CSTEEP, 323 Campion Hall, Boston College, Chestnut Hill, MA 02167); and various reports from FAIRTEST, 342 Broadway, Cambridge, MA 02139.

11. Extensive documentation on the failure of incentives—and of carrot-and-stick psychology, more generally—is contained in Alfie Kohn, *Punished by Rewards: The Trouble with Gold Stars, Incentive Plans, A's, Praise, and Other Bribes* (Boston: Houghton Mifflin, 1993); Edward L. Deci and Richard M. Ryan, *Intrinsic Motivation and Self-Determination in Human Behavior* (New York: Plenum, 1985); and Mark R. Lepper and David Greene, eds., *The Hidden Costs of Rewards: New Perspectives on the Psychology of Human Motivation* (Hillsdale, N.J.: Erlbaum, 1978). The phrase "control through seduction" appears in the Deci and Ryan book, p. 70. The other quotation about evaluation and rewards is from Judith M. Harackiewicz, George Manderlink, and Carol Sansone, "Rewarding Pinball Wizardry: Effects of Evaluation and Cue Value on Intrinsic Interest," *Journal of Personality and Social Psychology* 47 (1984), p. 293.

12. Not only do public officials frequently follow in lock-step with business on issues of educational policy, but they typically endorse a significant role for business in determining that policy. Donna Shalala, secretary of Health and Human Services under President Clinton, and widely regarded as a liberal Democrat, has said of business that "education needs this powerful voice" (quoted in Jonathan Weisman, "The New Player: Educators Watch with a Wary Eye as Business Gains Clout," *Teacher Magazine,* Oct. 1991, p. 11).

13. The Business Roundtable points approvingly to just such assignments in Fort Worth, Texas, claiming that they "have the effect of motivating students." See *A Business Leader's Guide to Setting Standards,* p. 21.

14. This paraphrase of a report released by the Committee for Economic Development appears in Catherine S. Manegold, "Study Says Schools Must Stress Academics," the *New York Times,* 23 Sept. 1994, p. A22.

CHAPTER FOURTEEN

The False Premises of School Choice Plans

Most critics of school choice proposals, in which students shop for an education and school districts must compete for their business, have emphasized the inequity of such plans, contending that they are recipes for making the rich districts richer and the poor districts poorer.

This argument needs to be taken seriously, but it is by no means the only problem with such proposals. The whole idea of school choice rests on a series of myths and misunderstandings.

• The contention that a marketplace model will improve the quality of schools contains two hidden premises: first, that every district already has what it needs to give children a better education, and only inertia or sheer laziness prevents this from happening; second, that all educators require is a swift kick—specifically, the threat of losing public funds—and they will get to work.

Neither assumption survives close inspection. Many districts are struggling to make do with inadequate resources—run-down buildings,

---

Originally published in *The Boston Globe* in 1993.

a scarcity of qualified teachers, and too few supplies. But even if this were not so, the idea that holding a gun to people's heads will motivate them to improve is psychologically naive, to say the least.

Fear typically creates anger and resentment. It leads people to switch into damage-control mode and act more cautiously. They do not think creatively and reach for excellence when they perceive themselves to be under threat.

• Choice plans reflect not only a misplaced acceptance of the value of external inducements in general but a blind faith in one inducement in particular: competition.

Our workplaces and classrooms are constructed on the myth that it makes sense to set people against one another so the success of each must come at someone else's expense. Yet hundreds of studies have shown that competition actually undermines the quality of task performance—to say nothing of its emotional costs. The more we must struggle to beat others, the more we handicap ourselves.

The reasons: competition causes anxiety, which undermines performance. It also makes people less interested in what they are doing for its own sake and more likely to see it as a means to an end (the end being victory) and therefore less likely to do their best over time.

Finally, competition is wasteful because people cannot cooperate with their rivals. If two school districts are fighting over the same students, for example, they are unlikely to exchange ideas and resources. The result is that both (and in the long run, the people they serve) are the losers.

• School choice plans misdiagnose the problem and offer a solution that is bound to backfire. But they also represent and underscore a philosophy that is troubling in its own right: the community be damned.

Selfishness is one of the reasons that schools are underfunded. Some people who have no children defiantly resist contributing to something from which they will not personally benefit. Some political philosophies have actually tried to make a virtue of this attitude.

Applying a marketplace mentality to education will just exacerbate this emphasis on self-interest, with parents encouraged to focus only on the improvement of their own children's situation. This is the very opposite of an invitation to work together to make schools more effective and inviting places for all.

• Finally, people who are sincerely committed to the concept of choice might do better to ask how much choice students have within their classrooms—that is, the extent to which children can participate in determining what they are learning and the principles by which their classes are guided.

The way a child learns to take responsibility for his or her actions is by being given responsibilities, not by having to follow someone else's rules all day. Learning becomes more engaging and children acquire moral and democratic skills when they are brought into the process of making choices and solving problems.

A sense of genuine self-determination results from playing a role in deciding how schooling happens, not from having one's parents decide where it happens. Turning education into one more commodity for sale does nothing to foster real choice. It simply invokes a comfortable faith in the magic of competition to make educational problems disappear.

CHAPTER FIFTEEN

Students Don't "Work"—
They Learn

September is a new beginning, a time for fresh starts. Consider, then, a resolution that you and your colleagues might make for this school year. *From now on, we will stop referring to what students do in school as "work."*

Importing the nomenclature of the workplace is something most of us do without thinking—which is in itself a good reason to reflect on the practice. Every time we talk about "homework" or "seat work" or "work habits," every time we describe the improvement in, or assessment of, a student's "work" in class, every time we urge children to "get to work" or even refer to "classroom *management*," we are using a metaphor with profound implications for the nature of schooling. In effect, we are equating what children do to figure things out with what adults do in offices and factories to earn money.

To be sure, there are parallels between workplaces and classrooms. In both settings, collaboration turns out to be more effective than pitting people against each other in a race to be Number One. In both

---

Originally published in *Education Week* in 1997.

places, it makes sense to have people participate in making decisions about what they are doing rather than simply trying to control them. In both places, problems are more likely to be solved by rethinking the value of the tasks than by using artificial inducements to try to "motivate" people to do those tasks.

Even the most enlightened businesses, however, are still quite different from what schools are about—or ought to be about. Managers may commit themselves to continuous improvement and try to make their employees' jobs more fulfilling, but the bottom line is that they are still focused on—well, on the bottom line. The emphasis is on results, on turning out a product, on quantifying improvement on a fixed series of measures such as sales volume or return on investment. The extent to which this mentality has taken hold in discussions about education is the extent to which our schools are in trouble.

In the course of learning, students frequently produce things, such as essays and art projects and lab write-ups, whose quality can be assessed. But these artifacts are just so many by-products of the act of making meaning. The process of learning is more important than the products that result. To use the language of "work"—or worse, to adopt a business-style approach to school reform—is to reverse those priorities.

In a learning environment, teachers want to help students engage with what they are doing to promote deeper understanding. Students' interests may therefore help shape the curriculum, and a growing facility with words and numbers derives from the process of finding answers to their own questions. Skillful educators tap students' natural curiosity and desire to become competent. They provide information about the success of these explorations and help students become more proficient learners. Not every student relishes every aspect of every task, of course, but the act of learning is ideally its own reward.

Things are very different in a classroom where students are put to work, as Hermine H. Marshall at San Francisco State University has persuasively argued in a decade's worth of monographs devoted to the difference between work and learning environments. In the former, the tasks come to be seen as—indeed, are often explicitly presented as—means to an end. What counts is the number of right answers, although even this may be seen as just a prerequisite to snagging a good grade. In fact, the grade may be a means to making the honor roll, which in turn may lead to special privileges or rewards provided at school or at home. With each additional inducement, the original act of learning is further devalued.

It is interesting to notice how commonly the advocates of extrinsic rewards also endorse (a) a view of education as something necessarily unpleasant, and (b) a curriculum that is in fact unappealing. A sour "take your medicine" traditionalism goes hand in hand with drill-and-skill lessons (some of which are aptly named "worksheets") and a reliance on incentives to induce students to do what they understandably have no interest in doing. Such is the legacy of seeing school as work.

"Measurable outcomes may be the least significant results of learning," as Linda McNeil of Rice University has observed, but measurable outcomes are the most significant results of work. Moreover, students are pressured to succeed because it is their "job" to do so; it is expected or demanded of them that they produce and perform.

It isn't hard to find schools that have undertaken this mission, where posters and bulletin boards exhort students to ever-greater success, which typically means higher standardized-test scores. (Many of these tests are normed, of course, so that success is defined as something that not everyone can achieve.) In such factory-like schools, you will often hear words like *performance* and *achievement,* but rarely words like *discovery* or *exploration* or *curiosity.*

Even those of us who do not recognize our own schools in this description may want to rethink the work metaphors that creep into our speech. We may wish to reconsider the extent to which learning is corrupted by talking about it as work—or by talking about learners as "workers," which amounts to the same thing. Even some progressive thinkers have given in to the latter temptation, intending to elevate the status of students but in fact compromising the integrity of what distinguishes classrooms from workplaces.

We are living in an age when education is described as an "investment," when school reform is justified by invoking the "need to be competitive in the twenty-first century." The implication here is that the central function of schools is to turn out adequately skilled employees who will show up on time and do whatever they're told so that corporations can triumph over their counterparts in other countries. (Interestingly, Catherine Lewis, in her recent book *Educating Hearts and Minds,* reports that "the metaphor of the school as a factory or workplace where children do 'work,' so common in American schools, was notably absent from the Japanese [elementary] schools" she visited.) But if it is repugnant to regard children primarily as future workers—or more broadly, as adults-in-the-making—it is worse to see what children do right now as work.

To get a sense of whether students view themselves as workers or as learners, we need only ask them (during class) what they are doing. "I'm doing my work" is one possible response; "I'm trying to figure out why the character in this story told her friend to go away" is something else altogether. Better yet, we might ask students *why* they are doing something, and then attend to the difference between "Because Ms. Taylor told us to" or "It's going to be on the test," on the one hand, and "Because I just don't get why this character would say that!" on the other.

Another way to judge the orientation of a classroom is to watch for the teacher's reaction to mistakes. Someone who manages students' work is likely to strive for zero defects: perfect papers and assignments that receive the maximum number of points. Someone who facilitates students' learning welcomes mistakes—first, because they are invaluable clues as to how the student is thinking, and second, because to do so creates a climate of safety that ultimately promotes more successful learning.

Moreover, a learning-oriented classroom is more likely to be characterized by the thoughtful exploration of complicated issues than by a curriculum based on memorizing right answers. As Hermine Marshall has observed, for students to see themselves as learning, "the tasks provided must be those that require higher-order thinking skills."

Does a rejection of the models, methods, and metaphors of work mean that school should be about play? In a word, no. False dichotomies are popular because they make choosing easy, and the "work versus play" polarity is a case in point. Learning is a third alternative, where the primary purpose is neither playlike enjoyment (although the process can be deeply satisfying) nor the worklike completion of error-free products (although the process can involve intense effort and concentration).

To challenge the work metaphor is not to abandon rigor or excellence. Rather, it is to insist that work is not the only activity that can be pursued rigorously—and play, for that matter, is not the only activity that can be experienced as pleasurable.

Of course, to talk about students' "projects" or "activities" instead of their "work" represents only a change in language. My objective here is not to add to the list of words we are not supposed to mention. But how we speak not only reflects the way we think, it contributes to it as well. Perhaps a thoughtful discussion about the hidden implications of workplace metaphors will invite us to consider changing what we do as well as what we say.

CHAPTER SIXTEEN

The Littlest Customers
TQM Goes to School

Every few years a new idea captures the imagination of educators. The journals are filled with breathless accounts of its importance, a cadre of consultants materializes to offer workshops, and a new vocabulary insinuates itself into discussions of familiar topics. The idea that currently fits that description is Total Quality Management (TQM), based on the work of the renowned statistical consultant W. Edwards Deming in corporate settings.[1]

Because I am raising concerns about the application of TQM to schools, I should begin by acknowledging not only my admiration for Deming but also my involvement with the movement he helped to set in motion. Some of my own writing is apparently regarded as relevant in these circles, and I have been invited to lecture at a number of Quality conferences, as well as to exchange ideas with Deming as part of a videotape series on his work. I mention these things only by way of emphasizing that I have some connection to the field I am discussing.

Originally published in *Educational Leadership* in 1993.

Not only am I enthusiastic about TQM in a business context, but I believe that many of its underlying values resonate with some of the best work in educational theory. Deming and his followers offer an essentially positive view of human nature, emphasizing people's fundamental desire to learn and challenge themselves. TQM advocates promote democratic environments and shared decision making. They stress the benefits of cooperation and the destructive consequences of competition. They insist that a climate of trust must replace one based on fear. And they urge the abolition of systems of rating, ranking, and behavioral manipulation, including grades.

While none of these ideas is new to education—indeed, each has been articulated by a variety of educational writers over the decades—we should be pleased to see them corroborated by people from other fields. But pointing out parallels in passing is very different from what is happening with TQM. Educators are attempting to transplant a model native to the business world, along with its methods and metaphors, to the classroom.

A MARKETPLACE MODEL IN THE CLASSROOM

Part of the problem, to be sure, is that some educators waving the Quality banner have either misunderstood Deming's work or drawn from it selectively to lend credibility to their own objectives. If TQM offers any imperative to schools, it is the need to abolish standardized tests (Holt, 1993; Rankin, 1992) and grades (Deming, 1991). Yet higher test scores are sometimes cited by self-styled proponents of TQM as the measure of their success at transforming a school or district (McLeod et al., 1992; Schmoker and Wilson, 1993)—or even used as the basis for redesigning the curriculum (Abernethy and Serfass, 1992). Likewise, there is reason to believe that the abolition of grades, admittedly a difficult feat, is not even on the agenda of many champions of Quality. (Some of them have moved to allow students to participate in determining their own grades [AASA, 1992] but seem to regard this modification of current practice as sufficient.) Moreover, the use of extrinsic motivators appears to be widespread among those who invoke Deming's name.

But my complaint goes deeper than a failure to understand the implications of Deming's ideas or to implement them properly. I believe that *a marketplace model, even correctly applied, does not belong in the classroom.* The difference between two management approaches (old and new, top-down and participative, Taylor and Deming) is less significant than the difference between *any* method for managing workers and what happens in classrooms.[2]

Notwithstanding Deming's admonition to eliminate slogans and exhortations, some articles about TQM and education consist of just that: a string of shibboleths about systems theory, profound knowledge, the need for vision and leadership, and so on. Of course, the repetition of favored phrases tells us nothing about how to make meaningful change, but at least no one will disapprove. By contrast, there is cause for grave concern when we come across pointed assertions that "quality is achieved . . . by acknowledging that education is a business" (McLeod et al., 1992) or "the modern school should look . . . like our best high-tech companies" (David Kearns, quoted in Blankstein, 1992). Likewise, when this philosophy is put into practice by enterprising teachers, the results verge on self-parody: second graders being instructed in the fine points of filling orders, pleasing customers, and turning out products to rigid specifications.

Something has gone terribly wrong here. But again the problem is not that proponents of Quality fail to understand Deming's work so much as that they fail to understand where that work belongs.

THE NOMENCLATURE
OF THE WORKPLACE

When the process of teaching children is forced onto the Procrustean bed of management theory, it is necessary to designate an educational counterpart for each role in a business setting. Because TQM is about satisfying customers, the first order of business is to figure out who should be called the *customer* of education. Some writers nominate students. Some insist that the word is best applied to parents or other adults in the community. Some say it depends on the situation.

That it is so difficult to agree on the educational correlative to a company's customer—one who *purchases* a product—should alert us to the possibility that the question is misconceived.[3] Attempting to answer it is about as sensible as trying to figure out which member of a family is most like a colonel and which is most like a lieutenant.

To talk about learning in terms of buying and selling not only reflects a warped view of the activity but contributes to the warping. To the best of my knowledge, only one individual has expressed misgivings in print about this use of language (see Sztajn, 1992). Most educators who have addressed themselves to the topic of TQM adopt the terminology uncritically—and in one case even suggest that anyone who resists it is suffering from "a fear of industrial models" (Rhodes, 1990b).

Other words borrowed from the manager's lexicon are no less disturbing than *customer.* Students are sometimes said to be *raw materials,* while parents are *suppliers.* USX ships steel to General Motors to be made into cars; Mom and Dad (having shed their status as customers) ship their children (ditto) to school to be processed into some other sort of commodity. Alternatively, teachers have been described as "delivering instruction" to students (Willis, 1993). All of these phrases have disturbing pedagogical implications.

The deafening clash of metaphors gets louder when students are also referred to as *workers* (Bonstingl, 1992; Schmoker and Wilson, 1993). This locution, perhaps the most troubling of all, represents the logical conclusion of a well-established trend of seeing education as an investment. It is probably not a coincidence that the rationale for adopting TQM in particular is often couched not in terms of how students can be helped to become self-directed, lifelong learners, but rather in terms of improving corporate competitiveness in global markets (Leonard, 1991; McLeod et al., 1992; Schmoker and Wilson, 1993).

Implicit in this perspective is the view of students as potential workers. But in the last few years we have witnessed a shift to something even more ominous: a view of students as *actual* workers. Businesspeople and politicians are not the only ones who describe the activities of schoolchildren in economic terms. Albert Shanker (quoted in Perry, 1988) declares that "we must start thinking of students as workers." William Glasser (1990), whose books have supported many educators in transforming schools into more humanistic places, insists that "the industrial analogy of workers and managers . . . is both accurate and appropriate."

Need we enumerate the respects in which the analogy is neither?

• Workers are adults. Most students are children, whose capacities and limits demand a developmentally appropriate set of strategies. Age differences not only inform what and how we teach, but also affect our response to inappropriate behavior.

• If workers are helped to acquire skills, this is intended as a way to build an effective organization; it is rarely a goal in its own right. By contrast, helping students to acquire skills, to become good learners and good people, is the very point of school.

• While it is undesirable for many reasons to manipulate workers with incentives (Kohn, 1993a, 1993b), they still have to be paid. Nothing, including grades, is analogous in a school setting.

• Most important, workers produce goods like automobiles and houses; they are hired to make things. The only thing students should be making is *meaning*. To turn the classroom into a workplace, through our practices or our parlance, is to put at risk the intellectual exploration and development that ought to be taking place there.

TEACHING BY THE NUMBERS?

What is striking about the articles and books on the application of TQM to education is their failure to address any fundamental questions about learning, per se, or even more remarkably, about curriculum. Incredibly, page after page written by educators enamored of business models typically contains not a single reference to whether the things we are teaching are worth learning—whether the curriculum is engaging and relevant to children's experiences. In fact, one influential introduction to the topic promotes TQM as "content-free, applicable to any instruction or structural reform" (AASA, 1992).

This is hardly the first time educators have been offered a package said to be compatible with any curriculum. That TQM takes the same approach should not be surprising, since its use in a corporate context is not dependent on what people in an organization are doing: whether a company manufactures medicine or missiles is of no consequence to consultants who talk about moving toward Quality.

At best, then, TQM offers little challenge to the curricular status quo and leaves students with the same material to learn. But if, as I suspect, TQM turns out not to be content-neutral in practice, its impact may actually be counterproductive. The premise of TQM seems to be that the trouble with organizations of all sorts, including schools, is a lack of data. Great importance is placed on the use of statistical control diagrams and other pictorial representations of quantitative information about performance. New converts to TQM frequently display examples of these tools, along with pride at having mastered them.

Is it really true that the principal problem with American classrooms is a lack of data? I think not, but we can put off this question to another day. Instead, let us consider the possible effect on the curriculum of this way of thinking. In academic social science, the questions addressed in a given discipline often seem to be selected on the basis of how well they lend themselves to the methodologies native to that field: the method drives the content. Similarly, it is entirely possible that TQM classrooms will incline toward the analysis of data and the assignment of tasks where progress can be easily quantified and analyzed. While Deming has said unequivocally that "the most important things we need to manage can't be measured" (quoted in Rhodes, 1990a; also see Deming, 1991), an emphasis on statistical analysis is likely to accelerate the tendency toward teaching by the numbers.

There is evidence, in fact, that this is already happening. In one case, proponents of systems thinking have talked about computer simulations of the actions of Shakespeare's characters to maximize "the use of precise numbers to talk about psychological motives" (Senge and Lannon-Kim, 1991). In another case, people committed to Quality have built into assessment instruments such measures as "the number of poems a student [has] memorized" (Harris and Harris, 1992). David Langford, a pioneer in the field, recently dismissed "the argument that much of what happens in the classroom is intangible and hence not subject to the statistical scrutiny TQM prescribes. 'It can all be measured,' he maintains" (Willis, 1993).

It was e.e. cummings who declared that "nothing measurable matters a good goddam." Even if we are not willing to go quite that far, it is hard to deny that much of what is worth learning cannot be reduced to numbers without doing violence to its substance. In fact, anyone sensitive to the tyranny of standardized testing should be just as skeptical about turning the process of children's intellectual creation and discovery into bars on a Pareto chart.

At the heart of Deming's approach is a repudiation of the use of numerical goals and mass inspection at the end of production. What we choose to quantify, and how we do so, is highly relevant within the Quality framework. But what are we to make of the assertion that "improving the system," for educators as well as managers, means trying to "narrow the amount of variation within it" (Blankstein, 1992)? Or that it means "removing inefficiencies" in the curriculum itself, or even worse, subjecting children to "frequent assessment of quality at every stage" (Schmoker and Wilson, 1993)?

BACK TO THE GOALS OF EDUCATION

Assuming that these writers have not misinterpreted the goals of TQM, the issue once again is whether such a system is consistent with our goals as educators. If we prefer to focus on process rather than product—if efficiency is a goal incommensurate with the act of discovery—then we have reason to question the appropriateness of TQM in a classroom setting. Nor will our concerns be allayed when some of the recommendations are modified. Even if students' performance isn't construed in terms of reducing variation and even if it isn't relentlessly quantified, there is no getting around the fact that the Quality model is designed to draw attention to performance in order to improve it.

Unfortunately, a performance focus is inherently problematic in a classroom. The work of leading motivation researchers (Ames, 1992; Dweck, 1986; Nicholls, 1989), none of which has been mentioned by defenders of TQM's role in education, converges on a single crucial distinction concerning how to think about what happens in schools. Variously framed as "mastery versus ability," "learning versus performance," and "task versus ego," the point is that there is an enormous difference between getting students to think about *what* they are doing, on the one hand, and *how well* they are doing (and therefore how good they are at doing it), on the other. The latter orientation does a great deal of harm.

Students who are overly concerned about how well they are doing may come to see learning as a means to an end and start to think that their performance, especially when they fail, is due to innate intelligence (or its absence): "I screwed up; therefore I'm stupid." That in turn leads them to assume there isn't much point to trying harder next time, which means they are unlikely to improve.

This is not to say that the worth of an assignment cannot be judged. There is a time to think about whether what one has done is good, and it is important to talk with others about the results of one's work. But research is clear that getting children to become preoccupied with their performance can:

- Interfere with their ability to remember things about the challenging tasks they just worked on (Graham and Golan, 1991)
- Undermine their ability to apply scientific principles to new situations (Dweck, 1986)
- Reduce the quality of their work as measured on tests of creativity (Butler, 1992)
- Increase their fear of failure (Heyman and Dweck, 1992)
- Undermine their interest in what they are doing (Ryan, 1982; Butler, 1987)

• Lead them to choose the easiest possible task in an effort to avoid the sort of challenge that might lead to failure (Harter, 1978; Elliott and Dweck, 1988)

Getting students to think about grades or performance on tests is a particularly potent way to inhibit creative thinking and conceptual learning (Grolnick and Ryan, 1987; Butler and Nisan, 1986). But the point here is that any sort of performance orientation can be detrimental—and TQM is unavoidably based on just such an orientation.

I do not fault the theorists or practitioners of corporate management for ignorance of these and other findings, because there is no reason to expect them to have thought carefully about how children learn. But why, then, are we looking to these people for guidance on educational practices?

When someone in the business world asks me for advice, I unhesitatingly recommend the work of Deming. Educators, though, would do better to turn to Dewey. Before we jump on the bandwagon carrying another corporate model into our schools, we need to ask some hard questions about the nature and purposes of education. No one can object to "quality" as an abstract concept, but if a set of practices revolving around that word requires us to treat students as customers or workers, then we should leave management practices to managers and get on with the challenge of educating.

Notes

1. It is worth noting that Deming pointedly distanced himself from much of what goes by the name of TQM. Nonetheless, I refer here to Deming's principles and the Quality movement inspired (if not always approved) by him more or less interchangeably. I do so for the sake of simplicity and because my concerns about using Deming's work in the classroom go well beyond the issue of whether the people citing that work are using it imprecisely.

2. Whether it belongs in any educational setting—for example, whether it is appropriate to managing the work of adults in a school or district—is a question worth pondering, but one that I will not attempt to deal with here. My concern is with teaching children.

3. It turned out that even as I was writing this article, W. Edwards Deming was proving himself far more reasonable than many Demingites. At a March 1993 seminar in Detroit, presumably in response to a question, he growled, "We don't have customers in education. Don't forget your horse sense" (quoted in Holt, 1994).

References

Abernethy, P. E., and R. W. Serfass. (Nov. 1992). "One District's Quality Improvement Story." *Educational Leadership:* 14–17.

American Association of School Administrators. (1992). *Creating Quality Schools.* Arlington, Va.: AASA.

Ames, C. (1992). "Classrooms: Goals, Structures, and Student Motivation." *Journal of Educational Psychology* 84: 261–271.

Blankstein, A. M. (Mar. 1992). "Lessons from Enlightened Corporations." *Educational Leadership:* 71–75.

Bonstingl, J. J. (1992). *Schools of Quality: An Introduction to Total Quality Management in Education.* Alexandria, Va.: ASCD.

Butler, R. (1987). "Task-Involving and Ego-Involving Properties of Evaluation." *Journal of Educational Psychology* 79: 474–482.

Butler, R. (1992). "What Young People Want to Know When." *Journal of Personality and Social Psychology* 62: 934–943.

Butler, R., and M. Nisan. (1986). "Effects of No Feedback, Task-Related Comments, and Grades on Intrinsic Motivation and Performance." *Journal of Educational Psychology* 78: 210–216.

Deming, W. E. (1991). "Foundation for Management of Quality in the Western World." Paper delivered in Osaka, Japan, 1989; revised 1991. Re printed in *An Introduction to Total Quality for Schools.* Arlington, Va.: AASA.

Dweck, C. S. (1986). "Motivational Processes Affecting Learning." *American Psychologist* 41: 1040–1048.

Elliott, E. S., and C. S. Dweck. (1988). "Goals: An Approach to Motivation and Achievement." *Journal of Personality and Social Psychology* 54: 5–12.

Glasser, W. (1990). *The Quality School: Managing Students Without Coercion.* New York: Harper and Row.

Graham, S., and S. Golan. (1991). "Motivational Influences on Cognition." *Journal of Educational Psychology* 83: 187–194.

Grolnick, W. S., and R. M. Ryan. (1987). "Autonomy in Children's Learning." *Journal of Personality and Social Psychology* 52: 890–898.

Harris, M. F., and R. C. Harris. (Nov. 1992). "Glasser Comes to a Rural School." *Educational Leadership:* 18–21.

Harter, S. (1978). "Pleasure Derived from Challenge and the Effects of Receiving Grades on Children's Difficulty Level Choices." *Child Development* 49: 788–799.

Heyman, G. D., and C. S. Dweck. (1992). "Achievement Goals and Intrinsic Motivation." *Motivation and Emotion* 16: 231–247.

Holt, M. (Jan. 1993). "The Educational Consequences of W. Edwards Deming." *Phi Delta Kappan:* 382–388.

Holt, M. (Sept. 1994). "Why Deming and OBE Don't Mix." *Educational Leadership:* 85–86.

Kohn, A. (Sept.–Oct. 1993a). "Why Incentive Plans Cannot Work." *Harvard Business Review:* 54–63.

Kohn, A. (1993b). *Punished by Rewards: The Trouble with Gold Stars, Incentive Plans, A's, Praise, and Other Bribes.* Boston: Houghton Mifflin.

Leonard, J. F. (1991). "Applying Deming's Principles to Our Schools." Reprinted in *An Introduction to Total Quality for Schools.* Arlington, Va.: AASA.

McLeod, W. B., B. A. Spencer, and L. T. Hairston. (1992). "Toward a System of Total Quality Management." *ERS Spectrum* 10, 2: 34–41.

Nicholls, J. G. (1989). *The Competitive Ethos and Democratic Education.* Cambridge, Mass.: Harvard University Press.

Perry, N. J. (Nov. 7, 1988). "Saving the Schools: How Business Can Help." *Fortune:* 42–56.

Rankin, S. C. (Sept. 1992). "Total Quality Management: Implications for Educational Assessment." *NASSP Bulletin:* 66–76.

Rhodes, L. A. (Nov. 1990a). "Why Quality Is Within Our Grasp . . . If We Reach." *The School Administrator:* 31–34.

Rhodes, L. A. (Dec. 1990b). "Beyond Your Beliefs: Quantum Leaps Toward Quality Schools." *The School Administrator:* 23–26.

Ryan, R. M. (1982). "Control and Information in the Intrapersonal Sphere." *Journal of Personality and Social Psychology* 43: 450–461.

Schmoker, M., and R. B. Wilson. (Jan. 1993). "Transforming Schools Through Total Quality Education." *Phi Delta Kappan:* 389–395.

Senge, P., and C. Lannon-Kim. (Nov. 1991). "Applying the Systems Approach in the Classroom." *The School Administrator:* 10–11.

Sztajn, P. (Nov. 1992). "A Matter of Metaphors." *Educational Leadership:* 35–37.

Willis, S. (Feb. 1993). "Creating 'Total Quality' Schools." *ASCD Update:* 1, 4–5.

PART FIVE

Lessons Learned

CHAPTER SEVENTEEN

Caring Kids

The Role of the Schools

E ducation worthy of the name is essentially educa-
tion of character," the philosopher Martin Buber told a gathering of
teachers in 1939.[1] In saying this, he presented a challenge more radical and unsettling than his audience may have realized. He did not
mean that schools should develop a unit on values or moral reasoning and glue it onto the existing curriculum. He did not mean that
problem children should be taught how to behave. He meant that the
very profession of teaching calls on us to try to produce not merely
good learners but good people.

Given that even the more modest task of producing good learners
seems impossibly ambitious—perhaps because of a misplaced emphasis on producing good test-takers—the prospect of taking Buber
seriously may seem positively utopian. But in the half-century since
his speech, the need for schools to play an active role in shaping character has only grown more pressing. That need is reflected not only in
the much-cited prevalence of teenage pregnancy and drug use but also

---

Originally published in *Phi Delta Kappan* in 1991.

in the evidence of rampant selfishness and competitiveness among young people.[2] At a tender age, children learn not to be tender. A dozen years of schooling often do nothing to promote generosity or a commitment to the welfare of others. To the contrary, students are graduated who think that being smart means looking out for Number One.

I want to argue, first, that something *can* be done to rectify this situation because nothing about "human nature" makes selfishness inevitable; second, that educators in particular *should* do something about the problem; and third, that psychological research, common sense, and the experience of an important pilot project in California offer specific guidance for helping children to grow into caring adults.

Much of what takes place in a classroom, including that which we have come to take for granted, emerges from a set of assumptions about the nature of human nature. Not only how children are disciplined, but the very fact that influencing their actions is viewed as "discipline" in the first place; not merely how we grade students, but the fact that we grade them at all; not simply how teachers and students interact, but the fact that interaction *between students* is rarely seen as integral to the process of learning—all of these facts ultimately rest on an implicit theory of what human beings are like.

Consider the fact that most conversations about changing the way children act in a classroom tend to focus on curbing negative behaviors rather than on promoting positive ones. In part, this emphasis simply reflects the urgency of preventing troublesome or even violent conduct. But this way of framing the issue may also tell us something about our view of what comes naturally to children, what they are capable of, and by extension, what lies at the core of our species. Likewise, it is no coincidence, I think, that the phrase "it's just human nature to be . . ." is invariably followed by such adjectives as selfish, competitive, lazy, aggressive, and so on. Very rarely do we hear someone protest, "Well, of course he was helpful. After all, it's just human nature to be generous."

The belief persists in this culture that our darker side is more pervasive, more persistent, and somehow more real than our capacity for what psychologists call "prosocial behavior." We seem to assume that people are naturally and primarily selfish and will act otherwise only if they are coerced into doing so and carefully monitored. The logical conclusion of this worldview is the assumption that generous and responsible behavior must be forced down the throats of children who would otherwise be inclined to care only about themselves.

A review of several hundred studies has convinced me that this cynicism is not realism. Human beings are not only selfish and self-centered, but also decent, able to feel—and prepared to try to relieve—the pain of others. I believe that it is as "natural" to help as it is to hurt, that concern for the well-being of others often cannot be reduced to self-interest, that social structures predicated on human selfishness have no claim to inevitability—or even prudence. This is not the place for rehearsing the arguments and data that support these conclusions—in part because I have recently done so at book length.[3] But I would like to mention a few recent findings from developmental psychology that speak to the question of whether educators can aim higher than producing a quiet classroom or a nondisruptive child.

To start at the beginning, newborns are more likely to cry—and to cry longer—when they are exposed to the sound of another infant's crying than when they hear other noises that are equally loud and sudden. In three sets of studies with infants ranging in age from eighteen to seventy-two hours, such crying seemed to be a spontaneous reaction rather than a mere vocal imitation.[4] In the view of Abraham Sagi and Martin Hoffman, who conducted one of the studies, this finding suggests the existence of "a rudimentary empathic distress reaction at birth."[5] Our species may be primed, in other words, to be discomfited by someone else's discomfort.

As an infant grows, this discomfort continues and takes more sophisticated forms. Marian Radke-Yarrow, Carolyn Zahn-Waxler, and their associates at the National Institute of Mental Health have been studying toddlers for nearly twenty years, having in effect deputized mothers as research assistants to collect data in the home instead of relying on brief (and possibly unrepresentative) observations in the laboratory. A ten- to fourteen–month-old child, they have found, can be expected to show signs of agitation and unhappiness in the presence of another person's distress, perhaps by crying or burying her head in her mother's lap. As a child develops the capacity to undertake more deliberate behavior, in the period between eighteen and twenty-four months, his response to distress will become more active: patting the head, fetching a toy, offering verbal expressions of sympathy, finding an adult to help, and so forth.[6]

I should add that, like all parents, researchers have also observed hostile and selfish actions on the part of children. To say that sympathy or helping behavior is pervasive and precocious is not to claim that every child is an angel or to deny that toddlers—particularly in a society preoccupied with possessiveness—will sometimes snatch back a toy ("Mine!") or throw it across the room. But it is to argue that the *antisocial* is no more basic or natural than the *prosocial.*

By the time children are of preschool age, comforting, sharing, and helping are regular occurrences. One study of preschoolers during free play discovered that sixty-seven of the seventy-seven children shared with, helped, or comforted another child at least once during only forty minutes of observation.[7] After counting such behaviors in similar experiments of her own, Arizona State University psychologist Nancy Eisenberg became curious about why children were acting this way. To find out, she came up with a technique that few research psychologists had thought to use: she *asked* the children.

Eisenberg and a colleague simply followed four– and five–year–olds around a preschool and watched for unprompted prosocial behavior. Each time such an act was observed, the child was asked why he or she did it. ("How come you gave that to John?") None of the children intended to conform to adult expectations or expressed any fear of punishment. Very few said that they expected to benefit in some way by helping—such as by impressing their peers. Among the most frequent explanations heard was the simple observation that the other child had needed help.[8] This, when you come right down to it, is the heart of altruism.[9] And it is enough to suggest that parents and educators hoping to raise a child who is responsive to the needs of others already have "an ally within the child," in Martin Hoffman's lovely phrase.

If we had to pick a logical setting in which to guide children toward caring about, empathizing with, and helping other people, it would be a place where they would regularly come into contact with their peers and where some sort of learning is already taking place. The school is such an obvious choice that one wonders how it could be that the active encouragement of prosocial values and behavior—apart from occasional exhortations to be polite—plays no part in the vast majority of American classrooms. This would seem to stem either from a lack of interest in the idea or from some objection to using the schools in particular for this purpose. Both factors probably play a role, but I will concentrate here on the latter and consider three specific reservations that parents, teachers, policymakers, and others may have—or at least may hear and thus need to answer—about classroom-based programs to help children develop a prosocial orientation.

The first objection is that an agenda concerned with social and moral issues amounts to teaching values—a dangerous business for a public institution. In response, we must concede that a prosocial agenda is indeed value-laden, but we should immediately add that the very same is true of the status quo. The teacher's presence and behavior, her choice of text, the order in which she presents ideas, and her tone of voice are as much part of the lesson as the curriculum itself. So, too, is a teacher's method of discipline or classroom management saturated in values, regardless of whether those values are transparent to the teacher. In short, to arrange our schools so that caring, sharing, helping, and empathizing are actively encouraged is not to introduce values into a neutral environment; it is to examine the values already in place and to consider trading them in for a new set.

It is sometimes said that moral concerns and social skills ought to be taught at home. I know of no one in the field of education or child development who disagrees. The problem is that such instruction—along with nurturance and warmth, someone to model altruism, opportunities to practice caring for others, and so forth—is not to be found in all homes. The school may need to provide what some children will not otherwise get. In any case, there is no conceivable danger in providing these values in both environments. Encouragement from more than one source to develop empathic relationships is a highly desirable form of redundancy.

The second concern one hears—and this one dovetails with the broader absence of interest in the prosocial realm—is the fear that children taught to care about others will be unable to look out for themselves when they are released into a heartless society. The idea that someone exposed to such a program will grow up gullible and spineless, destined to be victimized by mean-spirited individuals, can be traced back to the prejudice that selfishness and competitiveness are efficacious social strategies—a sterling example of what sociologist C. Wright Mills used to call "crackpot realism." In fact, those whose mantra is "look out for Number One" are actually at a greater disadvantage in any sort of society than those who are skilled at working with others and inclined to do so. Competition and the single-minded pursuit of narrowly conceived self-interest typically turn out to be counterproductive.

By contrast, a well-designed program of prosocial instruction will include training in cooperative conflict resolution and in methods of achieving one's goals that do not require the use of force or manipulation. But even without such a component, there is nothing about caring for others that implies not caring for or looking after oneself. A raft of research has established that assertiveness, healthy self-esteem, and popularity are all compatible with—and often even cor-relates of—a prosocial orientation.[10]

The final objection to teaching children to be caring individuals is that the time required to do so comes at the expense of attention to academics—a shift in priorities apt to be particularly unpopular at a time when we entertain ourselves by describing how much students don't know. In fact, though, there is absolutely no evidence to suggest that prosocial children—or the sort of learning experiences that help to create them—are mutually exclusive with academic achievement. To the contrary, the development of perspective taking—the capacity to imagine how someone else thinks, feels, or sees the world—tends to promote cognitive problem solving generally. In one study, the extent to which girls had these skills at age eight or nine was a powerful pre-dictor of performance on reading and spelling tests taken two years later—an even better predictor, in fact, than their original test scores.[11]

Not only are the ingredients of a prosocial orientation conducive to academic excellence, but the educational process itself does not re-quire us to choose between teaching children to think and teaching them to care. It is possible to integrate prosocial lessons into the reg-ular curriculum; as long as children are learning to read and spell and think critically, they may as well learn with texts that encourage per-spective taking. Indeed, to study literature or history by grappling with social and moral dilemmas is to invite a deeper engagement with those subjects. Meanwhile, literally hundreds of studies have shown that co-operative learning, which has an important place in a prosocial class-room, enhances achievement regardless of subject matter or age level.[12] So consistent and remarkable have these results been that schools and individual teachers often adopt models of cooperative learning pri-marily to strengthen academic performance. The development of prosocial values is realized as an unintended bonus.

Education of character in Buber's sense asks of teachers something more than the mere elimination of behavior problems in the class-room. The absence of such problems is often seen as an invitation to move past behavioral and social issues and get on with the business at hand, which is academic learning. I am arguing, by contrast, that be-havioral and social issues, values and character, are very much part of the business at hand. But whether we are talking about addressing misconduct or about taking the initiative to help students become more responsive to one another, a teacher can take any of several basic orientations. Here are four approaches to changing behaviors and attitudes, presented in ascending order of desirability.

1. Punishing. A reliance on the threat of punishment is a reasonably good indication that something is wrong in a classroom, since children have to be bullied into acting the way the teacher demands. Apart from the disagreeable nature of this style of interaction—which cannot be disguised, incidentally, by referring to punishment as "consequences"—it is an approach distinguished mostly by its ineffectiveness. Decades of research have established that children subjected to punitive discipline at home are *more* likely than their peers to break rules when they are away from home.

Isolating a child from his peers, humiliating her, giving him an F, loading her with extra homework, or even threatening to do any of these things can produce compliance in the short run. Over the long haul, however, this strategy is unproductive.

Why? First, at best, punishment teaches nothing about what one is supposed to do—only about what one is not supposed to do. There is an enormous difference between not beating up one's peers, on the one hand, and being helpful, on the other.

Second, the child's attention is not really focused on the intended lesson at all ("pushing people is bad"), much less on the rationale for this principle, but primarily on the punishment itself. Figuring out how to get away with the misbehavior, how to avoid detection by an authority, is a perfectly logical response. (Notice that the one who punishes becomes transformed in the child's eyes into a rule enforcer who is best avoided.) Social learning theory tells us that this attention to the punishment is also likely to *teach* the child to be punitive and thus exacerbate the behavior problems; a teacher's actions do indeed speak louder than words.

Finally, punishment breeds resistance and resentment. "The more you use power to try to control people, the less real influence you'll have on their lives," Thomas Gordon has written.[13] Since such influence is associated with helping children to develop good values, the use of power would seem ill-advised.

2. Bribing. There is no question that rewards are better than punishment. On the other hand, what these two methods share is probably more important than the respects in which they differ, and herein lies a tale that will be highly disconcerting to educators enamored of positive reinforcement. Psychological—and particularly develop-mental—theory and research have come a long way since the sim-plistic behaviorism of the last generation, but many well-meaning teachers continue to assume that what works for training the family pet must be appropriate for shaping children's actions and values as well.

Gold stars, smiley faces, trophies, certificates, high grades, extra re-cess time, candy, money, and even praise all share the feature of being "extrinsic" to whatever behavior is being rewarded. Like sticks, carrots are artificial attempts to manipulate behavior that offer children *no reason to continue acting in the desired way when there is no longer any goody to be gained.* Do rewards motivate students? Absolutely. They motivate students to get rewarded. What they fail to do is help chil-dren develop a commitment to being generous or respectful.

In fact, the news is even worse than this. Not only is bribing some-one to act in a particular way ultimately ineffective, but like the use of threats it can actually make things worse. Consider the effects of re-wards on achievement. Yale psychologist Robert Sternberg recently summed up what a growing number of motivation researchers now concede: "Nothing tends to undermine creativity quite like extrinsic motivators do. They also undermine intrinsic motivation: when you give extrinsic rewards for certain kinds of behavior, you tend to re-duce children's interest in performing those behaviors for their own sake."[14] Once we see ourselves as doing something in order to get a re-ward, we are less likely to want to continue doing it in the absence of a reward—even if we used to find it enjoyable.

Readers of the *Kappan* were first exposed to research demonstrat-ing this phenomenon more than fifteen years ago,[15] and the data have continued to accumulate since then, with some studies concentrating on how extrinsic motivators reduce intrinsic interest and others show-ing how they undermine performance, particularly on creative tasks.[16] A number of explanations have been proposed to account for these re-markably consistent findings. First, people who think of themselves as working for a reward feel controlled, and this lack of self-determination interferes with creativity. Second, rewards encourage "ego involve-ment" to the exclusion of "task involvement," and the latter is more predictive of achievement. Third, the promise of a reward is "tanta-mount to declaring that the activity is not worth doing for its own sake," as A. S. Neill put it;[17] indeed, anything construed as a prerequi-site to some other goal will probably be devalued as a result.

What is true for academic learning also applies to behavior. A little-known series of studies has pointed up the folly of trying to encourage prosocial behavior through the use of extrinsic incentives. Children who received rewards for donating to another child—and in another experiment, adults who were paid for helping a researcher—turned out to be less likely to describe themselves in words suggesting intrinsic motivation to help than were people who received nothing in return.[18] In another study, women offered money for answering a questionnaire were less likely to agree to a similar request two or three days later, when no money was involved, than were women who had not been paid for helping with the first survey.[19]

The implication is that when someone is rewarded for prosocial behavior, that person will tend to assume that the reward accounts for his or her actions and thus will be less likely to help once no one is around to hand out privileges or praise. Indeed, elementary school students whose mothers believed in using rewards to motivate them were less cooperative and generous than other children in a recent study.[20] Such findings are of more than theoretical interest given the popularity of Skinnerian techniques for promoting generosity in schools. A recent *New York Times* article described elementary schools where helpful children have their pictures posted in hallways, get to eat at a special table in the cafeteria, or even receive money.[21] Such contrivances may actually have the effect of undermining the very prosocial orientation that their designers hope to promote.

3. Encouraging commitment to values. To describe the limitations of the use of punishments and rewards is already to suggest a better way: the teacher's goal should not be simply to produce a given behavior—for example, to get a child to share a cookie or stop yelling—but to help that child see himself or herself as the kind of person who is responsible and caring. From this shift in self-concept will come lasting behaviors and values that are not contingent on the presence of someone to dispense threats or bribes. The child has made these behaviors and values his or her own.

A student manipulated by currently fashionable behavioral techniques, however, is unlikely to internalize the values underlying the desired behaviors. At the heart of "assertive discipline," for example, is control: "I want teachers to learn that they have to take charge," Lee Canter explained recently.[22] I don't. I want *children* to become responsible for what they do and for what kind of people they are. The teacher has a critical role to play in making sure that this happens; in criticizing manipulative approaches I am not suggesting that children be left alone to teach themselves responsibility. But the teacher ought to be guided less by the need to maintain control over the classroom than by the long-term objective of helping students to act responsibly because they understand that it is right to do so.

I will have more to say later about strategies for facilitating this internalization, but first I want to mention a version of this process that I believe is even more desirable—the ideal approach to helping children become good people.

4. Encouraging the group's commitment to values. What the first two approaches have in common is that they provide nothing more than extrinsic motivation. What the first two share with the third is that they address only the individual child. I propose that helpfulness and responsibility ought not to be taught in a vacuum but in the context of a community of people who learn and play and make decisions together. More precisely, the idea is not just to internalize good values *in* a community but to internalize, among other things, the value *of* community.

Perhaps the best way to crystallize what distinguishes each of these four approaches is to imagine the question that a child is encouraged to ask by each. An education based on punishment prompts the query, "What am I supposed to do, and what will happen to me if I don't do it?" An education based on rewards leads the child to ask, "What am I supposed to do, and what will I get for doing it?" When values have been internalized by the child, the question becomes, "What kind of person do I want to be?" And in the last instance the child wonders, "How do we want our classroom (or school) to be?"

Educators eager to have children think about how they want their classrooms to be—which is to say, educators who do not feel threatened at the prospect of inviting children to share some of the responsibility for creating norms and determining goals—need to think in terms of five broad categories: what they believe, what they say, what they do, how they relate to students, and how they encourage students to relate to one another. Let us consider each in turn.

What educators believe. The famous Pygmalion effect refers to the fact that a teacher's assumptions about a child's intellectual potential can affect that child's performance. Such self-fulfilling prophecies, however, are by no means limited to academics; they also operate powerfully on a child's actions and values. Write off a student as destructive or disruptive, and he or she is likely to "live down to" these expectations. Conversely—and here is the decisive point for anyone concerned with promoting generosity—attributing to a child the best possible motive that is consistent with the facts may set in motion an "auspicious" (rather than a vicious) circle. We help students develop good values by assuming whenever possible that they are already motivated by these values—rather than by explaining an ambiguous action in terms of a sinister desire to make trouble.

However, what we assume about a given student is also colored by our assumptions regarding human nature itself. While I am not aware of any research on this question, it seems reasonable to suppose that an educator who thinks that self-interest motivates everything we do will be suspicious of individual instances of generosity. Someone who takes for granted that a Hobbesian state of nature would exist in a classroom in the absence of a controlling adult to keep children in line, who believes that children need to be leaned on or "taught a lesson" or bribed to act responsibly, is likely to transfer these expectations to the individual child and produce an environment that fulfills them. The belief that children are actually quite anxious to please adults, that they may simply lack the skills to get what they need, that they will generally respond to a caring environment, can create a very different reality. What you believe matters.

What educators say. An immense body of research has shown that children are more likely to follow a rule if its rationale has been explained to them, and that, in general, discipline based on reason is more effective than the totalitarian approach captured by the T-shirt slogan "Because I'm the mommy, that's why." This finding applies not only to discouraging aggression but to promoting altruism. From preschool to high school, children should learn why—not merely be told that—helping others is good. Pointing out how their actions affect others sensitizes students to the needs and feelings of others and tacitly communicates a message of trust and responsibility. It implies that once children understand how their behavior makes other people feel, they can and will choose to do something about it.

How such explanations are framed also counts. First, the level of the discourse should be fitted to the child's ability to understand. Second, the concept of using reason does not preclude passion. A prohibition on hurting people, for example, should not be offered dispassionately but with an emotional charge to show that it matters. Third, prosocial activity should not be promoted on the basis of self-interest.

"Zachary, if you don't share your dump truck with Linda, she won't let you play with her dinosaur" has an undeniable appeal for a parent, but it is a strategy more likely to inculcate self-regarding shrewdness than genuine concern for others. The same goes for classroom exhortations and instruction.

A series of studies by Joan Grusec of the University of Toronto and her colleagues is also relevant. Her research provides a concrete alternative to the use of rewards or praise to elicit generosity. "Children who view their prosocial conduct as compliance with external authority will act prosocially only when they believe external pressures are present," she has written. Far preferable is for children to "come to believe that their prosocial behavior reflects values or dispositions in themselves."[23]

This result is best achieved by verbally attributing such values or dispositions to the child. In one experiment, in which children gave away some of their game winnings after watching a model do so, those who were told that they had made the donation "because you're the kind of person who likes to help other people" were subsequently more generous than those who were told that they had donated because they were expected to do so.[24] In another study, the likelihood of children's donating increased both when they were praised and when they were led to think of themselves as helpful people. But in a follow-up experiment, it was the latter group who turned out to be more generous than those who had received verbal reinforcement. In other words, praise increased generosity in a given setting but ceased to be effective outside of that setting, whereas children with an intrinsic impulse to be generous continued to act on that motivation in other circumstances.[25]

A study of adults drives home the point. Subjects who were told that a personality test showed that they were kind and thoughtful people were more likely to help a confederate who "accidentally" dropped a pile of cards than were those who were told that they were unusually intelligent or those given no feedback at all. This finding is important because it implies that being led to think of oneself as generous does not affect behavior merely because it is a kind of reinforcement or a mood enhancer; this label apparently encourages prosocial action because it helps to build a view of the self as altruistic.[26]

This is not to suggest that a teacher's every utterance must be—or can be—geared toward internalization. Simply making sure that a classroom is a safe environment conducive to learning can require the sort of behavioral interventions on a day-to-day basis that don't do much to strengthen a child's prosocial self-concept. But the more teachers attend to the latter, the fewer problems they are likely to have over the long run.

What educators do. Children of all ages, from before the time they can read until after the time they start seeking distance from adults, learn from what they see. Studies show that children who watched, even briefly, as someone donated to charity were themselves likely to donate more than other children—even if months had elapsed since their exposure to the model.[27] The extent to which a teacher expresses concern about people in distress and takes the initiative to help— which applies both to how the teacher treats the students themselves and to how he or she refers to people outside the classroom—can set a powerful example and be even more effective than didactic instruction in promoting a sense of caring in students.

There is no shortage of suggestions about how to devise lessons that address social and ethical issues, ranging from explicit training in perspective taking or moral reasoning to discussions about values that can, in turn, include either "clarification" of the beliefs that students already hold or old-fashioned lectures on character or morality. Most of the debate on the subject occurs between proponents of just such programs, each accusing the other of being relativistic or of seeking to indoctrinate. Far less consideration is given to the possibility of integrating such issues into the regular curriculum.

A distinction, though not a sharp one, can be made between teaching morality (or about morality) as such and helping children to be positively connected to others. The latter is my focus here, and some writers have argued that, particularly for younger children, it ought to be the primary focus in the schools, too. "Unless the young child has acquired a positive propensity towards other persons," says one educator, "subsequent moral education will become virtually impotent."[28]

As an alternative to special units devoted to one of these approaches, children can use texts in conventional subject areas that encourage perspective taking. This option should allay the concern that moral instruction will distract us from academics.

How educators relate to students. Preceding and underlying specific techniques for encouraging particular behaviors is the practice of nesting all kinds of discipline and instruction in the context of a warm, nurturant, and empathic relationship with students. Children whose parents are interested in and supportive of them usually distinguish themselves as socially competent and psychologically healthy on a range of measures, and there is no reason to think that the teacher-student relationship is any different.

Warm, caring, empathic adults do several things at once. They provide the child with a benevolent, safe place in which to act. (If a child's experience with others leaves him or her feeling threatened rather than safe, this is likely to foster psychological damage control at the expense of any inclination to help others.) I hope that few educators take seriously the absurd dictum that teachers should display no warmth until well into the school year—after firm control of the classroom has been won. Instead, teachers should establish themselves from the beginning as the students' allies, adults with whom they can work to solve the problems that emerge during the normal course of development. In meeting a child's emotional needs, we give him or her the emotional freedom to meet the needs of others.

How educators encourage students to relate to one another. Anyone interested in children as social beings must recognize the need to attend to the interactions among them in the classroom. In most American schools, children are forced to work either against one another (by competing) or apart from one another (by learning individually). The chance to work *with* one another, to learn social skills and caring, is left to happen by itself during recess, at lunch, or after school. This single fact goes a long way toward explaining why people in our society tend to regard others as potential obstacles to their own success. David Johnson and Roger Johnson of the University of Minnesota have emphasized that the relationship between student and student is at least as important as that between student and teacher or between student and curriculum. Their reference to student-student relationships is offered in the context of creating good learners, and it is all the more true in terms of creating good human beings.

How, specifically, should teachers encourage student interaction? First, students can be put in pairs or small groups so as to help one another learn. This concept, known as cooperative learning, embraces many disparate models for implementation: some depend on grades and other extrinsic incentives to ensure that students work together, some involve cooperation among as well as within groups, some provide for a strict division of labor in completing assignments. A substantial number of studies have found that cooperative learning of various types has the potential to help students feel good about themselves, feel good about each other, feel good about what they are learning, and learn more effectively.

Cooperation, by virtue of being an interaction in which two or more people work together for mutual benefit, is not itself an example of prosocial behavior as the term is usually used. Neither does its successful use presuppose the existence of prosocial motives in all children. Rather, by creating interdependence and a built-in incentive to help, cooperative learning *promotes* prosocial behavior. Having children learn from one another creates powerful bonds between them and sends a message very different from that sent by a classroom in which each child is on his or her own—or worse still, one in which the success of each is inversely related to the success of the others.[29]

In one study, fifth graders who studied grammar in cooperative learning groups were more likely to give away prize tokens to a stranger than were those who studied on their own; in another, kindergartners who participated in cooperative activities acted more prosocially than their peers in a traditional classroom.[30] But the consequences are not limited to generosity per se. Carefully structured cooperative learning also promotes a subjective sense of group identity, a greater acceptance of people who are different from oneself (in terms of ethnicity or ability level), and a more sophisticated ability to imagine other people's points of view.[31] Cooperation is an essentially humanizing experience that predisposes participants to take a benevolent view of others. It allows them to transcend egocentric and objectifying postures and encourages trust, sensitivity, open communication, and prosocial activity.

Second, teachers can move the idea of discipline not only away from punishments and rewards but also away from the premise of these strategies—namely, that teachers should simply be figuring out by themselves how to elicit compliance with a set of rules or goals that they alone devise. The realistic alternative is not for the teacher to abdicate responsibility for what happens in the classroom but rather to bring in (and guide) children so that they can play a role in making decisions about how their classroom is to be run and why. (Must hands always be raised or only during certain kinds of discussions? What is the best way for the class as a community to balance principles of fairness and the spontaneity that encourages participation?)

Discipline would thus be reconfigured as collaborative planning and mutual problem solving. Such an approach will be preferred by anyone who favors the idea of autonomy and democratic decision making—but it can also be argued that purely practical considerations recommend it, since children are more likely to follow rules that they have helped to create than rules dictated to them. This, of course, assumes that following rules is in itself a desirable goal. More broadly, educators need to ask themselves and each other about the ultimate objective of discipline. Even if one of the conventional programs of behavior control succeeded in keeping children quiet, do quiet children learn more effectively or merely make fewer demands on the teacher? (The Johnsons like to say that a principal walking through the school corridors should be concerned if he or she hears no sound coming from a classroom; this means that real learning probably is not taking place.) And which approach is most likely to help children come to care about one another?

To invite children to participate in making decisions not only about classroom procedures but also about pedagogical matters (what is to be learned, how, and why) and housekeeping matters (how to celebrate birthdays or decorate the walls) is to bring them into a process of discussion, an opportunity to cooperate and build consensus. To this extent, it is a chance for them to practice perspective-taking skills, to share and listen and help. In short, involving children in planning and decision making is a way of providing a framework for prosocial interactions that supports other such opportunities; it turns a routine issue into another chance to learn about and practice caring, and not so incidentally, thinking as well.[32]

Finally, educators can provide students with opportunities to be responsible for one another so they will learn (prosocial values and skills) by doing. Ideally this can include interaction with those of different ages. For an older child to guide someone younger is to experience firsthand what it is to be a helper and to be responsible for someone who is dependent on him or her. For the younger child, this cross-age interaction presents an opportunity to see a prosocial model who is not an adult.

One of the most exciting and innovative educational programs now in operation, the Child Development Project (CDP), is devoted specifically to helping children become more caring and responsible.[33] The experience of the CDP offers lessons in the systematic application of many of the ideas discussed here; indeed, I owe my formulation of some of these ideas to the work done by Eric Schaps, Marilyn Watson, and others involved with the project.

The CDP is the first long-term, comprehensive, school-based project in prosocial education. After being invited a decade ago to work in the San Ramon Valley (California) Unified School District, about thirty miles east of San Francisco, the staff carefully matched two sets of three elementary schools in the district for size and socioeconomic status. A coin flip then determined which of these sets would receive the program and which would serve as the comparison group. The first teachers were trained before the start of the 1982–83 school year. Staff researchers focused on a group of children in the experimental schools (then in kindergarten and now in junior high school) to assess whether their attitudes, behavior, and achievement differed significantly from those of their counterparts in the comparison schools. In the fall of 1988, the program was introduced into two elementary schools in nearby Hayward, a district more ethnically diverse than the white, affluent suburbs in San Ramon Valley, and Schaps is now seeking funding to take the program to eight more sites around the country.

"How do we want our classroom to be?" is exactly the question that the CDP would have children ask. Rejecting punishment and rewards in favor of strategies geared toward internalization of prosocial norms and values, the CDP invites teachers and students to work together to turn their classrooms into caring communities. The primary components of the program intended to bring this about are these:

- A version of cooperative learning that does not rely on grades or other extrinsic motivators

- The use of a literature-based reading program that stimulates discussion about values and offers examples of empathy and caring even as it develops verbal skills

- An approach to classroom management in which the emphasis is on developing intrinsic motives to participate productively and prosocially, in which teachers are encouraged to develop warm relationships with the children, and in which periodic class meetings are held so that children can play an active role in planning, assessing progress, and solving problems

- A variety of other features, including pairing children of different ages to work together, setting up community service projects to develop responsibility, giving periodic homework assignments specifically designed to be done (and to foster communication) with parents, and holding schoolwide activities that may involve whole families.

In their writings, members of the CDP staff have distinguished their way of teaching values from the approaches of better-known models. Unlike certain kinds of character education, the CDP approach emphasizes helping students to understand the reason for a given value rather than simply insisting that they accept it or behave in a certain way because they have been told to do so. Unlike purely child-centered approaches, however, the CDP is committed to the importance of adult socialization: the teacher's job is to teach, to guide, to enforce, to facilitate cooperation, to model behaviors—in short, to be much more than a passive bystander. Prosocial values come from a synthesis of adult inculcation and peer interaction, and these values—in contrast to the programs developed by some theorists in the area of moral reasoning—emphasize caring for others as well as applying principles of fairness.

Prior to the implementation of the CDP, students randomly selected from the three experimental and the three comparison schools proved to be similar not only demographically but also on a range of social attitudes, values, and skills. Once the program was implemented, however, structured interviews and observations turned up significant differences between students participating in the program and those in the comparison schools on some, though not all, measures.

Children taking part in the CDP engaged in a greater number of spontaneous prosocial behaviors in class, seemed better able to understand hypothetical conflict situations, and were more likely to take everyone's needs into account in dealing with such situations. They were more likely to believe that one has an obligation to speak up in a discussion even if one's position seems unlikely to prevail (which should answer those concerned about the assertiveness of caring children). While the CDP's emphasis has not required any sacrifice of conventional achievement (as measured by standardized test scores), neither has it given participants a consistent academic advantage over students in comparison schools. (In part this finding may be due to a ceiling effect: students in the district already score in the top 10 percent of California schoolchildren, so there is not much room for improvement.) By the time the CDP group reached sixth grade, though, they were outscoring their counterparts in the comparison schools on a measure of higher-order reading comprehension (essays written about stories and poems).

It remains to be seen whether and in what ways the values and behaviors of children from schools using the CDP will continue to distinguish them from those who attended comparison schools now that they are all in junior high school. But this pilot project provides real evidence for the larger point I am making here: it is both realistic and valuable to attend to what students learn in the classroom about getting along with their peers. Children can indeed be raised to work with, care for, and help one another. And schools must begin to play an integral role in that process.

Notes

1. Martin Buber, *Between Man and Man,* trans. by Ronald Gregor Smith (New York: Macmillan, 1965), p. 104.

2. Our society's current infatuation with the word *competitiveness,* which has leached into discussions about education, only exacerbates the problem by encouraging a confusion between two very different ideas: excellence and the desperate quest to triumph over other people.

3. Alfie Kohn, *The Brighter Side of Human Nature: Altruism and Empathy in Everyday Life* (New York: Basic Books, 1990).

4. Marvin L. Simner, "Newborn's Response to the Cry of Another Infant," *Developmental Psychology,* vol. 5, 1971, pp. 136–150; Abraham Sagi and Martin L. Hoffman, "Empathic Distress in the Newborn," *Developmental Psychology,* vol. 12, 1976, pp. 175–176; and Grace B. Martin and Russell D. Clark III, "Distress Crying in Neonates: Species and Peer Specificity," *Developmental Psychology,* vol. 18, 1982, pp. 3–9.

5. Sagi and Hoffman, p. 176.

6. See, for example, Carolyn Zahn-Waxler and Marian Radke-Yarrow, "The Development of Altruism: Alternative Research Strategies," in Nancy Eisenberg-Berg, ed., *The Development of Prosocial Behavior* (New York: Academic Press, 1982).

7. Marian Radke-Yarrow and Carolyn Zahn-Waxler, "Dimensions and Correlates of Prosocial Behavior in Young Children," *Child Development,* vol. 47, 1976, pp. 118–125.

8. Nancy Eisenberg-Berg and Cynthia Neal, "Children's Moral Reasoning About Their Own Spontaneous Prosocial Behavior," *Developmental Psychology,* vol. 15, 1979, pp. 228–229. Eisenberg and another colleague have observed that appeals to authority or punishment (which were completely absent here) are what one would expect if the children were at Lawrence Kohlberg's first stage of moral reasoning, and that the apparently altruistic needs-oriented explanations have often—and presumably unfairly—been

coded as stage 2, that is, as an immature, "preconventional" way of thinking about moral problems (see Nancy Eisenberg-Berg and Michael Hand, "The Relationship of Preschoolers' Reasoning About Prosocial Moral Conflicts to Prosocial Behavior," *Child Development*, vol. 50, 1979, pp. 356–363).

9. The tendency to define *altruism* so narrowly that only Mother Teresa would qualify for the label both reflects and perpetuates a cynical view of human nature. It would never occur to us to define *aggression* so as to exclude everything short of mass murder.

10. Kohn, chap. 3.

11. Norma Deitch Feshbach and Seymour Feshbach, "Affective Processes and Academic Achievement," *Child Development*, vol. 58, 1987, pp. 1335–1347. For more research on cognitive skills and perspective taking, see David W. Johnson and Frank P. Johnson, *Joining Together: Group Theory and Group Skills*, 3rd ed. (Englewood Cliffs, N.J.: Prentice-Hall, 1987), p. 244.

12. For example, see David Johnson et al., "Effects of Cooperative, Competitive, and Individualistic Goal Structures on Achievement: A Meta-Analysis," *Psychological Bulletin*, vol. 89, 1981, pp. 47–62; David W. Johnson and Roger T. Johnson, *Cooperation and Competition* (Edina, Minn.: Interaction Book Co., 1989), especially chap. 3; and Robert E. Slavin, *Cooperative Learning: Theory, Research, and Practice* (Englewood Cliffs, N.J.: Prentice-Hall, 1990), especially chap. 2.

13. Thomas Gordon, *Teaching Children Self-Discipline* (New York: Times Books, 1989), p. 7.

14. Robert J. Sternberg, "Prototypes of Competence and Incompetence," in Robert J. Sternberg and John Kolligian Jr., eds., *Competence Considered* (New Haven: Yale University Press, 1990), p. 144.

15. Mark R. Lepper and David Greene, "When Two Rewards Are Worse Than One: Effects of Extrinsic Rewards on Intrinsic Motivation," *Phi Delta Kappan*, Apr. 1975, pp. 565–566.

16. See, for example, Edward Deci and Richard Ryan, *Intrinsic Motivation and Self-Determination in Human Behavior* (New York: Plenum Press, 1985); Mark R. Lepper and David Greene, eds., *The Hidden Costs of Reward* (Hillsdale, N.J.: Erlbaum, 1978); and the work of John Nicholls, Teresa Amabile, Judith M. Harackiewicz, Mark Morgan, and Ruth Butler. I have reviewed some of this research in "Group Grade Grubbing Versus Cooperative *Learning*," *Educational Leadership*, Feb. 1991, pp. 83–87.

17. Quoted in Mark Morgan, "Reward-Induced Decrements and Increments in Intrinsic Motivation," *Review of Educational Research*, vol. 54, 1984, p. 5.

18. Cathleen L. Smith et al., "Children's Causal Attributions Regarding Help Giving," *Child Development*, vol. 50, 1979, pp. 203–210; and C. Daniel Bat-

son et al., "Buying Kindness: Effect of an Extrinsic Incentive for Helping on Perceived Altruism," *Personality and Social Psychology Bulletin,* vol. 4, 1978, pp. 86–91.

19. Miron Zuckerman, Michelle M. Lazzaro, and Diane Waldgeir, "Undermining Effects of the Foot-in-the-Door Technique with Extrinsic Rewards," *Journal of Applied Social Psychology,* vol. 9, 1979, pp. 292–296.

20. Richard A. Fabes et al., "Effects of Rewards on Children's Prosocial Motivation," *Developmental Psychology,* vol. 25, 1989, pp. 509–515.

21. Suzanne Daley, "Pendulum Is Swinging Back to the Teaching of Values in U.S. Schools," *New York Times,* Dec. 12, 1990, p. B–14.

22. Quoted in David Hill, "Order in the Classroom," *Teacher Magazine,* Apr. 1990, p. 77.

23. Joan E. Grusec and Theodore Dix, "The Socialization of Prosocial Behavior: Theory and Reality," in Carolyn Zahn-Waxler, E. Mark Cummings, and Ronald Iannotti, eds., *Altruism and Aggression: Biological and Social Origins* (Cambridge: Cambridge University Press, 1986), p. 220.

24. Joan E. Grusec et al., "Modeling, Direct Instruction, and Attributions: Effects on Altruism," *Developmental Psychology,* vol. 14, 1978, pp. 51–57.

25. Joan E. Grusec and Erica Redler, "Attribution, Reinforcement, and Altruism: A Developmental Analysis," *Developmental Psychology,* vol. 16, 1980, pp. 525–534.

26. Angelo Strenta and William DeJong, "The Effect of a Prosocial Label on Helping Behavior," *Social Psychology Quarterly,* vol. 44, 1981, pp. 142–147.

27. See James H. Bryan and Nancy H. Walbek, "Preaching and Practicing Generosity," *Child Development,* vol. 41, 1970, pp. 329–353; James H. Bryan and Perry London, "Altruistic Behavior by Children," *Psychological Bulletin,* vol. 72, 1970, pp. 200–211; Martin L. Hoffman, "Altruistic Behavior and the Parent-Child Relationship," *Journal of Personality and Social Psychology,* vol. 31, 1975, pp. 937–943; and Marian Radke-Yarrow, Phyllis M. Scott, and Carolyn Zahn-Waxler, "Learning Concern for Others," *Developmental Psychology,* vol. 8, 1973, pp. 240–260.

28. Ben Spiecker, "Psychopathy: The Incapacity to Have Moral Emotions," *Journal of Moral Education,* vol. 17, 1988, p. 103.

29. For an analysis of the harms of competition in the classroom and elsewhere, see Alfie Kohn, *No Contest: The Case Against Competition* (Boston: Houghton Mifflin, 1986).

30. David W. Johnson et al., "Effects of Cooperative Versus Individualized Instruction on Student Prosocial Behavior, Attitudes Toward Learning, and Achievement," *Journal of Educational Psychology,* vol. 68, 1976, pp. 446–452; and Bette Chambers, "Cooperative Learning in Kindergarten: Can It

Enhance Students' Perspective-Taking Ability and Prosocial Behaviour?" Unpublished manuscript, Concordia University, Montreal, 1990.

31. See, for example, the research cited in David W. Johnson and Roger T. Johnson, "The Socialization and Achievement Crisis: Are Cooperative Learning Experiences the Solution?" in Leonard Bickman, ed., *Applied Social Psychology Annual 4* (Beverly Hills, Calif.: Sage, 1983), p. 137; and Elliot Aronson and Diane Bridgeman, "Jigsaw Groups and the Desegregated Classroom: In Pursuit of Common Goals," *Personality and Social Psychology Bulletin,* vol. 5, 1979, p. 443.

32. Another classroom management issue is raised by Carolyn Zahn-Waxler. She warns that a teacher who routinely and efficiently takes care of a child in distress in order to preserve order in the classroom may unwittingly be teaching two lessons: (1) that "people do not react emotionally to upset in others"; and (2) that, "if someone is hurt, someone else who is in charge will handle it" ("Conclusions: Lessons from the Past and a Look to the Future," in Zahn-Waxler, Cummings, and Iannotti, eds., p. 310).

33. For more about the Child Development Project, see Alfie Kohn, "The ABC's of Caring," *Teacher Magazine,* Jan. 1990, pp. 52–58; and *The Brighter Side of Human Nature,* chap. 6. For accounts written by members of the staff, see Victor Battistich et al., "The Child Development Project: A Comprehensive Program for the Development of Prosocial Character," in William M. Kurtines and Jacob L. Gewirtz, eds., *Moral Behavior and Development: Advances in Theory, Research, and Applications* (Hillsdale, N.J.: Erlbaum, 1989); and Daniel Solomon et al., "Cooperative Learning as Part of a Comprehensive Classroom Program Designed to Promote Prosocial Development," in Shlomo Sharan, ed., *Cooperative Learning: Theory and Research* (New York: Praeger, 1990).

CHAPTER EIGHTEEN

Choices for Children
Why and How to Let Students Decide

*The essence of the demand for freedom is the need of condi-
tions which will enable an individual to make his own special contribution to a group interest, and to partake of its
activities in such ways that social guidance shall be a matter of his own mental attitude, and not a mere authoritative dictation of his acts.*

—*John Dewey,* Democracy and Education

Educators are painfully well acquainted with the phenomenon known as "burnout." Some days it seems that the bulbs have
gone out in most faculty lounges and administration buildings. But
what if, hypothetically speaking, this syndrome also affected students?
How would *they* talk and act? Teachers around the country to whom

---

Originally published in *Phi Delta Kappan* in 1993.

I have put this question immediately suggest such symptoms as disengagement and apathy—or conversely, thoughtlessness and aggression. Either tuning out or acting out might signal that a student was burning out. In both cases, he or she would presumably just go through the motions of learning, handing in uninspired work and counting the minutes or days until freedom.

Of course, no sooner is this sketch of a hypothetical student begun than we recognize it as a depiction of real life. The fact is that students act this way every day. But now let us ask what we know from research and experience in the workplace about the cause of burnout. The best predictor, it turns out, is not too much work, too little time, or too little compensation. Rather, it is powerlessness—a lack of control over what one is doing.

Combine that fact with the premise that there is no minimum age for burnout, and the conclusion that emerges is this: much of what is disturbing about students' attitudes and behavior may be a function of the fact that they have little to say about what happens to them all day. They are compelled to follow someone else's rules, study someone else's curriculum, and submit continually to someone else's evaluation. The mystery, really, is not that so many students are indifferent about what they have to do in school but that any of them are not.

To be sure, there is nothing new about the idea that students should be able to participate, individually and collectively, in making decisions. This conviction has long played a role in schools designated as progressive, democratic, open, free, experimental, or alternative; in educational philosophies called developmental, constructivist, holistic, or learner-centered; in specific innovations such as whole-language learning, discovery-based science, or authentic assessment; and in the daily practice of teachers whose natural instinct is to treat children with respect.

But if the concept is not exactly novel, neither do we usually take the time to tease this element out of various traditions and examine it in its own right. Why is it so important that children have a chance to make decisions about their learning? How might this opportunity be provided with regard to academic matters as well as other aspects of school life? What limits on students' right to choose are necessary, and what restrictions compromise the idea too deeply? Finally, what barriers might account for the fact that students so rarely feel a sense of self-determination today? A close inspection of these issues will re-

veal that the question of choice is both more complex and more compelling than many educators seem to assume.

Several years ago, a group of teachers from Florida traveled to what
was then the USSR to exchange information and ideas with their
Russian-speaking counterparts. What the Soviet teachers most wanted
from their guests was guidance on setting up and running democratic schools. Their questions on this topic were based on the assumption that a country like the United States, so committed to the idea of
democracy, surely must involve children in decision-making processes
from their earliest years.

The irony is enough to make us wince. As one survey of American
schools after another has confirmed, students are rarely invited to become active participants in their own education.[1] Schooling is typically about doing things *to* children, not working *with* them. An array
of punishments and rewards is used to enforce compliance with an
agenda that students rarely have any opportunity to influence.

Think about the rules posted on the wall of an elementary school
classroom, or the "rights and responsibilities" pamphlet distributed in
high schools, or the moral precepts that form the basis of a values or
character education program. In each case, students are almost never
involved in deliberating about such ideas; their job is basically to do
as they are told.

Moreover, consider the conventional response when something
goes wrong (as determined, of course, by the adults). Are two children
creating a commotion instead of sitting quietly? Separate them. Have
the desks become repositories for used chewing gum? Ban the stuff.
Do students come to class without having done the reading? Hit them
with a pop quiz. Again and again, the favorite motto of teachers and
administrators seems to be "Reach for the coercion" rather than engaging children in a conversation about the underlying causes of what
is happening and working together to negotiate a solution.

Earlier this year, the principal of a Brooklyn high school told a
New York Times reporter that he lived by "a simple proposition: This
is my house. I'm 46 years old. A 15–year-old is not going to dictate
to me how this school is run."[2] But even educators who recoil from
such a frank endorsement of autocracy may end up acting in accor-
dance with the same basic principle. I have met many elementary
teachers, for example, who make a point of assuring students that

"this is *our* classroom"—but proceed to decide unilaterally on almost everything that goes on in it, from grading policy to room decor.

As for the content of instruction, the educators who shape the curriculum rarely bother to consult those who are to be educated. There is plenty of enthusiasm about reforms such as outcome-based education but little concern about bringing students into the process of formulating the outcomes. There is spirited debate about "school choice"— an arrangement in which districts are compelled to compete for the business of parent-consumers—but much less talk about how much choice students have concerning what happens in their classrooms. Indeed, spontaneous, animated conversations about topics of interest to children, when they are allowed to occur at all, are soon snuffed out in order that the class can return to the prescribed lesson plan.

THE RATIONALE

To talk about the destructive effects of keeping students powerless is to describe the benefits of having a sense of self-determination.[3] Five such benefits seem particularly compelling.

1. Effects on general well-being. Many different fields of research have converged on the finding that it is desirable for people to experience a sense of control over their lives. These benefits reach into every corner of human existence, starting with our physical health and survival. One series of studies has shown that people who rarely become ill despite having to deal with considerable stress tend to be those who feel more control over what happens to them.[4] In another well-known experiment, nursing home residents who were able to make decisions about their environment not only became happier and more active but were also more likely to be alive a year and a half later than were other residents.[5]

The psychological benefits of control are, if anything, even more pronounced. All else being equal, emotional adjustment is better over time for people who experience a sense of self-determination; by contrast, few things lead more reliably to depression and other forms of psychological distress than a feeling of helplessness.[6] (One recent study showed that this was true in an educational setting: distress was inversely related to how much influence and autonomy teachers said they had with respect to school policy.[7]) Whereas rewards and punishments are notably ineffective at maintaining behavior change,[8] people are likely to persist at doing constructive things, like exercising, quitting smoking, or fighting cavities, when they have some choice about the specifics of such programs.[9] Laboratory experiments have also shown that individuals are better able to tolerate unpleasant sensations like noise, cold, or electric shock when they know they have the power to end them.[10]

Children are no exception to these rules, the studies show. One-year-old infants had fun with a noisy mechanical toy if they could make it start; it was less interesting, and sometimes even frightening, if they had no control over its action.[11] Elementary students had higher self-esteem and a greater feeling of academic competence when their teachers bolstered their sense of self-determination in the classroom.[12]

2. Effects on behavior and values. One is repeatedly struck by the absurd spectacle of adults insisting that children need to become self-disciplined or lamenting that "kids just don't take responsibility for their own behavior"—while spending their days ordering children around. The truth is, if we want children to *take* responsibility for their own behavior we must first *give* them responsibility, and plenty of it. The way a child learns how to make decisions is by making decisions, not by following directions. As Constance Kamii has written, "We cannot expect children to accept ready-made values and truths all the way through school, and then suddenly make choices in adulthood. Likewise, we cannot expect them to be manipulated with reward and punishment in school, and to have the courage of a Martin Luther King in adulthood.[13]

In fact, an emphasis on following instructions, respecting authority (regardless of whether that respect has been earned), and obeying the rules (regardless of whether they are reasonable) teaches a disturbing lesson. Stanley Milgram's famous experiment, in which ordinary people gave what they thought were terribly painful shocks to hapless strangers merely because they were told to do so, is not just a comment about "society" or "human nature." It is a cautionary tale about certain ways of teaching children. Indeed, an emphasis on obedience, with all the trappings of control that must be used for enforcing it, typically fails even on its own terms: children are less likely to comply with a rule when they have had no role in inventing or even discussing it. And if our goals are more ambitious—if we want children to make good values their own over the long haul—then there is no substitute for giving them the chance to become actively involved in deciding what kind of people they want to be and what kind of classroom or school they want to have.

To talk about the importance of choice is also to talk about democracy. At present, as Shelley Berman of Educators for Social Responsibility has drily noted, "we teach reading, writing, and math by [having students do] them, but we teach democracy by lecture."[14] I believe it is time to call the bluff of every educator who claims to prize democratic principles. Anyone who truly values democracy ought to be thinking about preparing students to participate in a democratic culture—or to transform a culture *into* a democracy, as the case may be. The only way this can happen, the only way children can acquire both the skills of decision making and the inclination to use them, is if we maximize their experiences with choice and negotiation.[15]

Ultimately, even virtues that appear to be quite different from an orientation toward participation or a capacity to make intelligent decisions turn out to depend on these things. For example, like many others, I am concerned about how we can help children to become generous, caring people who see themselves as part of a community.[16] But these values simply cannot be successfully promoted in the absence of choice. A jarring reminder of that fact was provided by a man who recalled being "taught that my highest duty was to help those in need" but added that he learned this lesson in the context of how important it was to "obey promptly the wishes and commands of my parents, teachers, and priests, and indeed of all adults. . . . Whatever they said was always right." The man who said that was Rudolf Höss, the commandant of Auschwitz.[17] A commitment to helping is important, but if the environment in which such values are taught emphasizes obedience rather than autonomy, all may be lost.

3. Effects on academic achievement. Every teacher who is told what material to cover, when to cover it, and how to evaluate children's performance is a teacher who knows that enthusiasm for one's work quickly evaporates in the face of being controlled. Not every teacher, however, realizes that exactly the same thing holds true for students: deprive them of self-determination and you have likely deprived them of motivation. If learning is a matter of following orders, students simply will not take to it in the way they would if they had some say about what they were doing. Not long ago, in a tenth grade geometry class whose teacher collaborates with students to decide about curriculum and grades, a student explained to me that being able to make such choices "leads to learning rather than just remembering."

The evidence to support that view is so compelling that it is frankly difficult to understand how anyone can talk about school reform without immediately addressing the question of how students can be given more say about what goes on in their classes. The classic Eight-Year Study, which should be required reading for everyone with an interest in education, provided data on this point more than half a century ago. After thirty high schools were encouraged to develop innovative programs whose "essential value was democracy,"[18] researchers found that the graduates of those schools did better in college than a matched comparison group from traditional schools. In fact, the students who were most successful tended to come from the schools that had departed most significantly from the conventional college-prep approach—the approach currently lauded by those calling for higher standards, more accountability, and getting back to basics.

Subsequent research has confirmed the conclusion:

• When second graders in Pittsburgh were given some choice about their learning, including the chance to decide which tasks they would work on at any given moment, they tended to "complete more learning tasks in less time."[19]

• When high school seniors in Minneapolis worked on chemistry problems without clear-cut instructions—that is, with the opportunity to decide for themselves how to find solutions—they "consistently produced better write-ups of experiments" and remembered the material better than those who had been told exactly what to do. They put in more time than they had to, spending "extra laboratory periods checking results that could have been accepted without extra work." Some of the students initially resisted having to make decisions about how to proceed, but these grumblers later "took great pride in being able to carry through an experiment on their own."[20]

• When preschoolers in Massachusetts were allowed to select the materials they used for making a collage, their work was judged more creative than the work of children who used exactly the same materials but did not get to choose them.[21]

• When college students in New York State had the chance to decide which of several puzzles they wanted to work on and how to allot their time to each of them, they were a lot more interested in working on such puzzles later than were students who were told what to do.[22]

• When teachers of inner-city black children were trained in a program designed to promote a sense of self-determination, the students in these classes missed less school and scored better on a national test of basic skills than those in conventional classrooms.[23]

• When second graders spent the year in a math classroom where textbooks and rewards were discarded in favor of an emphasis on "intellectual autonomy"—that is, where children working in groups took an active role in figuring out their own solutions to problems and were free to move around the classroom on their own initiative to get the materials they needed—they developed more sophisticated reasoning skills without falling behind on basic conceptual tasks.[24]

The evidence goes on and on. At least one recent study has found that children given more "opportunity to participate in decisions about schoolwork" score higher on standardized tests;[25] other research shows that they are more likely than those deprived of autonomy to continue working even on relatively uninteresting tasks.[26] There is no question about it: even if our only criterion is academic performance, choice works.

In a way, this conclusion shouldn't be surprising. Putting aside the value of particular programs that give students more discretion about what they are doing, the irrefutable fact is that students always have a choice about whether they will learn. We may be able to force them to complete an assignment, but we can't compel them to learn effectively or to care about what they are doing. The bottom line is that "teaching requires the consent of students, and discontent will not be chased away by the exercise of power."[27] No wonder that expanding the realm in which the learner's consent is sought tends to enhance learning.

4. Effects on teachers. Despite attitudinal barriers to creating democratic classrooms and schools, which I will discuss later, educators who are willing to share power may well find that they benefit directly from doing so. One's job becomes a good deal more interesting when it involves collaborating with students to decide what is going to happen. As one fifth grade teacher in upstate New York explained:

> I've been teaching for more than 30 years, and I would have been burned out long ago but for the fact that I involve my kids in designing the curriculum. I'll say to them, "What's the *most* exciting way we could study this next unit?" If we decide their first suggestion isn't feasible, I'll say, "Okay, what's the *next* most exciting way we could study this?" They always come up with good proposals, they're motivated because I'm using their ideas, and I never do the unit in the same way twice.[28]

Teachers also benefit in other ways from allowing students to be active participants in their learning. In such a classroom, according to the researchers involved in the second grade math project described earlier, the teacher is "freed from the chore of constantly monitoring and supervising the children's activity and [is] able to give her full attention to . . . interacting with the children" as they learn.[29]

5. Intrinsic value. Finally, it needs to be said that allowing people to make decisions about what happens to them is inherently preferable to controlling them. It is more respectful and consistent with basic values to which most of us claim to subscribe. Apart from the skills that will be useful for students to have in the future, they ought to have a chance to choose in the present. Children, after all, are not just adults-in-the-making. They are people whose current needs and rights and experiences must be taken seriously. Put it this way: students should not only be trained to live in a democracy when they grow up; they should also have the chance to live in one today.[30]

CHOOSING IN PRACTICE

Because quite a few programs and practices in which children can make meaningful choices have been described elsewhere, I will offer only a sampling of the ways this basic idea can be implemented. These suggestions can be grouped according to whether they are primarily concerned with academic decisions or with social and behavioral ones.

Academic issues. The four key realms in which students can make academic decisions are what, how, how well, and why they learn. *What* they learn is the most straightforward of these. Student participation here can range from choosing where in an assigned text to start reading to deciding what course to take. In between these examples is the question of what is to be read, not only by individual students but by the class as a whole. "Here are five books that the supply store has in stock," a fourth grade teacher may say to the class. "Why don't you flip through them during your free time this week, and we'll decide together on Friday which one to read next." (Of course, if students are not reading stories at all but making their way through worksheets and workbooks, basals and primers and dittos, then their capacity to participate in their education has been significantly curtailed from the start.)

Teachers may not always have the discretion to let students participate in deciding what topic to study. But even when compelled to teach a certain lesson, a teacher might open up a discussion in which members of the class try to figure out together why someone apparently thought the subject was important enough to be required. The next step would be to connect that topic to students' real-world concerns and interests. When teachers have themselves decided for one reason or another to exclude students from the selection of the subject matter, there is still room to give them choices about the specific questions within a general topic to be explored. A teacher might begin any unit, for example, by inviting children to discuss what they already know about the subject and what they would like to know.

The question of *how* students learn embraces a great many issues—beginning with whether to work alone, in small groups, or as a class—and including such incidental matters as where students will sit (or lie) while they work. (One teacher swears that achievement in her class improved markedly as soon as she gave students the right to find a favorite reading place and position.) And there are other choices as well: if a student has written a story, she ought to be able to decide whether to read it aloud and, if so, whether to answer her classmates' questions about it afterward and, if so, on whom to call.

Every day ought to include at least one block of time in which children can decide individually what to do: get a head start on homework, write in one's journal, work on an art project, or read a library book. Creative writing assignments offer plenty of opportunity for decisions to be made by the writers themselves. In expressing an idea or responding to a lesson, children sometimes can be allowed to decide what medium or genre they will use—whether they want to write a poem, an essay, or a play, or do a collage, painting, or sculpture. Mathematics lessons can be guided by quantitative issues of interest to students.

The entire constructivist tradition is predicated on the idea of student autonomy, which is to say, the chance for students to view learning as something "under their control rather than as disembodied, objectified, subject matter."[31] The same can be said about some (but not all) models of cooperative learning. One version, devised by Shlomo Sharan and his colleagues and known as Group Investigation, is based on the idea of active participation throughout the process. Students break a subject into specific questions, sort themselves into groups to explore these questions, plan and conduct an investigation, and figure out how to share what they have learned with the rest of the class.[32]

To talk about *how well* a student is doing is to raise the complicated issues of assessment and evaluation, the improvement of which has lately been of increasing concern to educators. But a key consideration in changing these systems, beyond whether judgments are based on sufficiently rich measures of student achievement, is the extent to which students themselves are involved in the process. Obviously, the chance to pick one of three possible essay questions for one's final paper does not begin to get at what is important here. Students ought to help determine the criteria by which their work will be judged and then play a role in weighing their work against those criteria. This achieves several things at once: it gives students more control over their education, it makes evaluation feel less punitive, and it provides an important learning experience in itself. Students can derive enormous intellectual benefits from thinking about what makes a story interesting, a mathematical proof elegant, or an argument convincing. More traditional approaches to testing can also be improved if students are consulted about what the test ought to cover and when it ought to be given; there is no need for teachers to decide these things on their own.

Last, and most frequently overlooked, is the need to involve students in talking about *why* they are learning. Few aspects of education are more important than the "participation of the learner in the formation of the purposes which direct his activities in the learning process," as Dewey put it.[33] Children should be given a voice not only about the means of learning but also about the ends, the why as well as the what. Even very young children are "curriculum theorists," according to John Nicholls, and there may be no better use of classroom time than a sustained conversation following someone's challenge: "Why do we gotta do this stuff?"[34]

Social and behavioral issues. School is about more than intellectual development; it is about learning to become a responsible, caring person who can make good choices and solve problems effectively. Thus educators must think about ways of helping students to take an active part in decisions that are only indirectly related to academics.

Is it necessary to raise one's hand before talking or to line up before walking through the school? How much noise is too much? How should the furniture be arranged in our room? Where might we take a field trip? These are the sorts of questions that children should be encouraged to ponder and argue about. In considering what kind of classroom or school each person wants to have, the point is to reach consensus on general guidelines or principles, not to formulate a list of rules. (Specific admonitions tend to invite legalistic thinking about their application and a preoccupation with enforcement that emphasizes punishment over problem solving.) Moreover, this process goes well beyond, and may even exclude, the practice of voting. What we want to promote are talking and listening, looking for alternatives and trying to reach agreement, solving problems together and making meaningful choices. Voting, which is an exercise in adversarial majoritarianism, often involves none of these acts. It may be the least objectionable method when a quarter of a billion people must govern themselves, but classroom teachers can do better.[35]

A structured opportunity for members of a class or school to meet and make decisions provides several advantages: it helps children feel respected by making it clear that their opinions matter; it builds a sense of belongingness and community; and it contributes to the development of social and cognitive skills such as perspective taking (imagining how the world looks to someone else), conflict resolution, and rational analysis.[36] Few contrasts in education are as striking as that between students participating in such meetings, taking responsibility for deciding how they want their classroom to be, and students sitting in rows, having been bribed or threatened into complying with an adult's rules.

Thus, when problems develop, the adage for teachers to keep in mind is "Bring the kids in on it." This approach may call for a class meeting, in the case of a conflict involving a number of students, or when only one or two are directly concerned, it could mean a conversation with just them. If a child is daydreaming and failing to complete assignments, or if two children cannot seem to be anywhere near each other without becoming nasty, the most successful (and respectful)[37] solutions are those that emerge after the teacher asks, "What do you think we can do about this?"

REASONABLE LIMITS

A number of writers and teachers who resist giving children the chance to make decisions have justified their opposition by erecting an enormous straw man called "absolute freedom" and counterposing it to the status quo. Since most of us do not relish the idea of children spending their time at school doing anything they please, deprived of structure or adult guidance, we are encouraged to settle for the controlling practices that now exist.

Not only is this a classic false dichotomy, but virtually every influential proponent of choice for students—as well as the programs that have put the idea into effect—proceeds from the assumption that there are indeed limits on the capacity and right of children to decide.

The scary specter of laissez-faire liberty that shows up in the rhetoric of traditionalists is not easy to locate in the real world. Nearly every essay on education by John Dewey, the father of progressive schooling, stresses the importance of adult guidance and derides the idea of "leaving a child to his own unguided fancies."[38] Even A. S. Neill, whose Summerhill school and philosophy lie at the outer edges of serious discussion about the issue, distinguished sharply between freedom and license, emphasizing repeatedly that "a child should not be permitted to violate the personal rights of others."[39] All reasonable adults, meanwhile, acknowledge that safety concerns will necessitate placing constraints on certain kinds of actions.

While agreement exists at a general level about the need to restrict students' choice, however, there is far less consensus about when and how to do so. The issues most frequently raised in support of such restrictions are not as simple as they first appear. Take the question of *age.* It goes without saying that a sixteen–year-old can approach a decision in a more sophisticated way than a six–year-old and therefore can usually be entrusted with more responsibility. But this fact is sometimes used to justify preventing younger children from making choices that are well within their capabilities. Moreover, the idea that we must wait until children are mature enough to handle responsibilities may set up a vicious circle: after all, it is experience with decisions that helps children become capable of handling them.[40]

A second rationale for restricting choice is *time:* if students were entitled to make decisions about, and had to agree on, everything they did, there would be no time to do anything else. True enough, and yet the heuristic value of such discussions is often overlooked in the rush to get on with the "real" lesson. In class meetings, for example, teachers would do well to remember that, at least to some extent, *the process is the point.* The idea isn't just to make a choice, reach a decision, and move on.

Of course, it is still true that there won't be time to hash out every matter; sometimes a teacher will need to request that students just do something. But a democratic approach doesn't demand that everything *is* actively chosen, only that it *can* be. As Deborah Meier has said, what matters is not whether a given issue is discussed but that it is discussable. Unavoidable time constraints should not be used to rationalize avoidable authoritarian practices.

Third, the importance of choice is often weighed against the fact that children need some *structure or limits* for their behavior, if not for their learning. Once again, this point may be accurate but does not justify much of what educators actually do. "The critical question," as Thomas Gordon has put it, "is not *whether* limits and rules are needed . . . but rather *who* sets them: the adults alone or the adults and kids—together."[41] Before depriving children of choice, then, an educator is obliged to demonstrate not that they need some structure but that there is some reason to exclude them from helping to shape that structure. The crucial difference between structures and limits, on the one hand, and control and coercion, on the other, has generally gone unrecognized.[42]

Fourth, and possibly most compelling, is the caution that the right to choose must give way to the needs and preferences of *other people*. Even the minimalist sort of liberalism articulated by Neill (in which one's connection to others is limited to not violating their rights) implies that people cannot do whatever they want. A more ambitious commitment to the value of community would seem to restrict choice even more severely. While each child ought to have more opportunity to make decisions than is typically allowed in American classrooms, such decisions must take into account their impact on the other people in the room. This may not feel like a burdensome restriction once a child has internalized a concern about others' well-being—but strictly speaking, one person's freedom to choose is always compromised by a set of obligations to others. At a recent town meeting of the long-standing experimental school-within-a-school program at Brookline (Massachusetts) High School, one student remarked that someone's choice to show up in class without having done the reading assignment adversely affects the quality of discussion for everyone. "It's not just 'You get out what you put into it,'" another girl added. "It's 'You get out what the class puts into it'"—and vice versa.

On closer examination, however, it seems clear that what must occasionally be restricted is not choice but *individual* choice. (It is an interesting reflection on our culture that we tend to see these as interchangeable.) To affirm the importance of community does not at all compromise the right to make decisions, per se, or the importance of involving everyone in a class or school in such a process. In fact, we might say that it is the integration of these two values, community and choice, that defines democracy.

I think we can conclude that, while some legitimate limits to the right to choose can be identified, the most commonly cited reasons for those limits may not automatically justify restrictions. But this discussion also raises questions about a conventional response to the matter of appropriate limits. Many people, understandably impatient with an either/or choice in which the possibilities are limited to freedom and its absence, assert that we need to find a happy medium between these two poles. This seems facile. For one thing, such a pronouncement offers no guidance about where on that continuum we should set up camp. For another, it overlooks the fact that the sensible alternative to two extremes may not be an intermediate point but a different way of thinking about the issue altogether. The interesting question here, for example, is not how *much* adults should limit the power of children to make decisions, but *how* they should get involved.

In a broad sense, that involvement may consist of suggesting the tasks, teaching the skills, supplying the resources—in short, providing the conditions under which students can choose productively and learn effectively. The teacher's role is to be a facilitator, but as Carolyn Edwards points out, this doesn't mean to "'mak[e] smooth or easy,' but rather to 'stimulate' [learning] by making problems more complex, involving, and arousing."[43] Notice the implication here: a democratic classroom is not one where the teacher has less work to do. There is no zero-sum game in which more responsibility for the children means less for the adults. Helping students to participate effectively takes talent and patience and hard work. "I'm in control of putting students in control," one teacher told me—a responsibility that demands more of an educator than simply telling students what to do.

Notice also that this role for the teacher does not always amount to being a voice for moderation or mainstream values—a conservative counterweight to students' reckless impulses. If, for example, children have been raised to assume that anyone who does something wrong must be forced to suffer a punitive consequence, they will be likely, left to their own devices, to spend their time deciding what should be done to a rule breaker. Here, the teacher might intervene to guide the discussion away from "Which punishment?" and toward the more radical question of whether an entirely different response— "Something has gone wrong; how can we solve this problem?"—might be more productive.

On a range of issues, adults can participate—and circumscribe children's choices—in fundamentally different ways. To wit:

• The teacher and the students may take turns at deciding something, each choosing on alternate weeks, for example, which book to read next. Or the responsibility can rotate between individual students, cooperative learning groups, the whole class, and the teacher.

• The teacher may offer suggestions and guidance, questions and criticism, but leave the final choice to students. Thus I have heard a third grade teacher advise her students that it might not be a good idea to go outside for recess on a day when there is slush on the ground, but then make it clear that it is up to each child to make the final decision for himself or herself. A high school teacher, meanwhile, suggests that it might make sense for the whole class to talk about the homework together, but offers them the option of discussing it in small groups if they prefer.

• The teacher can narrow the number of possibilities from which students are permitted to choose. He or she may want to do this to make sure that any material or text a student works with is likely to be of educational value and of approximately the right level of challenge. (On the other hand, neither of these goals always requires restricting children's choice.[44] And even when the teacher does decide to limit their options, she should explain her rationale for doing so and remain open to reasonable additions to her list. As a general rule, it is more important for children to have the chance to *generate* different possibilities than merely to select one possibility from among those that have been set before them.[45])

• The teacher may provide the parameters according to which decisions can be made, perhaps specifying the goal that has to be reached but inviting students to figure out how they want to get there. For example, "It's important to me that no one in here feels scared that other people will laugh at him for saying something stupid. How do you think we can prevent that from happening?" Or "I need some way at the end of this unit to see how much you understand. Think of a way you might be able to demonstrate what you've learned."

• A decision does not have to be thought of as something that teachers either make or turn over to students. Instead, it can be negotiated together. The emphasis here is on shared responsibility for deciding what gets learned and how the learning takes place. This process can become a lesson in itself—an opportunity to make arguments, solve problems, anticipate consequences, and take other people's needs into account—as well as a powerful contribution to motivation.

While well-meaning educators may offer very different prescriptions regarding the nature and scope of students' participation in decision making, I believe that certain ways of limiting participation are basically deceptive and best described as "pseudochoice." It is disturbing to find these tactics recommended not only by proponents of blatantly controlling classroom management programs, such as Assertive Discipline, but also by critics of such programs who purport to offer an enlightened alternative.

In the first version of pseudochoice, a student is offered a choice that is obviously loaded. "You can finish your math problems now or you can stay in during recess. Which would you prefer?" The problem here is not just that the number of options has been reduced to two, but that the second one is obviously something no student would select. The teacher is really saying, "Do what I tell you or you'll be punished," but he is attempting to camouflage this conventional use of coercion by pretending to offer the student a choice.

In a variation of this gambit, the student is punished after disobeying the teacher's command, but the punishment is presented as something the student asked for: "I see you've chosen to miss recess today." The appeal of this tactic is no mystery: it appears to relieve the teacher of responsibility for what she is about to do to the child. But it is a fundamentally dishonest attribution. Children may choose not to complete a math assignment,[46] but they certainly do not choose to miss recess; teachers do that *to* them. To the injury of punishment is added the insult of a kind of mind game whereby reality is redefined and children are told, in effect, that they chose to be punished. This gimmick uses the word *choice* as a bludgeon rather than giving children what they need, which is the opportunity to participate in making real decisions about what happens to them.[47]

Another kind of pseudochoice purports to let a student or a class make a decision even though there is only one choice that will be accepted. I recently heard a well-known educator and advocate for children reminisce about her experiences as a teacher. Recalling a student of hers who frequently and articulately challenged her authority, she commented with a smile, "I had to be a better negotiator than she was." This remark suggests that what had taken place was not negotiation at all but thinly disguised manipulation. As Nel Noddings has written, "We cannot enter into dialogue with children when we know that our decision is already made."[48]

If students are informed that they have made the "wrong" decision and must try again, they will realize they were not truly free to choose in the first place. But the last, and most insidious, variety of pseudo-choice tries to prevent students from figuring this out by encouraging them to think they had a say when the game was actually rigged. The "engineering of consent," as it has been called, seems to offer autonomy while providing "the assurance of order and conformity—a most seductive combination. Yet its appearance and its means should be understood for what they really are: a method of securing and solidifying the interests of those in power."[49] This description by educator James Beane might have been inspired by the behavior of politicians, but it is no less applicable to what goes on in schools. If we want students to learn how to choose, they must have the opportunity to make *real* choices.

BARRIERS

If we are to act on the arguments and evidence supporting the value of making students active participants in their education, we need to understand why more educators haven't already done so. I think the barriers to giving students more choice fall into three categories: structural impediments, resistance by teachers, and resistance by the students themselves.

Structural impediments. Classroom teachers frequently protest that they would love to open up the decision-making process but for the fact that a significant number of decisions are not theirs to give away or even to make themselves. Highly controlling schools and school districts may leave teachers very little discretion about either curricular or disciplinary issues. As Dewey noted, classrooms characterized by demands for "sheer obedience to the will of an adult" may sometimes imply a "situation [that] almost forced [that arrangement] upon the teacher," such as an absence of democracy or community among the educators themselves.[50] Even if controlling structures do not literally remove options from teachers, they may create a climate in which teachers do to children what is done to them. Often, teachers subject to rigid directives from above may find it easier not "to resist administrators but to increase controls on their students."[51]

Resistance by teachers. While structural constraints are sometimes very real, they can also be used as excuses to withhold power from students that teachers in any case are not inclined to share. The traditional instructional model sees the teacher as the king or queen of the classroom, and the fact is that monarchs do not always abdicate gracefully. On the basis of my own years as a teacher as well as my conversations with scores of others in the profession, I would argue that there is a certain reassurance and satisfaction to be taken from making unilateral decisions. No wonder many teachers who express relief at having "a good class this year" use the word *good* as parents of a newborn might talk about having "a good baby"—that is, one who is quiet, docile, and little trouble to manage.

Popular books about classroom life, as well as workshops and other forms of guidance offered to educators, typically take for granted that a teacher must secure control of the class. Hence the use of curricular materials, including basals and worksheets, that have the effect of keeping order.[52] And hence the popularity of manipulative measures such as punishments and rewards: their use can be traced back to the belief that there are exactly two possibilities: control or chaos. When students are allowed to make decisions, it is therefore only about matters that don't threaten the teacher's reign. More than once I have heard teachers pride themselves on letting students choose "when I don't really care what they end up with"—which is, of course, a far cry from a democratic process that helps students to become responsible decision makers.

If challenged, defenders of classroom autocracy may insist that a teacher must get control of the class *first* in order that students can be helped to become good learners and good people. Whether this is a sincerely held belief or just a rationalization for holding on to power, it is simply wrong. Control not only is unnecessary for fostering academic motivation; it also undermines its development, substituting reluctant compliance for the excitement that comes from the experience of self-determination. Likewise for the nonacademic realm: as one group of social scientists put it, the emphasis on control "endanger[s] the long-term enterprise of socialization itself."[53]

This is no mere academic speculation. Watch what happens when a teacher concerned about maintaining control of his classroom walks away for a few minutes or is absent for a day: the class is likely to erupt, just as a child raised by parents who emphasize strict discipline is apt to misbehave when he is away from home. It is in classrooms (and families) where participation is valued above adult control that students have the chance to learn *self*-control—and are more likely to keep working when the teacher or parent isn't around.

There is nothing surprising about the fact that teachers resist being told what they can teach and how they must manage their classrooms. The astonishing fact is that so many of these teachers treat their students in exactly the way they themselves find so offensive. Whatever the reason for this discrepancy, though, students must be permitted to make substantive decisions about learning and living together, and this will not happen until teachers and administrators understand that *control can't be the goal*—or even a technique. This recognition, in turn, may require reconsidering basic beliefs about human nature and motivation. A teacher convinced that children are egocentric little terrors who must be forced to attend to other people's needs is likely to prefer a model of tight control.[54] And control, in turn, produces exactly the sort of antisocial behavior that such a teacher expects, confirming the view that such tactics are needed.

Sometimes, however, the main barrier to giving children choices is a simple lack of gumption. Parting with power is not easy, if only because the results are less predictable than in a situation where we have control. Asking students to decide about even the simplest issues can be scary. An elementary teacher once told me how difficult it was for her to leave the classroom walls bare when her students showed up on the first day of school. If she had already decorated them, she realized, it was really *her* room they were entering. But it took several years before she found the courage to bring them into the process, a decision that ultimately made an enormous difference in how the children felt about coming to school—and also occasioned a natural and eagerly received lesson on fractions so that the students could measure and tack up the construction paper that they had chosen for *their* walls.

Student resistance. Finally, and most discouragingly, teachers sometimes find that their willingness to let students make decisions is met with an apparent reluctance on the part of the students. This is really not so surprising, given that most of them have been conditioned to accept a posture of passivity at school and sometimes at home. After a few years of being instructed to do what you're told, it is disconcerting to be invited—much less expected—to take responsibility for the way things are.[55]

This resistance takes three primary forms. The first is simply *refusing*: "That's your job to decide," students may protest. The second is *testing*: offering outrageous suggestions or responses to see if the teacher is really serious about the invitation to participate. The third is *parroting*: repeating what adults have said or guessing what this adult probably wants to hear. (Thus a fifth grader asked to suggest a guideline for class conduct may recite, "We should keep our hands and feet to ourselves.")

The key question is how we respond to these maneuvers. It can be tempting to conclude that students are either unable to handle the responsibility of making decisions or unworthy of having it. But our challenge is to persevere. As Selma Wassermann has written,

> I have heard teachers give it up after a single attempt, saying, "Children cannot behave responsibly," then remove all further opportunity for students to practice and grow in their responsible behavior. I have also heard teachers say, "Children cannot think for themselves," and proceed thereafter to do children's thinking for them. But these same teachers would *never* say, "These children cannot read by themselves," and thereafter remove any opportunity for them to learn to read.[56]

Specifically, the comment "That's your job" provides a teachable moment, a chance to engage students in a conversation about their experiences with being controlled and about when they have found learning to be most exciting. Outlandish ideas can be met with a sense of humor but also taken seriously: a student who is asked how school could be improved and replies that all the books should be thrown away may be saying something about her experience of the curriculum that we ignore at our peril. Finally, in the case of parroting, it can be hard even to recognize this tactic as a form of resistance—or as something undesirable. Getting our ideas to come out of their mouths is a ventriloquist's trick, not a sign of successful participation and student autonomy. It represents an invitation to ask students about their experiences with saying what they knew would please an adult and how different that feels from taking the risk of making a suggestion that someone might not like—and then emphasizing that the latter is what we are looking for here.

Of course, whether the last point is true—whether we really are looking for students who take risks and make decisions—is the first question that each of us must answer. The structural and attitudinal barriers erected by educators often seem impregnable, with the result that students continue to feel powerless and, to that extent, burned out. For decades, prescriptions have been offered to enhance student motivation and achievement. But these ideas are unlikely to make much of a difference so long as students are controlled and silenced.

It is not "utopian" or "naive" to think that learners can make responsible decisions about their own learning: those words best describe the belief that any group of people will do something effectively and enthusiastically when they are unable to make choices about what they are doing.

Notes

1. For example, see Charles E. Silberman, *Crisis in the Classroom: The Remaking of American Education* (New York: Random House, 1970); John I. Goodlad, *A Place Called School: Prospects for the Future* (New York: McGraw-Hill, 1984); Linda McNeil, *Contradictions of Control: School Structure and School Knowledge* (New York: Routledge & Kegan Paul, 1986); and the observations of William Glasser in much of his work.

2. Felicia R. Lee, "Disrespect Rules," *New York Times Education Life,* Apr. 4, 1993, p. 16.

3. Strictly speaking, as such thinkers as Jean-Paul Sartre and Viktor Frankl have pointed out, people are never entirely powerless. Deborah Meier applies this observation to an education context: "Even devalued and disrespected people remain powerful, but they are forced to exercise their powers in odd, distorted, and limited ways. . . . Children have been exercising their powers for years, without the formal right to do so. Ditto for teachers . . . [who] sabotage reforms—the best and the worst—when they feel imposed upon and helpless." See "The Kindergarten Tradition in the High School," in Kathe Jervis and Carol Montag, eds., *Progressive Education for the 1990s: Transforming Practice* (New York: Teachers College Press, 1991), pp. 140–141.

4. Suzanne C. Kobasa and her colleagues found that control, together with a deeply felt commitment to one's activities and the tendency to perceive change as a positive challenge, contributed to a profile of "hardiness" that provides significant protection against illness. See, for example, "Stressful Life Events, Personality, and Health: An Inquiry into Hardiness," *Journal of Personality and Social Psychology,* vol. 37, 1979, pp. 1–10. See also Robert A. Karasek et al., "Job Characteristics in Relation to the Prevalence of Myocardial Infarction in the U.S. Health Examination Survey (HES) and the Health and Nutrition Examination Survey (HANES)," *American Journal of Public Health,* vol. 78, 1988, pp. 910–916.

5. Judith Rodin and Ellen J. Langer, "Long-Term Effects of a Control-Relevant Intervention with the Institutionalized Aged," *Journal of Personality and So-*

cial Psychology, vol. 35, 1977, pp. 897–902. In another study, nursing home residents who were able to control (or at least predict) when a student would come visit them were not only happier and more hopeful but also physically healthier than those who received the same number of visits but on a random schedule. See Richard Schulz, "Effects of Control and Predictability on the Physical and Psychological Well-Being of the Institutionalized Aged," *Journal of Personality and Social Psychology,* vol. 33, 1976, pp. 563–573.

6. Martin Seligman's research on helplessness is central to this field of study. For a review of the relevant studies by him and others, see Shelley E. Taylor, *Positive Illusions: Creative Self-Deception and the Healthy Mind* (New York: Basic Books, 1989).

7. See Elizabeth Tuettemann and Keith F. Punch, "Teachers' Psychological Distress: The Ameliorating Effects of Control over the Work Environment," *Educational Review,* vol. 44, 1992, pp. 181–194.

8. See Alfie Kohn, *Punished by Rewards: The Trouble with Gold Stars, Incentive Plans, A's, Praise, and Other Bribes* (Boston: Houghton Mifflin, 1993).

9. Women who were told they could choose the particulars of an exercise program at a health club were more likely to continue attending over six weeks (and to declare their willingness to keep coming after that) than were women who were told their program was simply assigned to them—even though they too were actually assigned activities on the basis of the preferences they had expressed. See Carol E. Thompson and Leonard M. Wankel, "The Effects of Perceived Activity Choice upon Frequency of Exercise Behavior," *Journal of Applied Social Psychology,* vol. 10, 1980, pp. 436–443. A smoking cessation program that "focused attention on the individual's own efforts in smoking cessation" was more successful than one in which people followed a set of guidelines. See Judith M. Harackiewicz et al., "Attributional Processes in Behavior Change and Maintenance: Smoking Cessation and Continued Abstinence," *Journal of Consulting and Clinical Psychology,* vol. 55, 1987, pp. 372–378. Adolescent girls (but not boys) were more likely to continue using an anticavity fluoride rinse for nearly half a year when they were invited to make decisions about how the program was designed and monitored. See Joseph A. Burleson et al., "Effects of Decisional Control and Work Orientation on Persistence in Preventive Health Behavior," *Health Psychology,* vol. 9, 1990, pp. 1–17.

10. This research has been reviewed and evaluated by Suzanne C. Thompson, "Will It Hurt Less If I Can Control It? A Complex Answer to a Simple Question," *Psychological Bulletin,* vol. 90, 1981, pp. 89–101.

11. Megan R. Gunnar-Vongnechten, "Changing a Frightening Toy into a Pleasant

Toy by Allowing the Infant to Control Its Actions," *Developmental Psychology,* vol. 14, 1978, pp. 157–162.

12. Richard M. Ryan and Wendy S. Grolnick, "Origins and Pawns in the Classroom: Self-Report and Projective Assessment of Individual Differences in Children's Perceptions," *Journal of Personality and Social Psychology,* vol. 50, 1986, pp. 550–558.

13. Constance Kamii, "Toward Autonomy: The Importance of Critical Thinking and Choice Making," *School Psychology Review,* vol. 20, 1991, p. 387. In fact, the lessons of conformity that Kamii finds troubling are those that concern academic activities (such as having to "learn mathematics through blind obedience"), not just behavior.

14. Shelley Berman, "The Real Ropes Course: The Development of Social Consciousness," *ESR Journal,* 1990, p. 2. The authors of a classic text on high school teaching comment wryly that the American motto could be, "Let's have education *for* democracy, but let's be careful about democracy *in* education!" See Jean Dresden Grambs and John C. Carr, *Modern Methods in Secondary Education,* 4th ed. (New York: Holt, Rinehart & Winston, 1979), p. 71.

15. Citing several sources, Joseph D'Amico concludes that "children who have experiences in a school where they participate in making decisions are more likely to be . . . motivated to make decisions both in and out of school." See "Reviving Student Participation," *Educational Leadership,* Oct. 1980, pp. 44–46.

16. See Alfie Kohn, "Caring Kids: The Role of the Schools," *Phi Delta Kappan,* March 1991, pp. 496–506. (Reprinted in this volume as Chapter Seventeen.)

17. Höss is quoted in Alice Miller, *For Your Own Good: Hidden Cruelty in Child-Rearing and the Roots of Violence* (New York: Farrar, Straus & Giroux, 1984), pp. 67–68.

18. Kathy Irwin, "The Eight-Year Study," in Jervis and Montag, eds., p. 59. For a more comprehensive description of the study, see Wilford M. Aiken, *The Story of the Eight-Year Study* (New York: Harper, 1942); and Dean Chamberlin et al., *Did They Succeed in College?* (New York: Harper, 1942).

19. Margaret C. Wang and Billie Stiles, "An Investigation of Children's Concept of Self-Responsibility for Their School Learning," *American Educational Research Journal,* vol. 13, 1976, pp. 159–179. Unfortunately, task completion was the only outcome measured in this study.

20. Robert G. Rainey, "The Effects of Directed Versus Non-Directed Laboratory Work on High School Chemistry Achievement," *Journal of Research in Science Teaching,* vol. 3, 1965, pp. 286–292.

21. Teresa M. Amabile and Judith Gitomer, "Children's Artistic Creativity:

Effects of Choice in Task Materials," *Personality and Social Psychology Bulletin,* vol. 10, 1984, pp. 209–215.

22. Miron Zuckerman et al., "On the Importance of Self-Determination for Intrinsically Motivated Behavior," *Personality and Social Psychology Bulletin,* vol. 4, 1978, pp. 443–446. On the relation between choice and task involvement, see also John G. Nicholls, *The Competitive Ethos and Democratic Education* (Cambridge: Harvard University Press, 1989), p. 169.

23. Richard deCharms, "Personal Causation Training in the Schools," *Journal of Applied Social Psychology,* vol. 2, 1972, pp. 95–113.

24. For a description of the classroom structure in this year-long experiment, see Erna Yackel et al., "Small-Group Interactions as a Source of Learning Opportunities in Second-Grade Mathematics," *Journal for Research in Mathematics Education,* vol. 22, 1991, pp. 390–408. For a discussion of the results, see Paul Cobb et al., "Assessment of a Problem-Centered Second-Grade Mathematics Project," *Journal for Research in Mathematics Education,* vol. 22, 1991, pp. 3–29.

25. Ann K. Boggiano et al., "Helplessness Deficits in Students: The Role of Motivational Orientation," *Motivation and Emotion,* vol. 16, 1992, pp. 278–280. Informal reports from other researchers suggest that a more typical result from an intervention of this sort is an enhancement of conceptual thinking skills (along with intrinsic motivation and other psychological and social benefits) but no change on standardized test scores, which probably is a reflection of how little these scores really mean. It should be sufficient to be able to show people who care about these scores that giving students more choice about their learning has no detrimental effect on their performance on machine-scored tests while bringing about a variety of other advantages.

26. Three studies to this effect are cited in John Condry, "Enemies of Exploration: Self-Initiated Versus Other-Initiated Learning," *Journal of Personality and Social Psychology,* vol. 35, 1977, p. 466.

27. John Nicholls and Susan P. Hazzard, *Education as Adventure: Lessons from the Second Grade* (New York: Teachers College Press, 1993), p. 76.

28. Richard Lauricella is quoted in Thomas Lickona, *Educating for Character: How Our Schools Can Teach Respect and Responsibility* (New York: Bantam, 1991), p. 148. Presumably he does not mean to suggest that every aspect of a unit must be taught differently from one year to the next, only that an element that is changed on the basis of students' suggestions within a predictable structure can be invigorating for a teacher.

29. Yackel et al., p. 401.

30. This point is made forcefully by David Charnoff, "Democratic Schooling: Means or End?" *High School Journal,* vol. 64, 1981, pp. 170–175.

31. Paul Cobb et al., "Young Children's Emotional Acts While Engaged in Mathematical Problem Solving," in D. B. McLeod and V. M. Adams, eds., *Affect and Mathematical Problem Solving: A New Perspective* (New York: Springer-Verlag, 1989), p. 129.

32. See Yael Sharan and Shlomo Sharan, *Expanding Cooperative Learning Through Group Investigation* (New York: Teachers College Press, 1992). At its best, cooperative learning "gives students an active role in deciding about, planning, directing and controlling the content and pace of their learning activities. It changes the students' role from recipients of information to seekers, analyzers, and synthesizers of information. It transforms pupils from listeners into talkers and doers, from powerless pawns into participant citizens empowered to influence decisions about what they must do in school." See Shlomo Sharan, "Cooperative Learning: Problems and Promise," *The International Association for the Study of Cooperation in Education Newsletter,* Dec. 1986, p. 4.

33. John Dewey, *Experience and Education* (1938; reprint, New York: Collier, 1963), p. 67.

34. See Nicholls and Hazzard, especially pp. 182–184.

35. Sometimes elementary school students are asked to put their heads down when they raise their hands to register a preference. This strikes me as an apt metaphor for the whole enterprise of voting. "Who thinks we should take our field trip to the museum? Who prefers the zoo? Okay, the zoo wins, fifteen to twelve." About the best that can be said for this exercise is that it didn't take very long. Children have learned precious little about how to solve a problem, accommodate other people's preferences, or rethink their initial inclinations. Moreover, twelve children are now unlikely to feel very excited about the upcoming field trip. The same analysis applies on a schoolwide basis. The usual student council apparatus is deficient on three counts: most students are excluded from direct participation in decision making, some students are turned into losers since the representatives are chosen in a contest, and the council has little real power in any case. Educators interested in democratic values will discourage voting whenever possible; as the political philosopher Benjamin Barber has cogently argued, it is "the least significant act of citizenship in a democracy." See *Strong Democracy: Participatory Politics for a New Age* (Berkeley: University of California Press, 1984), p. 187.

36. My own thinking on how class meetings might be structured has been influenced primarily by the work of the Child Development Project. I can also recommend two other useful and very practical discussions of class

meetings: William Glasser, *Schools Without Failure* (New York: Harper and Row, 1969), chaps. 10–12; and Lickona, chap. 8.

37. "Democracy in the classroom . . . begins simply: with respect for the child as a person, someone who has a point of view and a right and a need to express it." See Thomas Lickona and Muffy Paradise, "Democracy in the Elementary School," in Ralph Mosher, ed., *Moral Education: A First Generation of Research and Development* (New York: Praeger, 1980), p. 325.

38. The quotation is from Dewey's *The School and Society* (Chicago: University of Chicago Press, 1990), p. 130.

39. "In Summerhill, a child is *not* allowed to do as he pleases," Neill added. See *Summerhill* (New York: Hart, 1960), pp. 308, 348.

40. On this point, see Lickona and Paradise, p. 323.

41. Thomas Gordon, *Teaching Children Self-Discipline* (New York: Times Books, 1989), p. 9.

42. This distinction is offered frequently in the work of Edward Deci and Richard Ryan. It seemed to be lost on several teachers at an alternative school program I visited recently who maintained that because today's students come from less structured home environments or are more conservative, it is appropriate to give them fewer choices about their learning.

43. Carolyn Edwards, "Partner, Nurturer, and Guide," in Carolyn Edwards et al., eds., *The Hundred Languages of Children: The Reggio Emilia Approach to Early Childhood Education* (Norwood, N.J.: Ablex, 1993), p. 157.

44. Indeed, children whose curiosity has not been killed by the use of rewards or other extrinsic controls typically select tasks of the right difficulty level for themselves. This finding "suggests that at least part of the teacher's difficult problem of matching tasks to children can be solved by providing children with more choices than they are typically offered." See Fred W. Danner and Edward Lonky, "A Cognitive-Developmental Approach to the Effects of Rewards on Intrinsic Motivation," *Child Development*, vol. 52, 1981, p. 1050.

45. A related restriction on choice that may be employed excessively is the practice of preventing students from altering an activity once they have selected it. They can choose, in other words, only among tasks that must be performed in a rigidly prescribed manner. Some critics have argued that this is a weakness of the Montessori method.

46. Even this assumption needs to be questioned, since a young child may lack the capacity for rational decision making or impulse control that is implicit in the suggestion that he made a choice. If so, the child needs help in developing these faculties, not punishment accompanied by blame. I have heard

some teachers reply to this point by insisting that if students are permitted to make choices, they must "take responsibility" for making a bad one. This approach, however, assumes that "taking responsibility" for a poor decision means being made to suffer for it rather than being part of a nonpunitive problem-solving process.

47. A nice discussion of this misuse of the idea of choice can be found in Vincent Crockenberg, "Assertive Discipline: A Dissent," *California Journal of Teacher Education,* vol. 9, 1982, especially pp. 65–70.

48. Nel Noddings, *The Challenge to Care in Schools* (New York: Teachers College Press, 1992), p. 23.

49. James A. Beane, *Affect in the Curriculum: Toward Democracy, Dignity, and Diversity* (New York: Teachers College Press, 1990), p. 35.

50. Dewey, *Experience and Education,* p. 55.

51. McNeil, p. 9. This phenomenon is not limited to schools, of course. There is evidence from the corporate world that the middle managers most likely to act in an autocratic fashion toward those below them in the hierarchy are those who are restricted and controlled themselves. See Rosabeth Moss Kanter, *Men and Women of the Corporation* (New York: Basic Books, 1977), pp. 189–190.

52. Despite the claim that discipline is "instrumental to mastering the content," the truth is often just the reverse: "many teachers . . . maintain discipline by the ways they present course content." The reduction of teaching to the transfer of disconnected facts and skills is the means; keeping a tight grip on student behavior is the end. See McNeil, pp. 157–158.

53. Phyllis C. Blumenfeld et al., "Teacher Talk and Student Thought," in John M. Levine and Margaret C. Wang, eds., *Teacher and Student Perceptions* (Hillsdale, N.J.: Erlbaum, 1983), p. 147.

54. A survey of more than three hundred parents found that those who inclined toward a negative view of human nature were more likely to prefer an authoritarian approach to child rearing. See Lawrence O. Clayton, "The Impact upon Child-Rearing Attitudes of Parental Views of the Nature of Humankind," *Journal of Psychology and Christianity,* vol. 4, no. 3, 1985, pp. 49–55. For an argument that the data do not support this negative view of human nature, see Alfie Kohn, *The Brighter Side of Human Nature: Altruism and Empathy in Everyday Life* (New York: Basic Books, 1990).

55. On this point, see Seth Kreisberg, "Educating for Democracy and Community," *ESR Journal,* 1992, p. 72; and Rheta DeVries, *Programs of Early Education: The Constructivist View* (New York: Longman, 1987), p. 379.

56. Selma Wasserman, "Children Working in Groups? It Doesn't Work!" *Childhood Education,* Summer 1989, p. 204.

CHAPTER NINETEEN

What to Look for in a Classroom

In describing the climate of a classroom, we are often guided by a certain set of values, a vision of what school *ought* to be like. We might begin with the premise, for example, that an ideal climate is one that promotes deep understanding, excitement about learning, and social as well as intellectual growth.

In such a classroom, students play an active role in decisions, teachers work *with* students rather than doing things *to* them, and the learners' interests and questions drive much of the curriculum. The environment supports children's desire to find out about things, facilitates the process of discovery, and in general meets children's needs. A school with this mission has a climate very different from one in which educators are mostly thinking about how they can make students work harder or follow directions.

Put another way, in a "doing to" classroom or school, the adults tend to focus on students' behavior in order to elicit compliance; the

---

Originally published in *Educational Leadership* in 1996.

preferred methods are punishments and rewards. In a "working with" environment, the focus is on students' underlying motives in order to help them develop positive values and a love of learning; the preferred methods include the creation of a caring community and a genuinely engaging curriculum.

WHAT DO YOU SEE?

When I conduct a workshop, I like to present a conceptual framework that contrasts these two approaches to education. I then invite workshop participants to list familiar practices that exemplify each of them. Participants work in groups, categorizing—and in the process, scrutinizing—various aspects of school life. (For example, if the faculty object to students' clothing, a "working with" response would be to invite students to meet and reflect together on how this problem might be solved. A "doing to" response would be to tell students what they may wear, or simply to force all of them to dress alike.)

These lists tend to grow quickly because there is no limit to the number of examples. And the exercise makes an important point: it is one thing to talk about a learner-centered classroom and something else again to specify exactly what such a place looks and sounds like. Here, then, is an abbreviated list (Table 19.1)—a crib sheet, if you will—that administrators, parents, and others can use to gauge the climate of a classroom and school.

Table 19.1. Learner-Centered or Not?

	Good Signs	Possible Reasons for Concern
Furniture	■ Chairs around tables to facilitate interaction ■ Comfortable areas for learning	■ Desks in rows or chairs all facing forward
Walls	■ Covered with students' projects ■ Evidence of student collaboration ■ Signs, exhibits, or lists created by students rather than teacher ■ Information about, and mementos of, those who spend time together in this classroom	■ Bare ■ Decorated with commercial posters ■ List of consequences for misbehavior ■ List of rules created by an adult ■ Sticker (or star) chart or other evidence that students are rewarded or ranked ■ Students' assignments displayed but they are (a) suspiciously flawless, or (b) only "the best" students' work, or (c) virtually all alike
Sounds	■ Frequent hum of activity and ideas being exchanged	■ Frequent periods of silence and/or teacher's voice the loudest or most often heard
Location of Teacher	■ Typically working with students so that it takes a moment to find him or her	■ Typically front and center
Teacher's Voice	■ Respectful, genuine, warm	■ Controlling and imperious ■ Condescending and saccharine-sweet

(continued on p. 280)

Table 19.1. Learner-Centered or Not? (*cont'd.*)

	Good Signs	Possible Reasons for Concern
Students' Reaction to Visitor	■ Welcoming; eager to explain or demonstrate what they're doing or to use visitor as a resource	■ Either unresponsive or hoping to be distracted from what they're doing
Class Discussion	■ Students often address one another directly ■ Emphasis on thoughtful exploration of complicated issues ■ Students ask questions at least as often as teacher does	■ All exchanges involve (or directed by) teacher; students wait to be called on ■ Emphasis on facts and right answers ■ Students race to be first to answer teacher's "Who can tell me?" queries
Tasks	■ Different activities take place simultaneously	■ All students usually do the same thing
Around the School	■ Inviting atmosphere ■ Students' projects fill hallway walls ■ Bathrooms in good condition ■ Faculty lounge warm and comfortable ■ Office staff welcoming toward visitors and students ■ Students helping in lunchroom, library, and with other school functions	■ Stark, institutional feel ■ Awards, trophies, and prizes displayed, suggesting emphasis on triumph rather than community

—⁓— **The Author**

Alfie Kohn, a former teacher turned author and lecturer, writes and speaks widely on human behavior, education, and social theory. Of his five previous books, the best known are *Punished by Rewards* and *No Contest: The Case Against Competition*. Kohn's criticisms of competition and rewards have helped to shape the thinking of educators—as well as parents and managers—across the country and abroad. (He has been described as the nation's leading critic of competition, but is quick to point out that there is not much competition for that title.) Kohn has appeared on more than two hundred TV and radio programs, including two recent appearances on *Oprah;* his work has been described on the front page of the *Wall Street Journal,* in *U.S. News and World Report,* the *Harvard Education Letter,* and dozens of other magazines and newspapers.

Kohn lectures widely at universities and to school faculties, parent groups, and corporations. He speaks at staff development seminars and serves as keynote speaker at national education conferences on a regular basis. He conducts workshops for teachers and administrators on various topics, including "Motivation from the Inside Out: Rethinking Rewards, Assessment, and Learning" and "Beyond Bribes and Threats: Realistic Alternatives to Controlling Students' Behavior." The latter corresponds to his 1996 book, *Beyond Discipline: From Compliance to Community,* which he describes as a modest attempt to overthrow the entire field of classroom management.

In addition to his articles in education journals and magazines, Kohn has contributed to publications ranging from *The Nation* to the *Harvard Business Review* ("Why Incentive Plans Cannot Work"). His efforts to make research in human behavior accessible to a general audience have also been published in *The Atlantic Monthly, Parents,* and *Psychology Today* (where he was a contributing editor).

Educated at Brown University and the University of Chicago, Kohn lives in the Boston area with his wife and daughter. He is at work on a new book for general readers, which will focus on "tougher standards, traditional classrooms, and other barriers to learning."

Also by Alfie Kohn

No Contest: The Case Against Competition

The Brighter Side of Human Nature: Altruism and Empathy in Everyday Life

You Know What They Say . . . : The Truth About Popular Beliefs

Punished by Rewards: The Trouble with Gold Stars, Incentive Plans, A's, Praise, and Other Bribes

Beyond Discipline: From Compliance to Community

⌁⌁ Index

A

ability grouping. *See* tracking
ability vs. effort, 156, 193
accountability, 197-98. *See also* control
achievement: attributed to ability vs. effort, 156; demanding, vs. supporting, 77-78, 198; effects on, of credentials focus, 93; effects on, of giving students choices, 254-56; effects on, of grades, 75-76; effects on, of previous failure, 154; effects on, of self-esteem, 140-42; effects on, of television viewing, 173-76; at meaningful vs. meaningless tasks, 153-54; of U.S. students, 151, 175; vs. learning, 78, 193-94, 221-22
Adler, Jerry, 149
advanced placement courses, 90
affective education. *See* social vs. academic objectives in education
altruism, 230, 246*n*9. *See also* helping
Ames, Carole, 193
Anderson, Daniel, 173, 180-83, 185-86
Armstrong, Thomas, 131
Assertive Discipline. *See* Canter, Lee
assertiveness: as compatible with helpfulness, 231-32; as skill vs. disposition, 4
assessment: impact on, of credentials emphasis, 91-92; motives for, 73-77; student involvement in, 258-59; suggestions for, 78-80. *See also* grades
Attention-Deficit Hyperactivity Disorder (ADHD): claims of biological basis for, 114, 121-22, 132-33; diagnostic status of, as dubious, 112-16;

as function of classroom organization, 117-20, 133-34*n*6; as function of parenting style, 120-21, 133; prevalence of, 111-12; recommended vs. typical treatment of, 128-31; use of behavior modification for, 131-32; use of drugs for, 123-30, 131
Augustine, St., 22
autonomy. *See* choices for students
awards. *See* competition; rewards vs. awards

B

back-to-basics. *See* traditional education
Barkley, Russell A., 118, 120, 125, 130
Beane, James, 94, 146-47, 151, 161*n*28, 266
behaviorism: and analysis of television viewing, 169-70; and character education, 26-33; and inattention to motives, 6; pervasiveness of, 69; and teaching of skills, 6
Bennett, William, 28, 31, 33, 42-43*n*59
Berman, Shelley, 254
Book It! program, 70
boredom in school, 97
Bosco, James, 129
"brain-based" education, 134*n*8
Branden, Nathaniel, 146
Brazelton, T. Berry, 167
Brecht, Bertolt, 36
Brooks, David, 29
Brown, Ronald T., 130
Brown University, 83
Buber, Martin, 227, 232